CH01521986

A Hand Book and Guide to Preston: Containing Historical Records, Topographical Description, Trade and Commerce, Public Buildings, Parks and Institutions, Churches and Chapels, the Environs and Their Attractions, Etc

William Pollard

BIBLIOLIFE

Copyright © BiblioLife, LLC

BiblioLife Reproduction Series: Our goal at BiblioLife is to help readers, educators and researchers by bringing back in print hard-to-find original publications at a reasonable price and, at the same time, preserve the legacy of literary history. The following book represents an authentic reproduction of the text as printed by the original publisher and may contain prior copyright references. While we have attempted to accurately maintain the integrity of the original work(s), from time to time there are problems with the original book scan that may result in minor errors in the reproduction, including imperfections such as missing and blurred pages, poor pictures, markings and other reproduction issues beyond our control. Because this work is culturally important, we have made it available as a part of our commitment to protecting, preserving and promoting the world's literature.

All of our books are in the "public domain" and some are derived from Open Source projects dedicated to digitizing historic literature. We believe that when we undertake the difficult task of re-creating them as attractive, readable and affordable books, we further the mutual goal of sharing these works with a larger audience. A portion of BiblioLife profits go back to Open Source projects in the form of a donation to the groups that do this important work around the world. If you would like to make a donation to these worthy Open Source projects, or would just like to get more information about these important initiatives, please visit www.bibliolife.com/opensource.

A HAND BOOK

AND

GUIDE TO PRESTON,

CONTAINING

*Historical Records—Topographical Description—Trade
and Commerce—Public Buildings—Parks, and
Institutions—Churches and Chapels—The
Environs and their attractions, &c.*

———◆———

By WILLIAM POLLARD,

Author of "THE GUILD MERCHANT OF 1842,"
"THE STANLEYS OF KNOWSLEY," &c.

———◆———

PRESTON:
H. OAKEY, CAXTON HOUSE, 36, FISHERGATE.
MDCCCLXXXII.

PREFACE.

T HE great "Wizard of the North"—the immortal author of
"Waverley," whose magnificent genius and magic pen called
into existence the most splendid productions of the literature of
his age—was wont to say that the preface was the only part of his
works that gave him any trouble. To him, evolving a gorgeous
romance was a delight; to indite a preface, a torture. On one occasion
he wished the preface to his work to be placed at the end; because, he
said, his experience had convinced him, that, in the majority of
instances, the reader perused the last pages first.

Far be it from the author of this modest effort, to place
himself for one moment in the same category with Sir Walter Scott, to
whom indeed, he is less even than an evanescent shadow. But in
common with the illustrious novelist, he feels the difficulty of writing
even his humble preface. The compilation of this unpretending volume
—for he claims for it the merit only of a compilation—has been to him
a labour of love. To trace the early history, the rise and the gradual
development, to its present increasing prosperity; to mark the
vicissitudes, the romantic incidents, the varied episodes, which constitute
the memorable past of Preston one of absorbing interest—was to him a
task of delight.

If the reader is afforded but a tithe of the pleasure in perusing
it that the author has experienced in compiling it, the latter will be
amply rewarded.

The author is indebted to many local celebrities for the
information necessary to produce this work; amongst whom he begs to
tender his especial acknowledgments to Mr. William Dobson and to
Mr. Charles Hardwick. In reference to the former, his charming
"Rambles by the Ribble" ought to be in the hands of all who value
exquisite scenic delineation with profound thought; whilst Mr.
Hardwick's valuable production possesses a county as well as a local
interest. The author also expresses his indebtedness to Mr. Porter's
"History of the Fylde," and to Mr. Hewitson's "Stonyhurst College,
Present and Past." To each and all of these gentlemen, the author
tenders his grateful obligations.

CONTENTS.

HISTORICAL RECORDS :—

TOPOGRAPHICAL DESCRIPTION :—.

TRADE AND COMMERCE :—

PUBLIC BUILDINGS, PARKS & INSTITUTIONS

HISTORICAL RECORDS.

THE ROMAN OCCUPATION OF BRITAIN.

IT may be affirmed, with a confidence not weakened by doubt or misgiving, that Preston is associated with some of the most interesting and memorable events in English history. From the earliest ages, dating back to the Roman occupation of Britain, and the succeeding Saxon and Danish periods, the concurrent testimony of the most reliable historians bears ample witness to the borough having been conspicuously identified with many of the remarkable passages in past and contemporary times. Nor can there be any question that during the successive internal convulsions which devastated the country in the early and middle ages, Preston was one of the chief centres where the contending armies of the time engaged in their sanguinary conflicts, and in turn won and lost their bloody battles. During the Scottish Invasion, in the reign of the Edwards; the Civil War in the time of Charles the First; the period of the Commonwealth to the Restoration; the Revolution in 1688, which led to the abdication of James the Second, and the final overthrow of the Stuarts ; or the Rebellion of 1715 in the interests of the Pretender ; Preston was the scene of some of the most deadly struggles which the history of the country records.

That Preston was one of the principal stations during the Roman Invasion, admits of no doubt, for the Roman roads and other discoveries in the locality, which in succession have been made, abundantly testify to the fact. Roman remains have from time to time been found in and about the town, and notably within a comparatively recent period, at Cuerdale, on the banks of the Ribble, near Walton-le-Dale, which, according to archæological authorities, places the Roman occupation at this point beyond dispute. The discovery of what was regarded as a Roman station at Walton-le-Dale, caused the Lancashire and Cheshire Historic Society to visit Preston in the year 1856, and on that occasion the members of the Society inspected the station at Walton. Relics of various kinds were discovered in the neighbourhood of the valley of the Ribble when excavating for the foundations of the two railway bridges which now cross the river. These include wild deer and rhinoceros skulls, the bones of oxen, canoes, &c. Roman remains have likewise been discovered in the Fylde, near the river Wyre ; also at Kirkham and Poulton. Amongst them were two copper coins of Hadrian, found near the Church at Poulton, and a large medal of Germanicus, in a garden behind the Market Place. A copper coin of Domitian was also discovered near the Skippool, at its junction with the river Wyre, and these discoveries have led to the inference that the Roman vessels were beached in that locality. So recently as the year 1840, a number of bricklayers discovered about four hundred silver coins near Rossall Point. These valuables consisted of the coins of Trajan, Hadrian, Vespasian, Titus, Domitian, Antoninas, Serverus, Caracalla, Sabina, and Faustina. The neighbourhood of Walton-le-Dale is specially distinguished as the locality where these Roman relics have on repeated occasions been discovered. About forty years ago the remains of a Roman station were discovered in what is known as the Lower Road, in Walton. A fortified camp was also found in the same neighbourhood, whilst axes, spear heads, and other weapons of ancient warfare have at intervals been found in abundance. On a comparatively recent occasion, when excavations were being made for the foundations of a new weaving shed at Walton for Mr. Calvert, the remains of a Roman road were discovered. Similar Roman roads from Preston to Lancaster, over Fulwood Moor, Cadley, Broughton, and Barton, have likewise been traced. The above are only a few of the many illustrations which might be cited in support of the theory of numerous historians, and by common consent admitted to be authentic, that the various roads in the neighbourhood of Preston, to which allusion has been made, were of Roman or ancient British construction, and that the relics which in successive ages have been unearthed, afford irrefragable evidence that Preston was an important station during the Roman occupation of Britain.

THE SAXON AND DANISH PERIODS.

Historical records and discoveries lead to the conclusion, not to be resisted, that from the Saxon period to the Conquest, Preston was on several occasions the theatre of the numerous struggles which took place between the ancient Britons and the Saxon and Danish invaders, following on the departure of the Romans. As in the case of the Roman period, the several "finds" of Saxon remains establish this historical fact as beyond dispute or cavil. One of the most important of these discoveries was that at Cuerdale, in the year 1840, when an exceptionally large and valuable amount of treasure was found. This interesting discovery was the result of a severe storm and floods, which materially disturbed the alluvial soil on the south bank of the Ribble. The repair of the river bank became necessary, and it was while the repairs were

in progress that the discovery was made. The spade of
one of the workmen struck upon a decayed wooden box,
which on being broken open disclosed a very large
number of silver coins and other valuable articles. On
examining the box in which the treasure had been
secreted, it was found to contain a lining of lead, the
conclusion arrived at being that this lining had to a
certain extent protected the contents from the action of
air and water. The coins had been methodically placed
in the box, and several of them, more especially those in
the centre of the box, were only slightly discoloured,
some of them, indeed, having the appearance of being
almost fresh from the mint. The box is believed originally to have contained about 10,000 coins. The treasure
was, some time after the discovery, claimed on behalf of
the Queen as Duchess of Lancaster, but not before many
of the coins, which included silver rings and bars, had, by
questionable means, got into the hands of collectors and
others. Several of them were ultimately sent to the
British Museum, the Institution for the Diffusion of
Knowledge, Preston; and museums in other parts of the
country, where they have ever since been on exhibition
for the inspection of the public. The whole treasure,
exclusive of the coins dispersed before the "find" was
taken possession of on behalf of the Queen, is said to
have weighed 1,265 ounces, consisting of 6,800 coins,
weighing 304 ounces; 16 ingots of silver, 132 ounces;
bars of silver, $725\frac{1}{2}$ ounces; and a number of manufactured articles, consisting of rings, armlets, and chains
which weighed $103\frac{1}{2}$ ounces. They included English
and French coins, together with several others of an uncertain character as to country. The English and French
coins bore dates varying from the years 814 to 928, the
English coins shewing several of the Saxon Kings, including Ethelstan, Ethelred, Eadward, and Alfred; and
the French coins representing Louis, Carolus, Carloman
Eudes, Lambert, and Berengarius. From the dates of
the coins it is the opinion of Mr. Hawkins, who formerly
held the office of Vice-President of the Numismatic

Society, that the treasure was deposited about the year
910, soon after the battle of Wodensfield in Gloucester-
shire. This, however, is rendered highly improbable
from the date of the coins themselves, and the Danish
antiquary, Worsaae, in some observations on the treasure,
observes:—"To judge from the coins, which, with a few
exceptions, were minted between the years 815 and 930,
the treasure must have been buried in the first half of
the tenth century, or almost a hundred years before the
time of Canute the Great." The discovery of these coins
is a strong indication that one of the Saxon conflicts
must have taken place in the locality, and amongst other
authorities who favour this view is the Rev. John Clay,
formerly chaplain of the House of Correction at Preston,
and well known for his enthusiasm in antiquarian re-
search. Mr. Clay, amongst his other labours, delivered
several interesting lectures on the historical incidents
connected with the valley of the Ribble, and in one of
these he says:—"That some of the contests involved in
their campaigns took place in Lancashire, may be inferred from what I have already mentioned—the erection
in 912 of a fort at Manchester, to curb the predatory
propensities of the Northumbrian Danes. In old maps
the scenes of ancient battles are noted by a pair of crossed
swords; and this mark appears on the map given by
Whitaker in his History of Whalley, on the site of the
discovery at Cuerdale." Mr. C. Hardwick, in his exhaustive and highly interesting History of Preston, observes
that "from the time of Athelstan, Preston appears to
have risen into a most important provincial town,
although little is known respecting its actual condition
during the succeeding one hundred and fifty years. It is
described, however, on the Doomsday Survey (1080) as
the chief town of the hundred, with six carucates of tax-
able land. The same document further adds, that all the
villages in Amounderness, together with three churches,
belonged to Preston." During the visit of the Lancashire and Cheshire Historic Society just named, they also
repaired to Castle Hill, Penwortham, where they caused

certain excavations to be made, with the result that ancient remains of a very interesting character were likewise found at this spot. These consisted, amongst others, of the relics of what appeared to have been a human habitation, covering a superficial area of about 250 yards. It was discovered that this residence had been paved with a series of boulders, and afterwards strewed with weeds and other vegetable matter. Upon the surface lay several beams of timber. The whole was covered with what appeared to have formed a roof, composed of "wattles and thatch." The vegetable compost which they met with contained a large quantity of bones, which seemed chiefly to be the remains of wild deer, and oxen, and smaller animals. There were likewise amongst them numerous jaw-bones of the wild boar. Outside the boundary of the house one half of an oaken canoe paddle was also found. Several articles in metal were likewise discovered. One of these was a Roman padlock key. Three nails of peculiar form were found, one of which resembled those found in the Roman station at Walton. Beads in bone were also found, and were reconciled with the Saxon occupation of a Roman outpost. Pieces of leather were likewise found, which appeared to have formed portions of sandals, or other covering for the feet, the several pieces of leather resembling, in shape, the sole of a foot. The conclusion at which the Society arrived on the completion of their inspection was that the subterranean structure was Saxon in character, and that in all probability it had at some period been "a royal residence."

THE CONQUEST TO HENRY THE THIRD.

From the period of the Conquest to the reign of Henry the First, there are few historical events with which Preston is identified, but shortly after that monarch came to the throne, and during the reign of succeeding sovereigns, the borough held a prominent place in the annals of the country. History records that the first charter granted to the town, empowering the burgesses to hold a "Guild Merchant, with Hanse and other customs belonging to such Guild," was granted in the reign of Henry the First; and that another charter was granted in the reign of Henry the Second, which conferred upon the inhabitants "similar privileges, liberties, and free customs as were then enjoyed by the burgesses of Newcastle-on-Tyne." This last named-charter seems to have been confirmed by King John, who further accorded the privileges of "the whole toll of the wapentake hundred of Amounderness and a free fair at Preston, at the Assumption of St. Mary, to last for eight days." The charter also grants "the right of pasturage in the forest which is called Fille Wode, and out of the forest itself so much wood as they shall want towards building their town." Ancient records state that in the fourth year of the reign of King John, letters patent of presentation to the church of Preston, directed to the archidiaconal officials of Richmond, were delivered to Master Peter Russiniol, and that on the death of this ecclesiastic, Henry the Third presented the living to Henry, nephew to the Bishop of Winchester. The rights of pasturage on Fulwood Moor, which had been granted to the burgesses by the charter of King John, were confirmed by Henry the Third; and a further charter, granted in the thirty-seventh year of Henry's reign, confirmed to the burgesses the right, in future, to the lands alluded to, consisting of three hundred and twenty-four acres, and which were afterwards called Preston Moor. This last-named grant was the result of a complaint on behalf of the crown, to the effect that the inhabitants of Preston had trenched upon crown lands and privileges in the forest and enclosure of Fulwood. Some curiously quaint and interesting documents relating to the ecclesiastical affairs of the parish were issued during Henry the Third's time. In the seventh year of his reign the King made an order, " commanding Roger Gernet to permit the vassals of the nephew of the Bishop of Winchester, parson of the church of Preston, to have reasonable estoves in the hay of Preston, to repair their houses and enclosures, and to have the other necessaries which the demesne vassels of the crown were accustomed to have in the time of King John during the wars between him and his barons."

HENRY THE EIGHTH TÓ THE DISSOLUTION
OF THE MONASTERIES.

Down to the present day Preston retains its character —one of the foremost before the Reformation—as one of the chief Roman Catholic centres in the country, although within the last one or two decades it has been ascertained that the Roman Catholic population is not, relatively, so numerous as it was in the earlier portion of the present century. Nevertheless, some of the oldest and most distinguished Roman Catholic families in England remain specially identified with Preston and its immediate surroundings. In the early ages there were two monasteries in Preston. One of these, called the Franciscan Convent of Grey Friars, was founded in 1221, by Edmund, Earl of Lancaster, son of Henry the Third. It was situated on the west side of Friargate, and is thus described by Leland:—"The Grey Frere's College in the north-west side of the Towne of Preston, in Amundreness, was sett in the soile of a gentleman caulid Prestun, and a Brother or Sunne of his confirmed the first graunt of the site of the House, and one of these two was after a great man of possessions, and Viscount of Gurmaston, as I hard say in Ireland. Diverse of the Prestuns were buried yn this House. But the original and great builder of this House was Edmund, erle of Lancastre, sunne to Henry the thyrde." Several members of the Sherburne and Dalton families, well known in Preston, are said to have been buried in the grounds of the monastery. During successive ages this religious retreat has undergone many mutations, but the historical interest attaching to its site remains unfaded. On the dissolution of the monasteries in the reign of Henry the Eighth, the site was granted to Thomas Holcroft, and Baines, in his History of Lancashire, states that it became, in the first instance, the residence of the Breres, of Hammerton, in Bowland, of which Oliver Breres, recorder, and one of the Council named in the charter of Elizabeth, was a member. It was subsequently converted into a house of correction, to which use it continued to be applied until the existing prison at the bottom of Church Street was erected, in the year 1790. When it ceased to be a gaol it was converted into cottages, and at the present time the whole of the site is covered by the large establishment known as Stevenson's foundry. If the spirits of the monastic dead, who in bye-gone ages worshipped at this sacred shrine, could now revisit our terrestrial scene, might they not exclaim with Shakespeare's Danish Prince—

" To what base uses we may return, Horatio !"

Whittle, in his History of Preston, states that " in 1823 the remains of a number of coffins and human bones were thrown up on digging near the old Friargate ; and also a large stone, octagon in shape, which must have been the base of a column belonging to the convent." St. Mary Magdalen was the name of the other monastic establishment existing in Preston. This Institution appears to have been founded towards the end of the thirteenth century, the site being on the Maudlands. Baines, in his History of Lancashire, states that it was used as a temporary residence for the Cistercian Monks, while their magnificent abbey in Furness was building. Five skeletons and numerous detached human bones were discovered by workmen in 1836, when excavations were being made for the foundation of new streets on the Maudland estate. Also when excavations were in progress for the foundations of St. Walburge's Roman Catholic Church—one of the noblest specimens of ecclesiastical architecture which the town possesses—said to occupy the precise site on which the ancient Monastery formerly stood, a stone coffin and several skeletons were met with. St. Mary Magdalene's was an eleemosynary as well as a religious institution.

THE SCOTTISH INVASION.

Preston will ever be remembered in history as being
the arena where some of the most deadly struggles took
place during the Scottish invasion in the reigns of the
Edwards. In the year 1306, Edward the First, on his
visit to Scotland, during the progress of the war, passed
through Preston, where he halted and remained for some
hours. During his stay in the town, he issued a proclamation, dated the 2nd of July, 1306, appointing the
Archbishop of York, and the Bishop of Coventry and
Lichfield, his wardens, during his absence in Scotland.
Edward the Third likewise paid a visit to Scotland during
the prosecution of the war, and like his predecessor, the
first Edward, he also halted at Preston, where he materially added to the strength of his army. Hollinshed, in
his records of the Scottish wars of the period, states that
in the year 1323, about the time when the Scots were
engaged in their incursions into the northern counties
from Scotland, with Robert Bruce at the head of the
Scotch armies, " Bruce entered into England by Carlisle
kept on his way through Cumberland, Westmoreland, and
Lancaster, which town he burnt, as he had done others
in the counties he had passed through, and after three
weeks and three days, he returned into Scotland without
engaging." One of the most sanguinary of the engagements which took place in the neighbourhood of Preston
during the prolonged continuance of the struggle, was
that which was fought on the banks of the Ribble, in
Edward the Second's reign. In this encounter, one Adam
de Banistre espoused the cause of the King, and his full
prerogative. He was opposed by the Earl of Lancaster on
the part of the Barons. Banistre was at the head of an
army containing about eight hundred men; and against him
were about six hundred of the Earl's knights and vassals
In the early part of the engagement, Banistre's forces
overpowered those of his opponent, who were numerically
less than Banistre's, but on the Earl's army being rein-
forced, his opponent was defeated with great slaughter

Banistre and the remnant of his followers made a precipitate retreat, Banistre for some time succeeding in concealing himself, but being eventually discovered by the Earl's troops, he again made a desperate resistance on being called upon to surrender, killing several of his assailants, and wounding others. He at length fell in the engagement, and his head was sent as a trophy to the Earl of Lancaster. The record of the engagement adds that the Earl's followers, after the battle, entered the hundred of Leyland on the south of the Ribble, and levied contributions upon the inhabitants to a large amount, besides committing many disgraceful excesses.

THE FIRST PARLIAMENTARY ELECTION.
SEAT OF LAW FOR THE COUNTY.

Apart from the stirring events incident to the Scottish invasion, with which Preston was conspicuously identified, the town had several privileges conferred upon it during the Edwardian period, which are not without historical interest. In the reign of Edward the Second, letters patent were granted for the "paviage of the town of Preston," with powers to collect tolls, whilst a rate on merchandise was granted for a similiar purpose by the "good Duke of Lancaster," as he was called. In the twenty-third year of Edward the First's reign, the first parliamentary election for Preston took place, when the members elected were William Fitz Paul and Adam Russell. This was in the year 1295, so that Preston has returned members to parliament for a period of nearly six hundred years, the parliamentary enfranchisement of the borough taking effect a little more than two hundred years after the Norman Conquest. This was the first election as appears by the local records, but there are some historians who incline to the belief that the borough sent representatives to parliament at a period anterior to the above date. In the reign of Edward the Third, in the year 1323, the tithes of "Fulwood, Merescough, and Hyde

Park," were restored to the vicars of Preston and Lancaster; and in 1362, being the thirty-fifth year of the same
King's reign, we read that the "church and lordship of
Preston were held in *capite* by John of Gaunt, Duke of
Lancaster;" and it is further recorded that "the high
altar, with its appurtenances, was computed to be worth
five hundred marks at that time." Edward the Third
created Henry, Earl of Lancaster, Duke of Lancaster, in
return for the services he had rendered to the King when
in the French wars. In the same reign, the county of
Lancaster was made a palatinate, under John of Gaunt, who
married the daughter of Henry, and succeeded to the Duke-
dom. On that occasion, as will be seen from what follows
Preston would have been made the county town had not the
circumstance recorded below interposed to prevent it
John of Gaunt being the fourth son of Edward the Third
the powers conferred under the palatinate provided that
"Law was to be administered by the officers and ministers
of the Duke, and under his seal, and anciently all offences
were said to be against his peace, his sword, and dignity,'
and not, as at present, against "the Queen, her crown
and dignity." Speaking of Preston in connection with
this subject of the palatinate, Mr. Baines says that the
house of Lancaster held Preston "in high estimation
and nothing but the local situation of their baronia
castle on the banks of the Lune, prevented them from
establishing the capital of the county where it ought to
have been fixed—on the banks of the Ribble." Practically
the entire business of the county is conducted at Preston
All the offices of law in connection with the palatinate
are still at Preston. The meetings of the county magis
trates are also held at Preston, which is likewise the head
quarters of the county constabulary force, and recently an
extensive block of new county buildings have been erected
in the town for the transaction of the general business of
the palatinate.*

---

* See description of building under head of "Public Buildings."

PRESTON THE RICHEST "ROYAL BOROUGH" IN THE COUNTY.

In 1343, Preston appears to have been the richest "royal borough" in the county. In that year, Edward the Third imposed a tax on merchandise and moveable property. The document imposing the tax states that the "ninth part of the goods of the men dwelling in the borough of Preston," was six pounds, seventeen shillings, and four pence, [equal, however, to about one hundred pounds of coinage of the present day.] That the total value of the moveable goods of the inhabitants of the "wealthiest borough in Lancashire," in the fourteenth century should have been the modest sum of nine hundred pounds is a study for the antiquarian enquirer. The ninth part for Wigan was five pounds, nine shillings, and fourpence; for Lancaster, six pounds, thirteen shillings, and sixpence; and for Liverpool, six pounds, sixteen shillings, and seven-pence. These were the only "royal boroughs" in Lanca-shire. The record adds, as showing the comparative insignificance of the "capital of the cotton manufacture," that Manchester at that period did not possess sufficient trade to render it liable to the tax on merchandise and moveable property. About this time the streets of Preston appear to have been the scene of an unusually degrading exhibition, when the subordinate of a church dignitary was the innocent victim. In his History of Cheshire, Ormerod records that Sir William de Clifton, exasperated at the Abbot of Vale Royal, Cheshire, in consequence of some dispute respecting the church at Preston, avenged himself by flogging the secretary of the obnoxious ecclesiastic through the streets of the town. According to Dr. Kuerdon, the first Guild was held in the reign of Edward the Third, namely, in the year 1329, two years after Edward came to the throne.

THE MANOR OF WALTON-LE-D, LE AND
THE HOGHTON FAMILY.

From the close of the reign of Edward the Third, in

1377, to the accession of Elizabeth, in 1558, a period approaching two hundred years, no events in which Preston was specially concerned or interested took place, although the celebrated and prolonged "Wars of the Roses" had been fought, and the Reformation brought about and completed within the interval.   During Elizabeth's reign, when, in 1588, the country was threatened with the invasion of the Spanish Armada, the lieutenants of the various counties received orders from the Queen to levy men for the defence of the country. On that occasion, the gentry, magistrates, and freeholders of the county of Lancaster, were summoned "at their utmost peril, to meet Lord Strange, at Preston, on the 13th of July, 1588."   In this Queen's reign, Camden, the historian, describes Preston as "a large, and for these parts, handsome and populous town, so called from religious persons, as much as to say Priests' Town.   Preston is vulgarly called Preston in Andernesse, for Acmundessenesse, for so the Saxons called this part of the country, which runs out with a long compass between *Ribill* and *Cocar*, and forms a promontary resembling a nose, and afterwᵃrds called Agmonderness."   The manor of Walton-le-Dale came into the possession of the ancestors of the present Sir Charles de Hoghton, during the reign of Elizabeth, in consequence of a family quarrel, which terminated fatally.   Mr. Hardwick narrates the circumstances as follow:—" A feud," he states, "had existed for some years between the families of Mr. Hoghton, of Lea, in the parish of Preston, and Langton, Baron of Walton and Newton, in Makerfield.   The latter, desirous of avenging some past indignity, made cause with a widow Singleton, whose cattle had been impounded by his rival.   The baron assembled about eighty of his tenants and retainers, marched them to the residence of Mr. Hoghton, and challenged that gentlemen and his friends to combat.   Finding his house surrounded by his enemies, Mr. Hoghton sallied forth at the head of about thirty followers.   A regular battle ensued, in which Mr. Hoghton and his retainer Richard Baldwin, lost their lives.   A magisterial investigation of the affair took place at Preston, when the parties were committed for trial, at the following assizes, for wilful murder. Through the influence of the Earl of Derby, who solicited the interest of the high treasurer, Burleigh, a petition from forty-seven of the belligerants, soliciting the Queen's pardon, was favourably received. Another petition from the widow of the deceased Mr. Hoghton, concurring in its prayer, was likewïse forwarded. Through this joint effort, a pardon was obtained for the combative baron. In order to effect this compromise, however, Langton entered into an engagement, by which he transferred to the heir of his late rival, as some compensation for the loss of his parent, the valuable manor and estate of Walton-le-Dale."

THE FIRST OF THE LANCASHIRE BARONETS.

THE LANCASHIRE WITCHES.

JAMES THE FIRST AT PRESTON.

The heads of several families residing in Lancashire, and in the neighbourhood of Preston, were included amongst the first of the baronets, when that hereditary honour and title was first instituted by James the First, in the year 1616. Amongst them were the following knights, namely, Sir Richard Hoghton, of Hoghton Tower ; Sir Thomas Gerard, of Bryn ; and Sir Richard Molyneux, of Sefton. The term "Lancashire Witches" has long been identified with the popular proverb which recognises the fair sex of the county as possessing exceptionally personal attractions, but the probability is that the sex themselves would repudiate any sort of connexion with the "Lancashire Witches" of King James's time. In his day the belief in demonology and witchcraft attained to dimensions of the most superstitious and dangerous character, and Lancashire, in common with many other counties, was the scene of the witches' devices and incantations. In the year 1612, no less than nineteen of the Lancashire Witches were tried at the Lancaster

Assizes.   Seven of them were the "Witches of Samlesbury," near Preston, and the other twelve, the "Witches
of Pendle Forest," near Whalley.   On the trial, the
Samlesbury Witches were acquitted in consequence of
the evidence against them not being conclusive, but ten
of the witches of Pendle Forest were convicted and
hanged, King James declaring that "those detestible
slaves of the Duiel, the witches or enchanters" were
unworthy of the royal clemency.   In the year 1617, on
his return from Scotland, James, halted at Preston, and
remained several days in the neighbourhood, during which
time he paid visits to many gentlemen of the county,
including William, Earl of Derby, then residing at
Lathom House; Sir Thomas Gerard, of Ashton Hall;
Edward Tildesley, Esq., of Myerscough; and Sir Richard
Hoghton, Bart., of Hoghton Tower, where he made a
prolonged stay of several days.   The visit took place in
the month of August, the King, on the 15th of that
month, being entertained by the Mayor and Corporation
of Preston, at a banquet at the Town Hall.   The royal
visit to Hoghton Tower was kept up with considerable
pomp, very large numbers of the nobility and gentry,
accompanying the King as his suite, which also included
three judges of the Court of King's Bench.   The guests
invited to meet His Majesty, likewise included, amongst
others, Sir Edward Mosley, M.P., for Preston, in the
years 1614, 1620, and 1623; Sir Edmund Trafford, High
Sheriff of the county; Richard Towneley, of Towneley;
Ralph Assheton, of Whalley; Nicholas Girlington, of
Thurnham Castle; Richard Sherburne, of Stonyhurst;
Richard Shuttleworth, of Gawthorpe; William Anderton,
of Anderton, "Mayor of the Ceremonies" at Preston; in
addition to about one hundred other gentlemen of Lancashire.   It is a generally accepted tradition that during
this visit to Hoghton Tower the King knighted the loin
of beef, at one of the banquets at Sir Richard Hoghton's
table, and that it has ever since been called the Sirloin.

CHARLES THE FIRST AND THE CIVIL WAR.

During the long and memorable Civil Wars caused by the disputes between the King and the Parliament, in the reign of Charles the First, Preston was on several occasions the battle field between the contending parties, the town at one time being held on behalf of the King, and at another time for the Parliament. Amongst the members of the "long parliament," which was elected, during the continuance of the war. in 1640, Richard Shuttleworth Esq., and Thomas Standish Esq., were the representatives for Preston. They had both been elected only a few months previously, as members of the future parliament, which the King dissolved, after it had sat three weeks, in consequence of its refusal to levy additional taxes for the purpose of supplying the King's pecuniary wants. The last elected parliament, however, appeared at first to be no more submissive to the King than that which had preceded it, and one of its first acts was to order the Chancellor of the Duchy of Lancaster to remove several gentlemen from their position as commissioners of peace within the county, on account of their supposed attachment to the cause of the King and the royal prerogative, and to appoint others in their places. Amongst those removed were Sir Gilbert Hoghton, of Hoghton Tower; Alexander Rigby, of Preston, M.P., for Wigan; William Farington. of Leyland; Orlando Bridgman, M.P., for Wigan; and several others. Those who replaced the dismissed commissioners included Richard Shuttleworth and Thomas Standish, the two members for Preston; Sir Thomas Stanley, Bart., and other Lancashire gentlemen, whose sympathies were known to be with the parliament. When the breach between the King and the parliament became so wide as to preclude any chance of reconciliation, the King left for York, where he issued his "commission of array." Simultaneously with this step on the part of Charles, Lord Strange, by his majesty's authority, called upon the men of Lancashire to arm in the cause of their King; and Sir John Girlington then high Sheriff, in obedience to the King's command, called a meeting at Preston, "for the purpose of promulgating a petition from Lancashire, and the King's answer together with his declarations." At this meeting, which was held on Preston Moor, there were present Lord Strange, Lord Molyneux, Mr. William Farington, of Leyland; Mr. Tildesley, of Myrescough; and several other gentlemen of the county, adherents of the royal cause; Mr. Richard Shuttleworth, one of the members for Preston; and Mr. Rigby, member for Wigan; and several other supporters of the parliament, were likewise in attendance. The entire number of persons present were estimated at about five thousand. It is recorded that Mr. Rigby, in a letter to the Speaker of the House of Commons, under date June 24, 1642, narrating what took place at the meeting, and the significant demonstration which characterised it, stated that "when Sir John Girlington, the high sheriff, exhibited the commission of array, and exclaimed 'for the King!' 'for the King!' about four hundred joined in the cry, and the remainder 'prayed for the King *and the parliament.*'" It is added that Mr. Rigby, and his colleagues "advised them not to suffer themselves to be drawn into armes without directions from parliament, and so dismissed the assembly." The following quaint comments on the meeting by Mr. Rigby, will be read with a special interest as affecting the critical position in which Preston was at the moment placed, as respects its safety :—

"Sir George Middleton, and Master Thomas Tildesley, of Mierscough, and Master Thomas Prestwiche, whose wives are Popish recusants, and Master William Farington, a Justice of Peace, were in our judgments, the most busie and active, and they assisted, countenanced, and abetted the Sheriffe in all the aforesaid passages, and therein pressed and urged him forward, who of himself was thereunto sufficiently inclined; and while these things were in acting upon the moor, Will Sumpner, servant to Master William Farington, who during his late Deputy Lieutenancy, had placed in a private house in Preston, about 13 barrels of gunpowder and some quantity of match, did secretly convey about 6 barrels thereof in Packcloaths upon Packhorses, and the next morning about six of the clocke, and before we had notice in whose house that Powder

and Match was lodged, the Sheriffe did convey away out of the
Towne and Liberties of Preston the residue of the said Powder and
Match, which being made knowne to me, I forthwith repayred to
the Sheriffe, and shewed him the order of the Lords and Commóns,
made the 10th of May last, for disposing of the Magazines, and
also a deputation from the Lord Wharton, authorising his Deputy
Lieutenants, or any 2 or more of them, to dispose of the Magazines
of Lancashire, and then desired him to cause that powder to be
returned to Preston, but he answered that he would not returne it,
but would keepe it and defend it with the power of the county,
and the Sheriffe and Sir George Middleton then said that that
order should not be obeyed, and I thought it not meet for so small
a quantity of Powder and Match, though indeed a very considerable quantity for the time and place, to endeavour a returne thereof by force, so that it now remaineth unknowne to me where they
(who took it) have disposed it ; in the last place I make bold to
present my opinion that the Malignant party could not, by any
passage at the assembling on Preston Moor, distinguish that the
affections of any considerable part thereof enclined unto them, and
I verily believe that we lost not, but gained by that day's work,
for the safety and peace of the King and Kingdome."

The first actual outbreak of the war between the King's
troops and the parliamentary forces, is popularly believed to
have been at Manchester, in July 1642, although there is
a conflict of testimony on this point. However that may
be Preston was, in a very few months afterwards, fixed
upon as a scene of the struggle, which had now extended
to several parts of the country, for on the 10th of
December, the royalists of the county met at Preston "for
the purpose of recruiting the King's forces, and raising the
supplies for their support." At this meeting it was
resolved that four hundred horse and two thousand foot
soldiers should be raised, and the sum of £8700 levied on
the county. The war was now being prosecuted in
different parts of Lancashire, and at the close of the year
the royalists held the towns of Preston, Lancaster, Wigan,
Liverpool, and Warrington, whilst the parliamentary
forces had possession of Manchester, Bolton, Rochdale, and
Blackburn. The first, and one of the most deadly battles
fought at Preston during the war was at the beginning of
the year 1643, when the town was beseiged by the parliamentary forces, at the head of which was Major General
Sir John Seaton, who was sent to Preston by Sir Thomas

Fairfax, the parliamentary general, whose head quarters
were at Manchester. It was on the 10th of February
that the attack was made on the town, which was then
fortified with both inner and outer walls of brick. The
parliamentary attacking forces consisted of "about nine
hundred or a thousand Firemen, horse and foot, and about
six hundred Billmen, Halbudiers, and Clubmen." The
town was resolutely defended by a strong garrison of the
royalists, but after an engagement of two hours the royalists were completly defeated, and the parliamentary troops
held possession of the town. Captain Booth, on this
occasion, was one of the most distinguished officers of the
parliamentary forces. Heading the men under his command, he resolutely dashed forward, and scaling the outer
wall, called out to his troops "Follow me, or give me up
for ever!" The outer wall having been carried, the inner
defences were now attempted to be maintained and held
by the garrison within, and a close and desperate encounter between the contending forces took place, the royalists
maintaining their ground with "push of pike" and sword
in hand. Whilst this part of the siege was going forward
Major General Sir John Seaton was storming the defences
on the eastern side of the town, which he eventually
entered at Church street, and the royalists having now
been dislodged from every point of defence, including the
tower of the Parish Church, the capture of the town was
complete, after terrible slaughter, in which several distinguished leaders of both sides fell. Included in the killed
was Adam Morte, the Mayor of the borough, who was
mortally wounded whilst assisting in defending the garrison against the attack of the division of the parliamentary
troops, under the command of Colonel Holland. The
Mayor's son also fell during the engagement, whilst fighting by his father's side. The Mayor was amongst the
most resolute and determined in resisting the attacks of
the besiegers, and declared during the engagement, that
"he would fire the town, rather than surrender it into
the hands of rebels." Captain Hoghton, brother to
Sir Gilbert Hoghton, Sergeant-Major Parvey, and Doc-

tor Thomas Westby, were amongst the royalists who
fell. A large r˙ ˙nber of prisoners were taken, many of
them belonging to families of distinction connected with
Preston. They included Mr. Anderton, of Clayton, the
commander of the garrison; Captains Farington and
Preston; the son of Sir John Talbot; Mr. Blundell of
Crosby; Mr. Richard Fleetwood, Mr. Thomas Hoghton,
and Captain Hoghton, nephews to Sir Gilbert Hoghton;
Mr. R. Laughton, Mr. John Waltham, Mr. William Selby,
Mr. Abbot, and Mr. Mansley. Lady Hoghton, and Lady
Girlington, wife of the high Sheriff, were also amongst the
prisoners. Sir Gilbert Hoghton, and Mr. Towneley, of
Towneley, both effected their escape. The historians of the
time record that the capture of Preston was regarded by the
parliamentary party as of great importance, as its possession
by the puritans interrupted the communications between
the royalists of Carlisle and Newcastle, with their friends
in the south parts of Lancashire and the western counties.
The capture of Preston was followed up, a few days afterwards, by the besieging of Hoghton Tower, the residence
of Sir Gilbert Hoghton. This was easily effected, as the
occupiers of the mansion quickly "surrendered at discretion," but it was a disastrous surrender for the captors.
They had not been long in possession of the Tower, and
the ordnance, ammunition, and arms which it contained,
when the building suddenly blew up, by which about
sixty of the parliamentary troops were killed and wounded,
Captain Starkie, who had been sent by Sir John Seaton,
to besiege the Tower, being amongst those who were
killed. It was asserted by the puritans that the defeated
occupants of the Tower had secretly laid a train to destroy
the building, but this was denied on the part of the royalists, and the generally accepted belief at the period was
that whilst in possession of the place the parliamentary
troops were drinking and smoking, and that a spark or
lighted match had accidentally fallen amongst powder.
The parliamentary forces held Preston for a few weeks only
after the siege, having in turn been dislodged by the
royalists, under the Earl of Derby, (until recently Lord

Strange,) on the 21st of March. The occupation of the town by the King's troops was brought about by events which had just taken place at Lancaster. The Earl of Derby had marched his forces by way of Kirkham to Lancaster, where he burnt ninety houses, and about as many barns and out-buildings. Hearing of this, a body of the parliamentary forces were dispatched from Preston to relieve Lancaster, but arrived too late to save the town, where, however, they remained. On the approach of the troops from Preston, the Earl of Derby drew off his forces from Lancaster, and knowing that Preston was then in a defenceless state, he appeared before the town on the 21st of March, and summoned the garrison to surrender it to the King's troops. This request was refused by the Mayor, Edmund Werden, Esq , on which the Earl gave orders for the immediate storming of the defences. The leaders of the assaults, which were made at three distinct points, were Captain Edward Rosthorne, Captain Radcliffe, and Captain Chisnall, and after an hour's fighting, the garrison yielded, and the royal troops once more took possession of the town. In this engagement, eighty of the parliamentary troops are said to have fallen, Captain W. Shuttleworth, and Captain Ashworth being amongst the killed. Between three and four hundred prisoners were taken. A royalist version of the siege states that "after the said towne was taken, his Lordship had especial care to preserve the place, and only gave command that the houses of those who had betrayed the towne before should be responsall to his Majestie for their masters' treason, whose goods his Lordship ordered to be seized, and equally divided among the soldiers. The next morning being March 22nd, the whole country came in with apparent joy, and made signal proof of their good affections to his Majestie, flinging up their hats and shout- ing out, "God bless the King and the Earl of Derby !' It is added that the Earl of Derby secured the parliamen- tary magazine at Preston, but that fearing the probability of the place being again transferred by the vicissitude of war to the parliamentary forces, he destroyed the defence:

and military works, and after compelling Blackburn to surrender, he left for Manchester. The adherents of the King, in Lancashire more especially, during the war were constantly identified with popery, by the parliamentary and puritan party, as is shown by one of the war tracts which were repeatedly issued by the puritans. One of these publications circulated immediately after the re-occupation of Preston by the royalists, says "the Earl of Derby, the Lord Molineux, Sir Gilbert Hoghton, Colonell Tildesley, with all the other great Papists in this county, issued out of Preston, and on Wednesday now came to Ribchester with eleven troops of horse, 700 foot, and an infinite number of club men, in all conceived to be 5,000." The royalists were defeated during the Whalley and Ribchester expedition, on which the Earl of Derby and his troops made a retreat in the direction of Lathom, and subsequently again fell back upon Preston ; "whither also," we are told, " the Manchester forces, giving neither themselves nor their enemies any rest, followed them close, still driving the Earl thence also, and made him fly either to Hornby Castle or else to the Queen into the north, his forces being driven at least eight miles from Preston." The next occasion on which Preston figured in the conflict was in the month of August, 1644, when an engagement between the parliamentary forces and a body of royalists took place near the Ribble Bridge at Walton, when the royalists were defeated. The war continued in various parts of the country, and notably in Lancashire, until the summer of 1646, when the royalists having been defeated at various points, the King surrendered himself. This was followed by parliament resolving to compound with "delinquents, papists, and spies" for their sequestered estates in order to raise the required funds to meet the expenses of such a costly and prolonged war. In accordance with this legislative decision, a Lancashire committee of sequestration amongst others was appointed, and the sittings of this committee were, as a rule, held at Preston. Amongst those who compounded for their estates were several royalist families in and around Preston, whose descendants remain at the present time connected with the locality. It is an ancient adage—although of questionable morality—that "all is fair in war," but many will be of opinion that in this instance the action of parliament was exceptionally unjust, and morally degrading to the legislative assembly, eminently disreputable, indeed, when we read that the estates of Roman Catholics were subjected to these sequestrations whether they were adherents of the King's cause or the opposite. Nothing could more painfully illustrate the religious bitterness, not to say fanatical zeal and prejudice, which characterised the period. Although on the surrender, and subsequent imprisonment of the King, the prolonged conflict appeared to have arrived at its close, there were those amongst the English and Scotch royalists who were bent upon making another effort to regain the supremacy of the royal cause, and an organisation to effect this object having been formed with Lancashire as one centre of its operations, the parliament appointed a special committee of Lancashire to be formed for the defence of the county, and this committee ordered levies to be made for that purpose, at meetings which were held at Preston, Bolton, and other places. The renewed struggle between the royalists and the parliamentary party commenced in 1648, and Lancashire amongst other counties, was the scene of the contests which followed upon it. On the 17th of August an engagement took place on Ribbleton Moor between a body of English and Scotch royalists, under the command of Sir Marmaduke Langdale, and some puritan parliamentary troops, headed by Cromwell, when the latter defeated the royalists. At that time a large body of royalist forces, under the supreme command of the Duke of Hamilton, were quartered in Preston, and also in the neighbourhood of Walton, on the banks of the river Darwen, and after the encounter on Ribbleton Moor, the battle was continued in the streets of Preston, when the royalists were again overpowered, and compelled to make a hasty retreat in the direction of the Ribble bridge at Walton. The conflict was for the second time renewed, the royalist forces having been increased by large detachments from their main body stationed in the neighbourhood of Walton and the river Darwen. This engagement was attended with great loss of life on both sides, but was more especially disastrous to the royalists, who were completely routed. The historical details of this engagement state that at the end of the lane leading from Preston to the bridge at Walton, which was at that period "very narrow and deep," Cromwell narrowly escaped death from the huge stones which the royalists hurled at him and his troops from the higher ground. On the evening of the battle, Cromwell dispatched the following letter to the "Committee of Lancashire" then sitting at Manchester :—

'*For the Honourable Committee of Lancashire sitting at Manchester. (I desire the Commander of the Forces there to open this Letter if it come not to their hands.)*"

"'Preston,' 17th August, 1648.

'Gentlemen,—It hath pleased God, this day, to shew His great power by making the Army successful against the common enemy.

"We lay last night at Mr Sherburn's, of Stonyhurst, nine miles from Preston, which was within three miles of the Scots quarters. We advanced betimes next morning towards Preston, with a desire to engage the Enemy ; and by that time our Forlorn had engaged the enemy, we were about four miles from Preston, and thereupon we advanced with the whole army ; and the Enemy being drawn out on a Moor betwixt us and the Town, the Armies on both sides engaged ; and *after a very sharp dispute, continuing for three or four hours, it pleased God to enable us to give them a defeat ; which I hope we shall improve, by God's assistance, to their utter ruin ;* and in this service your countrymen have not the least share.

"We cannot be particular, having not time to take account of the slain and prisoners ; but we can assure you we have many prisoners, and many of those of quality ; and many slain ; and the Army so dissipated 'as I say.' The principal part whereof, with Duke Hamilton, is on south side Ribble and Darwen Bridge, and we lying with the greatest part of the Army close to them ; nothing hindering the ruin of that part of the Enemy's Army but the night. It shall be our care that they shall not pass over any ford beneath the Bridge, to go Northward, or to come betwixt us and Whalley.

'We understand Colonel-General Ashton's are at Whalley ; we have seven troops of horse or dragoons that we believe lie at Clitheroe. This night I have sent order to them expressly to march to

Whalley, to join to those companies ; that so we may endeavour the ruin of this Enemy.   You perceive by this letter how things stand. By this means the Enemy is broken : and most of their Horse having gone Northwards, and we having sent a considerable party at the very heel of them : and the Enemy having lost almost all his ammunition, and near four-thousand arms, so that the greatest part of the Foot are naked ;—therefore, in order to perfecting this work, we desire you to raise your County ; and to improve your forces to the total ruin of that Enemy, which way soever they go ; and if you shall accordingly do your part, doubt not of their total ruin.

" We thought fit to speed this to you ; to the end you may not be troubled if they shall march towards you, but improve your interest as aforesaid, *that you may give glory to God for this unspeakable mercy.*   This is all at present from,

" Your very humble servant,

OLIVER CROMWELL."

In another dispatch to the Speaker of the House of Commons a few days afterwards, Cromwell details the subsequent successes of his forces in Wigan and Warrington, in the early part of his dispatch, describing the Preston engagement in the following terms :—

" *To the Honourable William Lenthall, Esquire, Speaker of the House of Commons :*

" *These*—

" ' Warrington,' 20th August, 1648.

" Sir,—*I have sent up this Gentlemen to give you an account of the great and good hand of God towards you,* in the late victory obtained against the Enemy in these parts.

" After the conjunction of that party which I brought with me out of Wales with the Northern Forces about Knaresborough and Wetherby,—bearing that the Enemy was advanced with their Army into Lancashire, we marched the next day, being the 13th of this instant August, to Otley (having cast off our Train, and sent it to Knaresborough, because of the difficulty of marching therewith through Craven, and to the end we might with more expedition attend the Enemys' motion) : and on the 14th to Skipton ; the 15th to Gisborne ; the 16th to Hodder Bridge over Ribble ; where we held a council of war.   At which we had in consideration, Whether we should march to Whalley that night, and so on, to interpose between the Enemy and his further progress into Lancashire and so southward,—which we had some advertisement the Enemy intended, and ' we are ' since confirmed that they intended for London itself: Or whether to march immediately over the said Bridge, there being no other betwixt that and Preston, and there engage the Enemy,—who we did believe would stand his ground, because we had information that the Irish Forces under Monro lately come out of Ireland, which consisted of Twelve-hundred horse and Fifteen-hundred foot, were on their march towards Lancashi.e to join them.

'It was thought that to engage the Enemy to fight was our business ; and the reason aforesaid giving us hopes that our marching on the North side of Ribble would effect it, it was resolved we should march over the Bridge ; which accordingly we did ; and that night quartered the whole Army in the field by Stonyhurst Hall, being Mr. Sherburn's house, a place nine miles distant from Preston. Very early the next morning we marched towards Preston ; having intelligence that the Enemy was drawing together thereabouts from all his out-quarters, we drew out a Forlorn of about two-hundred horse and four-hundred foot, the horse commanded by Major Smithson, the foot by Major Pownel. Our Forlorn of horse marched, within a mile ' to' where the Enemy was drawn up,—in the enclosed grounds by Preston, on that side next us ; and there, upon a Moor, about half a mile distant from the Enemy's Army, met with their Scouts and Outguard ; and did behave themselves with that valour and courage as made their Guards (which consisted both of horse and foot) to quit their ground ; and took divers prisoners ; holding this dispute with them until our Forlorn of foot came up for their justification ; and by these we had opportunity to bring up our whole Army.

'So soon as our foot and horse were come up, we resolved that night to engage them if we could ; and therefore, advancing with our Forlorn, and putting the rest of our Army into as good a posture as the ground would bear (which was totally inconvenient for our horse, being all enclosure and miry ground), we pressed upon them. The regiments of foot were ordered as followeth. There being a Lane, very deep and ill, on to the Enemy's Army, and leading to the Town, we commanded two regiments of horse, the first whereof was Colonel Harrison's and next was my own, to charge up that Lane ; and on either side of them advanced the ' Main '-battle,— which were Lieutenant-Colonel Reade's, Colonel Dean's and Colonel Pride's on the right; Colonel Bright's and my Lord General's on the left; and Colonel Ashton with the Lancashire regiments in reserve. We ordered Colonel Thornhaugh's and Colonel Twistleton's regiments of horse on the right; and one regiment in reserve for the Lane ; and the remaining horse on the left :—so that, at last, we came to a Hedge-dispute ; the greatest of the impression from the Enemy being upon our left wing, and upon the ' Main'-battle on both sides the Lane, and upon our horse in the Lane : in all which places the Enemy were forced from their ground, after four hours dispute ;—until we came to the Town ; into which four troops of my own regiment first entered ; and, being well seconded by Colonel Harrison's regiment, charged the Enemy in the Town, and cleared the streets.

" There came no band of your foot to fight that day but did it with in-
credible valour and resolution ; among which Colonel Bright's, my
Lord General's, Lieutenànt-Colonel Reade's and Colonel Ashton's
had the greatest work ; they often coming to push of pike and to
close firing, and always making the Enemy to recoil. And indeed
*I must needs say, God was as much seen in the valour of the
officers and soldiers of these before-mentioned as in any action
that hath been performed ;* the Enemy making, though he was still
worsted, very stiff and sturdy resistance. Colonel Dean's and
Colonel Pride's outwinging the enemy, could not come to so much
share of the action ; the Enemy shogging down towards the Bridge ;
and keeping almost all in reserve, that so he might bring fresh
hands often to fight. Which we not knowing, and lest we should
be outwinged, 'we' placed those two regiments to enlarge our
right wing ; this was the cause they had not at that time so great
a share in that action.

" At the last the Enemy was put into disorder; many men slain, many
prisoners taken : the Duke, with most of the Scots horse and foot,
retreated over the Bridge ; where,—after a very hot dispute betwixt the Lancashire regiments, part of my Lord General's, and
them, being often at push of pike,—they were beaten from the
Bridge ; and our horse and foot, following them killed many, and
took divers prisoners ; and we possessed the Bridge over Darwen
'also,' and a few houses there ; the Enemy being driven up within
musket-shot of us where we lay that night,—we not being able to
attempt farther upon the Enemy, the night preventing us. In this
posture did the Enemy and we lie most part of that night. Upon
entering the Town, many of the Enemy's horse fled towards Lancaster ; in the chase of whom went divers of our horse, who pursued them near ten miles, and had execution of them, and took
about five-hundred horse and many prisoners. We possessed in
this Fight very much of the Enemy's ammunition ; I believe they
lost four or five thousand arms. The number of slain we judge to
be about a thousand ; the prisoners we took were about four
thousand.

" In the night the Duke was drawing off his Army towards Wigan ; we
were so wearied with the dispute that we did not so well attend the
Enemy's going off as might have been ; by means whereof the
Enemy was gotten at least three miles with his rear, before ours
got to them. I ordered Colonel Thornhaugh to command two or
three regiments of horse to follow the Enemy, if it were possible
to make him stand till we could bring up the Army. The
Enemy marched away seven or eight thousand foot and about four-
thousand horse ; we followed him with about three-thousand foot
and two-thousand five-hundred horse and dragoons; and, in this
prosecution, that worthy Gentleman, Colonel Thornhaugh, pressing
too boldly, was slain, being run into the body and thigh and head
by the Enemy's lancers. And give me leave to say, he was a man
as faithful and gallant in your service as any ; and one who often

heretofore lost blood in your quarrel, and now his last. He hath left some behind him to inherit a father's honour; and a sad Widow;—both now the interest of the Commonwealth.

"Our horse still prosecuted the Enemy; killing and taking divers all the way. At last the Enemy drew up within three miles of Wigan; and by that time our Army was come up, they drew off again, and recovered Wigan before we could attempt any thing upon them. We lay that night in the field close by the Enemy; being very dirty and weary, and having marched twelve miles of such ground as I never rode in all my life, the day being very wet. We had some skirmishing, that night, with the Enemy, near the Town; where we took General Van Druske and a Colonel, and killed some principal Officers, and took about a hundred prisoners; where I also received a letter from Duke Hamilton, for civil usage towards his kinsman Colonel Hamilton, whom he left wounded there. We took also Colonel Hurry and Lieutenant-Colonel Innes, sometimes in your service. The next morning the Enemy marched towards Warrington, and we at the heels of them. The Town of Wigan, a great and poor Town, and very Malignant, were plundered almost to their skins by them.

We could not engage the Enemy until we came within three miles of Warrington; and there the Enemy made a stand, at a place near Winwick. We held them in some dispute till our Army came up; they maintaining the Pass with great resolution for many hours: ours and theirs coming to push of pike and very close charges,—which forced us to give ground; *but our men, by the blessing of God, quickly recovered it, and charging very home upon them, beat them from their standing; where we killed about a thousand of them, and took, as we believe, about two thousand prisoners;* and prosecuted them home to Warrington Town; where they possessed the Bridge, which had a strong barricado and a work upon it, formerly made very defensive. As soon as we came thither, I received a message from General Baillie, desiring some capitulation. To which I yielded. Considering the strength of the Pass, and that I could not go over the River 'Mersey' within ten miles of Warrington with the Army, I gave him these terms: That he should surrender himself and all his officers and soldiers prisoners of war, with all his arms and ammunition and horses, to me; I giving quarter for life, and promising civil usage. Which accordingly is done: and the Commissioners deputed by me have received, and are receiving, all the arms and ammunition; which will be as they tell me, about Four-thousand complete arms; and as many prisoners; and thus you have their Infantry totally ruined. What Colonels and Officers are with General Baillie, I have not yet received the list.

"The Duke is marching with his remaining Horse, which are about three-thousand, towards Nantwich; where the Gentlemen of the County have taken about five-hundred of them; of which they sent me word this day. The country will scarce suffer any of my

men to pass, except they have my hand-' writing;' telling them,
They are Scots. They bring in and kill divers of them, as they
light upon them. Most of the Nobility of Scotland are with the
Duke. If I had a thousand horse that could but trot thirty miles,
I should not doubt but to give a very good account of them : but
truly we are so harrassed and haggled out in this business, that we
are not able to do more than walk ' at ' an easy pace after them.—
I have sent post to my Lord Grey, to Sir Henry Cholmely and Sir
Edward Rhodes to gather all together, with speed, for their prosecution ; as likewise to acquaint the Governor of Stafford therewith.

" I hear Monro is about Cumberland with the horse that ran away, and
his ' own ' Irish horse and foot, which are a considerable body. I
have left Colonel Ashton's three regiments of foot, with seven
troops of horse (six of Lancashire and one of Cumberland), at
Preston ; and ordered Colonel Scroop with five troops of horse and
two troops of dragoons, ' and ' with two regiments of foot (Colonel
Lascelles's and Colonel Wastell's), to embody with them ; *and
have ordered them to put their prisoners to the sword if the Scots
shall presume to advance upon them,* because they cannot bring
them off with security.

" *Thus you have a Narrative of the particulars of the success which
God hath given you :* which I could hardly at this time have done,
considering the multiplicity of business ; but truly, when I was
once engaged in it, *I could hardly tell how to say less, there being
so much of God in it*; and I am not willing to say more, lest there
should seem to be any of man. Only give me leave to add one
word, shewing the disparity of forces on both sides ; that so you
may see, and all the world acknowledge *the great hand of God in
this business.* The Scots Army could not be less than twelve-
thousand effective foot, well-armed, and five-thousand horse ;
Langdale not less than two-thousand five-hundred foot, and fifteen-
hundred horse : in all Twenty-one Thousand ;—and truly very few
of their foot but were as well armed if not better than yours, and
at divers disputes did fight two or three hours before they would
quit their ground. Yours were about two-thousand five-hundred
horse and dragoons of your old Army ; about four-thousand foot of
your old Army ; also about sixteen-hundred Lancashire foot, and
about five-hundred Lancashire horse : in all about Eight-thousand
Six-hundred. *You see by computation about two-thousand of
the Enemy slain ?* betwixt *eight and nine-thousand prisoners ;*
besides what are lurking in hedges and private places, which the
Country daily bring in or destroy. Where Langdale and his broken
forces are, I know not ; but they are exceedingly shattered.

" *Surely Sir, this is nothing but the hand of God ; and wherever anything in this world is exalted, or exalts itself, God will pull it down ;
for this is the day wherein He alone will be exalted. It is not fit
for me to give advice, nor to say a word what use you should make
of this ;—more than to pray you, and all that acknowledge God,
That they would exalt him,—and not hate His people, who are as*

the apple of His eye, and for whom even Kings shall be reproved; and that you would take courage to do the work of the Lord, in fulfilling the end of your Magistracy, in seeking the peace and welfare of this Land,—that all that will live peaceably may have countenance from you, *and they that are incapable and will not leave troubling the Land may speedily be destroyed out of the Land. And if you take courage in this, God will bless you; and good men will stand by you; and God will have glory, and the Land will have happiness* by you in despite of all your enemies. Which shall be the prayer of,

" Your most humble and faithful servant,

"OLIVER CROMWELL."

The italics in the above remarkable documents are the author's own. Reading them between the lines there would seem to have been on the part of Cromwell, a grim desire and yearning to reconcile wholesale human slaughter with the merciful attributes of the Deity, a theory which it is scarcely possible to believe that even the puritan contemporaries of the period would endorse. Still it would perhaps be unjust to hold Cromwell only personally responsible for the revolting and barbarous sentiments and feelings which his dispatches unquestionably reveal. He must be regarded in a great measure as typical of the age in which he lived, when those with whom he was associated had been accustomed to esteem practical piety and the exercise of the christian virtues as compatible with the unlimited destruction of human life when worldly gains were to be attained thereby. It will scarcely be looked upon as an exaggeration to say that the constant invocation of the name of the Supreme, by Cromwell and his followers, and the unctuous cant which characterised their professions, have come to be regarded by successive ages as one of the most repulsive phases of these puritan times.

LOCAL RELICS OF THE CIVIL WAR.

The archives of the Corporation of Preston contain the following entry in reference to this battle:—

" Memorandum.

" Decimo Septimo die Augustie, 1648, 24 Car.

'That Henry Blundell, gent., being mayor of this town of Preston, the
daie and yeare aforesaid, Oliver Cromwell, lieutenant-general of
the forces of the parliament of England, with an army of about
10,000 at the most, (whereof 1500 were Lancashire men, under the
command of Colonel Ralph Assheton, of Middleton), fought a
battaill in and about Preston aforesaid, and overthrew Duke
Hamilton, general of the Scots, consisting of about 26,000, and of
English Sir Marmaduke Langdale and his forces joined with the
Scots, about 4,000 ; took all their ammunition, about 3,000
prisoners, killed many with very small losse to the parliament
army ; and in their pursuit towards Lancaster, Wigan, Warrington,
and divers other places in Cheshire, Staffordshire, and Nottingham-
shire, took the said Duke and Langdale, with many Scottish earls
and lords, and about 10,000 prisoners more, all being taken" (or)
"slayne, few escaping, and all their treasure and plunder taken.
This performed in lesse than one week."

At different periods within the present century numerous relics of the memorable struggle just referred to have
been discovered in the locality of the battle. Several
iron cannon-balls have from time to time been picked up
on Killingsough Farm, at Fulwood. Several bullets have
likewise been found in the immediate neighbourhood of
the site in Ribbleton, where the engagement took place,
some of them so recently as 1856. When the strawberry
garden, near Walton Bridge, was first laid out, several
coins and human remains were found. Two cannon
balls, weighing between eight and nine pounds each,
were found some years ago close to Darwen Bridge.
Bullets have likewise been found on " Walton Flats,"
together with a sword and a small dagger, which may
now be seen in the museum in Cross Street. Whittle, in
his History of Preston, records that on the 22nd of
October, 1831, "An ancient iron boot, was found at
Ingol, near Preston, by Mr. Simpson, Sedan Carrier, with
the initials engraved on it of O. C. 1648, supposed to be
the identical boot of Oliver Cromwell, or belonging to
one of the numerous body of men he commanded when at
Preston, during the civil war." Mr. Whittle also
records that " on the 11th day of April, 1812, a gentleman,

near Fulwood Moor, was making a hole in the floor of the house, when to his surprise he discovered a little below the surface, a quantity of silver coins, of various sizes. They consisted of those of Edward the Fourth, nearly defaced; Charles the First, James the First, and Elizabeth, in a fine state of preservation; also a coin of Philip the Fourth of Spain."

CROMWELL AND THE COMMONWEALTH.

Little more than four months after the great Lancashire War, Charles the First was tried and executed, namely in January, 1649, the tragical event forming a well known page in English history; and after this came the Commonwealth and the reign of Cromwell, accompanied by further intestine troubles looming in the immediate future, when Preston declared against the Lord Protector, and in favour of the Royalist cause. Notwithstanding the abolition by law of Monarchy in England; the Scotch immediately after Charles's execution, proclaimed the late King's son by the title of Charles the Second, and in July 1649, within six months afterwards, the Corporation of Preston, following the example of the Scotch, also proclaimed him at the Market Cross. In 1651 Charles the Second, with the Scottish Royalists, under the command of the new Duke of Hamilton and Lesley, and numbering fourteen thousand men, marched into England, arriving in Lancashire in August. On the evening of the 12th of that month the King stayed at Ashton Hall, near Lancaster; and on the following day he spent the night at Myerscough Lodge, near Preston. Continuing his journey southwards the King, after crossing over the Ribble Bridge at Preston, proceeded to Euxton Hall, the seat of the Anderton family; and on the 15th he was the guest of Sir William Gerard, of Bryn. On nearing the Mersey at Warrington an engagement took place between the Scottish Army, and a detachment of cavalry belonging to the Commonwealth, in which the

latter were defeated. The Earl of Derby now came upon
the scene, having along with Sir Thomas Tildesley, and
a number of officers, landed from the Isle of Man, at the
mouth of the Wyre, near Fleetwood, with about sixty
horse and two hundred and fifty foot soldiers. At Preston,
the Earl raised 600 horse, and on the evening of the 24th
of August a skirmish took place near Preston, between
the royalist and the parliamentary troops, followed on
the 25th by a great battle at Wigan Lane, between the
Earl of Derby, at the head of 1500 troops, and Colonel
Lilburne, commanding the parliamentary forces. This
was a most disastrous engagement for the royalists, who
were defeated with terrible slaughter, Major-General
Sir Thomas Tildesley, one of the Earl's chief officers,
being amongst the killed, and the Earl himself slightly
wounded. As the career of the "great Stanley," as this
James, the seventh Earl of Derby, has been called, must
ever be interesting to Preston, with which his family
have so long been identified, another version of the
memorable engagement at Wigan Lane, will not be out
of place, inasmuch as it puts a varied complexion upon
the relative strength of the contending forces. The
authority from which we quote states that when the
Earl proceeded to Preston he had only 500 troops in all,
including the 300 which he had brought over with him
from the Isle of Man. "With this weak force", says the
writer, "he advanced, on the 25th of August, to Wigan,
with the intention of taking up his quarters there. Here
however, he was unexpectedly attacked the next day by
Colonel Lilbourne, who was at the head of an overwhelming force of 3000 horse and foot, 1800 being
Dragoons, whom Cromwell had sent to hang upon the
King's rear. This was the occasion of the well-known battle
of Wigan Lane. It will easily be believed that in this
fearfully unequal conflict, the Earl and his little army
were worsted; but notwithstanding the immense odds
against him, he fought for two hours, performing
prodigies of valour, and receiving, in this sanguinary
engagement seven shots in his breastplate, thirteen cuts

in his beaver, five or six wounds on his arms and shoulders, and had two horses killed under him. It is little less than miraculous, that twice he dashed through the whole body of the enemy, and on making a third attempt, was overwhelmed with numbers, several of the officers of his force, including Lord Witherington, Sir Thomas Tildesley, and other gentlemen, being killed. The Earl, having succeeded in mounting a third horse, fought his way through the ranks of the enemy, in company with his faithful Governor Greenalgh, and five other officers." His lordship's escape, at the close of this momentous struggle is thus graphically described. "On his third charge, upon the fall of Lord Witherington, his lordship mounted his horse, and being seconded by six gentlemen of the party, he, with them, fought his way through a great body of the enemy, into the town, where his lordship, quitting his horse, leapt in at a door that stood open, and suddenly shutting it before the enemy could reach it, the woman of the house kept it shut so long till his lordship was conveyed to a place of privacy, where he lay concealed for many hours, notwithstanding the most industrious search of the enemy." The house above alluded to, is said to have been then, and for several years afterwards known by the name of "the Dog" public house, in which there was a brass plate with the arms of "Man" upon it, round which was the inscription "Honi soit qui mal y pense" with an intimation that that was the house into which Lord Derby fled after the battle of Wigan Lane, the day after he left Preston. About two months afterwards the Earl of Derby was arrested in Cheshire, on his way to Knowsley, and having been tried at Chester on a charge of high treason, was beheaded at Bolton on the 15th of October. The library at Knowsley contains the chair in which the Earl sat when he was beheaded, and which, some years ago, was presented to the fourteenth earl, father of the present earl. The chair is composed of oak, and has a low carved back, with spiral spindles. The chair was presented by Mr. Hardcastle, of Bolton, whose family had

had it in their possession for several generations, and on a brass plate on the chair is the following inscription:—
"This chair of the great Earl of Derby, at his martyrdom, was presented by James Hardcastle, of Bolton-le-moors, to the Right Hon. Edward Geoffrey. Earl of Derby."

THE PRETENDER, AND THE REBEL FORCES AT PRESTON.

We must pass from this period to a date several years subsequent to the downfall of the Commonwealth and the Restoration, before finding Preston identified with any specially striking events in the history of the country. It may, however, be recorded that when James the Second visited Chester previous to his expulsion from the throne, the Corporation of Preston sent a deputation of their body to present an Address to him. It should like- wise be added—but little to the credit of the municipal authorities of the time—that in 1684, the Corporation entertained the notorious Judge Jeffries, on his return from the Lancaster Assizes. During the early part of the reign of George the First, in the year 1715, when the rebellion broke out consequent on the partisans of the Stuarts in Scotland and the north of England pro- claiming the Pretender, the Chevalier de St. George, son of James the Second, King, by the title of James the Third, Preston was the scene and centre of several demonstrations and warlike engagements. The rebel forces, numbering, in cavalry and infantry, about one thousand six hundred men, arrived in Preston from the north, on the 9th and 10th of November, and on the last named day the Pretender was proclaimed King at the Market Cross, and it is stated that the Rev. Mr. Paul who had joined the rebel army at Lancaster, on this occasion read prayers three times for the heir of the Stuarts, as the lawful monarch of Britain. Sir Henry Hoghton, at that time member for Preston, espoused the cause of the reigning monarch, at the head of six hundred militia. During the struggle Patten House, in Church Street, then the property of Sir Edward Stanley was taken possession of by the King's troops, and it was from this mansion that the rebels met with their most disastrous losses during the engagements that took place, and which terminated with that on the 12th of November, when the rebel chiefs becoming convinced that they could not any longer resist the King's troops, offers were made on behalf of the insurgents to surrender the town, on condition that the reigning monarch's General would recommend them to the King's mercy. The reply of General Wills was that "he would not treat with rebels, for that they had killed several of the King's subjects, and they must expect to undergo the same fate. If they laid down their arms, and submitted prisoners at discretion, he would prevent the soldiers cutting them in pieces, until he had further orders, and that he would give them but an hour to consider it." Subsequently a treaty of capitulation was entered into between some of the leaders of the rebels and General Wills on the part of the King, but this coming to the ears of Colonel Mackintosh, one of the rebel generals, who with the Earl of Derwentwater, had been delivered into General Wills's hands as hostages, Colonel Mackintosh gave it as his opinion to Wills that the Highlanders would never submit without a struggle. "Go back to your people again," replied the General, "and I will attack the town; and the consequence will be that I will not spare one man of you." The rebel commanders and their troops, however, eventually surrendered, the swords of the officers being received by Lord Forrester in the churchyard, while those of Lord Derwentwater, Lord Widdrington, Lord Kenmure, Lord Carnworth, and several other lords, were delivered to him at the Mitre Inn, then in the Market Place. The highlanders also laid down their arms in the Market Place, and it is stated, were imprisoned for about a month in the church, where it is recorded, "they took what care of themselves they could, unripping all the linings from the seats and pews, and making thereof breeches and hose to defend themselves from the extremity of the weather." During their confinement in the church they were fed on bread and water at the cost of the inhabitants. A writer of the period gives some interesting particulars relating to the course pursued at that time by the then Vicar of Preston. He says:—"During the time that the rebels were in Preston, in 1715, the daring zeal of the Vicar, the Rev. Samuel Peploe, B.D., for the reigning sovereign, was the subject of general conversation, and he daily read the prayers for the King, on one occasion even in the presence of his Majesty's rival. It is also reported that a rebel soldier, forgetful of his allegiance to a higher power, once approached the Vicar during divine service, and drawing his bayonet threatened Peploe's life if he dared to read the prayer for the Elector of Hanover. With an undaunted courage, characteristic of the man, Peploe replied, "Soldier, do your duty, and I will do mine." The firmness of his tone and the dignity of his manner awed the rebel, who silently retired, and the alarmed congregation proceeded with their devotions. When this anecdote was related to George the First, he was so much affected by the heroism of his whig supporter, that he exclaimed in his broken German, with considerable emphasis "Peep-low, Peep-low; by——! he shall Peep-high —he shall be a Bishop.; a royal determination punctually performed." The Vicar, in fact, was created Warden of Manchester, in 1718, and in 1726, eight years afterwards he succeeded Bishop Jaskell, as Bishop of Chester.

TRIAL AND EXECUTION OF THE REBELS.

The noblemen and gentlemen who had surrendered and become prisoners, were temporarily confined under guard at several of the inns in the town, including the Mitre, the White Bull, and the Windmill. They were subsequently removed in custody to London where the following Earls and Barons were impeached and tried before their Peers, on a charge of high treason, Robert, Earl of Carnworth ; William, Earl of Nithsdale

James, Earl of Derwentwater; George, Earl of Wintoun; William, Lord Widdrington; William, Viscount Kenmure; and William, Lord Nairn. They were all found guilty, and sentence of death was passed upon them, but two of the Earls—Earls Wintoun and Nithsdale—subsequently escaped from the Tower. The King's pardon was extended to the Earl of Carnworth and Lords Nairn and Widdrington, but the sentence on the Earl of Derwentwater and Lord Kenmure was carried out, both being beheaded on Tower Hill. Large numbers of the rebels were removed and tried at Lancaster and Chester, several of them being convicted, and afterwards put to death, Preston being the scene of the execution of many of them. These included Major Navin, and Captains Lockhart, Shaftoe, and Erskine, who were shot at Preston in December, 1715. On the 28th of January, 1716, Richard Shuttleworth, of Preston; Roger Muncaster, of Garstang, attorney; Thomas Coope, of Walton-le-Dale; and William Butler and William Arkwright, were hanged on Gallows Hill, Preston; and on the 9th of February, Richard Chorley, Esq., James Drummond, William Black, Donald McDonald, John Howard, Berry Kennedy, and John Rowbottom were also hanged on the same spot. A century after these executions the remains of some of the victims appear to have been unearthed, for it is recorded that "on cutting through the Gallows Hill, in May, 1817, the workmen discovered two coffins, in which the headless bodies of two of the rebel chiefs executed here, were, no doubt, deposited. According to tradition, the heads were cut off at the time of execution, and exposed on poles in front of the town hall." Twenty-seven others were likewise hanged at Lancaster, Wigan, Manchester, Garstang, Liverpool, and Tyburn. Amongst those hanged at Lancaster were Captain Bruce, John Winckley, Thomas Shuttleworth, and George Hodson. The Rev. Mr. Paul, who read prayers at the Obelisk at Preston on behalf of the Pretender, was amongst the rebels executed at Tyburn. In a letter written by a "gentleman in Preston to his friend in the King's camp at Perth," in reference to the execution at Preston of Major Nairn, Captain Lockhart, Mr. Shaftoe, and Mr. Erskine, the writer says:

" It was not without great difficulty and much intercession, that the first two" (Nairn and Lockhart) "were allowed each a coffin, and a Christian, decent burial ; but these, for what reasons I know not, were refused to the other two. When they came to the place of execution, Major Nairn, who was to be shot first, desired his face might not be covered, and to have the liberty to give the word of command, but he was refused. After he was shot, Captain Lockhart would not suffer any of the common soldiers to touch his friend's body, but, with his own hands, and the help of the two other gentlemen, laid Major Nairn in his coffin, and with the greatest composure of mind, performed the last offices to his dear companion : After which he was shot, and the two others performed the like to his body. Then the others were shot, and laid together without a coffin, in a pit digged for that purpose. Which tragical scene being thus finished, Mr. Nairn and Mr. Lockhart were decently buried."

The cost of the executions at Preston and other places in Lancashire, is set out in the following grim and unique document :—

" The charge of Executing 34 rebels.

	£	s.	d.
" Jan. 27, 1715. Erecting gallows, and paid for materialls, hurdle, fire, cart, &c., on executing Shuttleworth and 4 more at Preston, and setting up his head, &c.	12	0	4
" Feb. 9. Disbursements on executing old Mr. Chorley, and setting up a head, &c.	5	10	6
" Besides the undersheriffs.			
" Feb. 10. Charge at Wigan on executing Blundell, &c....	7	1	2
" Besides the undersheriffs.			
" Feb. 11. Charge at Manchester on executing Syddall, &c.	8	10	0
" Besides the undersheriffs.			
" Feb. 16 and 18. Charge at Garstang and Lancaster on executing 4 at either place	22	0	1
" Besides the undersheriffs.			
" Feb. 25. Charge of executing Bennet and 3 more at Leverpoole..:.......	10	3	0
" Payd the two executioners	60	0	3
" Payd for horses to carry the executioners to the severall places of execution and their travelling charges	7	10	0
	£132	15	8

Several other persons in high positions in Lancashire were also tried at the time, as rebels, but the trials resulted in either acquittal or reprieve. It is a noteworthy fact that many of them were members of the old Roman Catholic Lancashire families, very closely connected with Preston, and whose representatives are well known at the present day. The gentlemen arraigned and tried were Ralph Standish, Esq., of Standish ; Francis Anderton, Esq., of Lostock ; John Dalton, Esq.; Richard Towneley, Esq., of Towneley ; Edward Tildesley, Esq., of the Lodge, Myrescough ; and Gabriel Hesketh, and his son, Cuthbert Hesketh. In the year 1745, during the reign of George the Second, when Prince Charles Edward, Son of the Pretender, caused his father to be proclaimed King in several of the Scotch towns, and some of the northern towns of England, he arrived at Preston on the 27th of November, when the proclamation was read, and on that occasion Mr. Towneley, amongst others, joined the Prince's standard, being, it was stated, the first gentleman of position and standing in England who had taken that step. The utter failure of the Prince's expedition forms one of the most prominent chapters in the country's history. With that failure the last hopes of the Stuarts were for ever effaced, and since that time no great national event, in which Preston was specially concerned, has happened.

THE GUILD CHARTERS.

Reference has already been made in the foregoing pages to the several charters which have from time to time been granted, conferring upon Preston its special Guild, and electoral and municipal privileges. It may be added that the Guild and other charters, originally granted to the town by the first Henry, were confirmed by successive monarchs down to the time of Henry the Fifth. But the principal charter, granted in 1565, was by Elizabeth, conferring a great variety of privileges, embracing those connected with the election of the corporation and the mayor. In this charter the names of the first mayor, bailiffs, and members of the council, nominated by the crown, are given, the mayor being Evan Walle, and the bailiffs, Richard Banester and William Robson. They are to continue in office until the election of their successors "at the feast of St. Wilfrid, Archbishop, next ensuing." Under this charter the mayor is also appointed "Clerk to the market, coroner within the said borough, and the liberties and precincts thereof." The charter next provides for the election of the future mayors and other officers, "in the week next before the feast of St. Wilfrid, Archbishop." The charter also confirms the right and privilege of the burgesses to hold a Guild Merchant, one of its clauses running as follows:—"Moreover, we have granted, and by these, for ourselves, our heirs and successors, we have confirmed to the aforesaid mayor, bailiffs, and burgesses of the said borough of Preston, and their successors, that the said mayor, bailiffs, and burgesses, and their successors, shall have a Gild Merchant in the aforesaid borough, with all the liberties and free customs appertaining to such a Gild, as they have hitherto enjoyed."

In 1673, Charles the Second granted a second charter, but subsequently he dispossessed the town of the privileges which it conferred, having, it was believed, been induced to take this step by the advice of the unpopular and notorious Jeffries. In the year 1684, however, Charles granted another charter which restored all the ancient privileges. The last charter is of comparatively modern date, being in the year 1828, and granted by George the Fourth. By this charter every alderman was made a borough magistrate, and the mayor's predecessor in office, and the senior aldermen were authorised to sit as coroners. This made the twelfth charter granted to the town. These various charters conferred upon the inhabitants many exclusive privileges. Under several of them no person was allowed to engage in trade in the town, unless he was enrolled as a freeman and burgess; and in several instances fines were inflicted upon numerous tradesmen who had commenced business not being "freemen or burgesses." In course of time however, these exclusive privileges were gradually relaxed, and they were altogether abolished on the passing of the Municipal Reform Act, in the year 1835.

CURIOUS CORPORATION BYE-LAWS.

Some of the quaint and amusing bye-laws of the Corporation, in force at a former period, are worth recording. Amongst other requirements of the municipality the inhabitants were under orders to prevent their "children, servantes, or familie, or anie of them beinge above the age of seaven years, to plaie in the open streetes of this toune, at anie game or plaie whatsoever, or to sit at the doors or in the streete." The penalty for any infringement of this bye-law was four-pence. A councillor for not attending the mayor when summoned was fined twelve-pence. It would appear that at this time visiting Preston must have been attended with its inconveniences and risks, for by one of these bye-laws it was provided that if any householder of the town or liberties thereof admitted any "strangers or foreigners" who should appear to the council "noe fytt person to inhabitte within the same," the "stranger" was required to leave the town within a month after notice given. The householder was called upon to see that this order was carried out, or to give security that the "stranger" or "foreigner," or any of his family should not become chargeable to the town, or to pay the sum of six shillings and eight-pence per week during the time that they remained. Another of these curious bye-laws provided that all publicans were to be compelled to sell "a full quart of the best beer or ale for a penny," the penalty for not complying with this bye-law being six shillings and eightpence. A further bye-law stipulated that no person should be permitted to tipple or drink in any ale house for a longer period than "one hour at a sitting;" the penalty for infringing this bye-law being three shillings and fourpence. It was also rather dangerous and costly in these days for householders

to allow illegitimate children to be brought into the world
in their dwellings, for one of the bye-laws provided that
"any person permitting a bastard to be born in any of
their houses" should be called upon to give security that
it should not become chargeable to the town. The
municipal authorities of the period would thus seem to
have been impressed with the obligation of providing
for the moral and social condition of the inhabitants,
although they appear to have been the patrons of that
practice of cock-fighting, which at the time was a popular
sporting amusement, and nowhere more so than in
Preston. It is recorded that in 1650 the ricketty condition of the town's cock-pit came under discussion at a
meeting of the council, the result of the discussion being
that the then building, described as "goods belonging to
the Towne" should be removed "in regard it would fall
downe, and so bee a grat charge to repaire, being in great
ruyne and decay for want of reparacons." It was resolved
that it should be re-erected "in such convenient place as
they (the bailiffs) should think fitt nere unto the Towne
hall to be employed for the publique use of this Towne."

THE EARL OF DERBY AS MAYOR OF PRESTON.

Preston has the honour of being the birth place of
the eleventh and twelfth Earls of Derby. The former
was the son of Sir Thomas Stanley, Bart., M.P. for
Preston, in the parliament of 1695, who married the
daughter of Thomas Patten, Esq., M.P. for Preston, in
the parliament of 1688, and by that marriage succeeded
to a considerable property in the neighbourhood of
Preston, including the family mansion, Patten House, in
Church Street, which was for many years afterwards the
frequent residence of the Stanley family, and during the
Guilds, races, and other festive occasions, the scene of
much hospitality. Edward, the eleventh Earl, was born
at his father's residence at Preston, in 1689. He was for
some time an alderman of the borough, and served the

office of mayor, in the year 1741-2, when in his fifty-second year, and only five years before he became Earl of Derby. The massive silver punch bowl, still used by the corporation on festive occasions, was given by the Earl in 1742, after his resignation of the office of alderman. In 1714, he married Elizabeth, daughter and heiress of Robert Hesketh, of Rufford Hall, the ancestor of the present Sir Thomas Hesketh. By this marriage he had issue, James, Lord Stanley, born in 1717. This Lord Stanley married the daughter and co-heiress of Hugh Smith, Esq., of Weald Hall, Essex, on which he assumed the name of Smith-Stanley. By this marriage he had issue Edward Smith Stanley, besides three daughters. In the year 1771, during the lifetime of his father, the eleventh Earl, Lord Stanley died. The Earl himself died on the 23rd of February, 1776, aged 87 years, when his grand-son, Edward Smith Stanley, succeeded him as twelfth Earl of Derby, being then only in his twenty-fourth year. Lord Stanley, or Lord Strange, the twelfth Earl's father, resided a great deal at the family mansion, in Preston, and it was here where the future Earl, Edward Smith Stanley, was born, and where he likewise resided for a considerable time after his birth, having been a pupil at the Preston Grammar School. Although, about ten years after succeeding to the title, when thirty-one years of age, he filled the office of Chancellor of the Duchy of Lancaster, in the Duke of Portland's adminis-tration, in 1783, and was again appointed to that office about twenty-three years afterwards, on the formation of the government, in which Lord Grey and Lord Holland were members, political life had few attractions for him. He took more pleasure in the splendid hospitalities of the social and private circle. In his day horse racing and cock fighting were popular and fashionable, confined to no one class of the community, but shared in and enjoyed by all. In connection with these sports the Earl was for several years closely identified with Preston. He was reputed to have one of the best studs, and the best breeds of cocks of any nobleman in the country. In the

enjoyment of the latter sport he was passionately enthusiastic, personally attending the several "mains" and race
meetings at Preston, where he erected a cock-pit at his
own expense, and maintained a noble and liberal hospitality at his residence, Patten House, where he was always
surrounded during the race week, by a brilliant circle of
the aristocracy of the county.   General Yates, whose
breed of cocks was considered equal to that of his Lordship, was almost uniformly his opponent, and as much as
one and two thousand guineas were often staked upon
the issue of each main, by his Lordship and the General.

MEMBERS OF PARLIAMENT FOR PRESTON, 1225 to 1882.

It has already been stated that the first recorded
parliamentary election for Preston took place in 1295,
and the town appears to have sent representatives to the
House of Commons until the year 1326, in the reign of
Edward the Second.   Between the last-named date and
1547—a period of 221 years—the town was without
representatives.   This arose in consequence of the burgesses of Preston having allowed their right of parliamentary representation to remain in abeyance for the
period above named.   Financial considerations would
seem to have had much to do with this determination of
the burgesses and those who might otherwise have
been aspirants for parliamentary honours.   In those days
members were paid, the remuneration being the modest
sum of four shillings per day for knights of the shire, and
two shillings per day for borough members.   It should,
however, be stated that these sums were equal in value to
about ten times the amount which that coin represents
in the present day.   But the expenses of the journey to
and from London must have been considerable, as we are
informed that in the reign of Edward the Third the time
allowed to members of parliament for travelling between
Lancashire and London was from five to eight days;
"according to the state of the weather."   It must, there-

fore, be concluded that those who might, under other circumstances, have been desirous of becoming parliamentary representatives, considered that the expense of undertaking the duties outweighed the honour. The representation of the borough was, however, resumed in 1547, being the first year of the short reign of Edward the Sixth, and from that time to the present day, several well known townsmen, and members of distinguished Lancashire families have, in turn, represented the town. Amongst these may be named various members of the Stanley family, one of whom was James Stanley, who represented the town in 1688, and Sir Thomas Stanley, who sat for the borough in the parliament of 1695. Members of the Gerard, Sherburne, Dalton, Shuttleworth, Standish, Fleetwood, Hoghton, Hesketh, Burgoyne, Hornby, Horrocks, and Townley Parker families, must also be included amongst those who have represented the borough.

In the year 1796, on the dissolution of Parliament, and immediately after attaining his majority, Edward, the thirteenth Earl of Derby, grandfather of the present Earl, was elected a member of Parliament for the borough of Preston, under circumstances which it may be interesting here to record. For several years before this election, extending, indeed, to an antecedent period of nearly half a century, the Derby family and the Corporation had been constantly at issue, as to whether the former or the latter should nominate the members for Preston, and the contests were always severe, invariably resulting, however, in the election of the Earl's nominees, against those of the Corporation. For nearly thirty years, namely, from 1768 to 1795, the borough was, with one exception, exclusively represented by General Burgoyne (who, while a subaltern in a marching regiment, stationed in Preston, contracted a secret marriage with Lady Charlotte Stanley, a daughter of the eleventh Earl of Derby), and Sir Henry Hoghton, Bart., the candidates in the interests of the Derby family. The exception to which we have alluded was, that on the death of General Burgoyne, in 1792, he was succeeded in the representation by

Mr. William Cunliffe Shawe, who, like his predecessors, came into Parliament under the Whig or Derby interest. We have already stated that at the general election, in 1796, the subject of our present notice, then Lord Stanley, became a candidate, in conjunction with Sir Henry Philip Hoghton, Mr. Shawe having retired. The Corporation, on this occasion, made a determined stand against the Derby interest, bringing forward as their candidate in the Tory, and, as they expressed it, the "manufacturing interest," Mr. John Horrocks, the head of the now wide-world-known and celebrated manufacturing firm of Horrocks, Miller, & Co. Mr. Horrocks at that time employed a considerable number of workpeople in the town, and was a gentleman of much wealth and local influence. The contest was an exceedingly severe one, and personal and party feeling ran very high. The poll was kept open for eleven days, during the first eight of which Mr. Horrocks was each day at the head. On the ninth day, however, he fell to the second; on the tenth he was at the bottom of the poll; and on the morning of the eleventh, he retired, when the numbers were—Stanley, 772; Hoghton, 756; Horrocks, 742. At this election the first Lord Abinger, chief Baron of the Exchequer, but at that time plain Mr. Scarlett, acted as "assistant" to the Mayor, and was paid 200 guineas for his services. A memorandum appears in the books of the Corporation, to the effect that that body borrowed the money from Mr. Pedder, a banker, and gave a bond for the amount. In order to show the intensity of the hostile feeling which at this time existed between the Derby family and the Corporation, in reference to the representation of the borough, we quote the following extract from an able and interesting little work, on the "History of the Parliamentary Representation of Preston, during the last hundred years," by William Dobson :—

"While," says the author, "the Derbyite nominees were the members' they were never, except one of them on a single occasion, solicited to take charge of any of the numerous addresses, which the Corporation were accustomed to present to the throne. Mr. Blackburne, the Tory member for the county, was always selected to be the medium of the corporate filicitations reaching the ears of royalty. Not merely was the feeling of hostility between the rival competitors for political influence carried into the business of the town, but even into its pleasures, and for six years, from 1786 to 1791, races were held under the auspices of each party, the Corporation races being held on Preston Moor; the Earl of Derby's races, as an opposition meeting, on Fulwood Moor, a lease of which had been obtained from the Duchy of Lancaster. The political differences which divided the town extended even to sedan chairs. The coats of the chairmen had collars of the colour of one or other of the two great parties, and as the ladies were equally warm in their political sympathies as the rougher sex, they showed their predilection, not only in the ribbons they wore, but in the choice of their sedans. A lady of the family of Pedder, or Starkie, or Gorst, would have walked home in a thunderstorm before she would have been carried in a Derby or Burgoyne chair, while the wives and damsels of the Shaws, the Hornbys, and the Whiteheads, would have missed going to the best ball of the season, rather than have been taken there in a Corporation sedan."

In the next election, which took place in 1802, Lord Stanley was again elected member for Preston, but under circumstances altogether dissimilar to those which we have just recorded. There were two reasons why it was deemed advisable that a different state of things to that which had so long existed should prevail. On the one hand the election struggles between the Corporation and the Derby interests respectively, had involved the former in certain expenses which, if not actually illegal, were at least not creditable to a public body; while, on the other hand, the influence of Mr. Horrocks had so largely increased, in consequence of his energy and enterprise in extending the cotton trade in the town, that a compromise between the two parties was recommended, and ultimately carried into effect; the terms of arrangement being that the Derby family should nominate one member, and the Corporation and manufacturing interest the other, and that each should support the other in carrying out the bargain. This questionable arrangement, which we must say, displayed an absence of political dignity on both sides, inasmuch as parties diametrically opposed to each other were now to work together against any independent candidate whose views might be in accord with

either of the coalition candidates, was nevertheless gravely
reduced to writing, and signed by the " high contracting
parties," for it is recorded in Baines's History of Lancashire that " this coalition was made through the inter-
vention of Thomas Butterworth Bagley, Esq., of Hope,
near Manchester, and ratified by the signatures of eleven
gentlemen in Preston, the leaders of the parties, to a
written agreement prepared for the purpose." Under it
Lord Stanley, the Whig, and Mr. John Horrocks, the
Tory, were returned unopposed at the election in 1802,
Sir Henry Hoghton having retired. Mr. John Horrocks,
however, died in 1804, when he was succeeded by his
brother, Mr. Samuel Horrocks. The next election was
in 1806, when Lord Stanley and Mr. Samuel Horrocks
were again elected under the "compact"; and in the following year, 1807, when the Parliament was dissolved,
they a third time presented themselves, and were, as before, returned unopposed. The absence of high political
principle involved in this arrangement was often
severely commented upon by the journalists of the time,
and one writer, referring to the position of Lord Stanley
and Mr. Horrocks under the terms to which they respec-
spectively became parties, somewhat satirically remarks,
" Although they scarcely ever voted on the same side in
the House of Commons, they had in Preston one committee, they canvassed together, and, strange as it would
now seem, subscribed their names to the same address."
This remarkable " coalition," however, although several
times assailed by independent candidates and their friends,
who did not approve of such a Whig and Tory combination, was successful at every general election which took
place after the agreement, and it was only in the year
1826, when the late Earl of Derby, then Mr. Stanley,
first became a candidate for Preston, that it was broken
through.

    Some of the most advanced and noted radicals have at
different periods contested the representation of the town.
In 1820, on the death of George the Third, Mr. Henry
Hunt, in conjunction with Mr. Williams, afterwards Mr.

Justice Williams, were candidates, but on that occasion were defeated by the coalition candidates, Horrocks and Hornby. In 1826, William Cobbett, the typical "Jacobin" of the day, opposed the late Earl of Derby, when, as the Hon. E. G. Stanley, he first came forward. Cobbett, however, was defeated by an overwhelming majority, after a contest which lasted fifteen days. Mr. Henry Hunt again came forward in December, 1830, in opposition to the Hon. E. G. Stanley, who presented himself for re-election on having been appointed Chief Secretary for Ireland in Earl Grey's Government.

Having so accepted office, he vacated his seat for Preston, and again presented himself for re-election. This was the most memorable event appertaining to Mr. Stanley's election experiences, and unexpectedly severed his political connexion with Preston. In a few days after his address had been issued, the friends and supporters of Mr. Hunt, the extreme Radical, again put forward his name; but Mr. Stanley's committee looked upon the opposition without any feelings of apprehension as to the safety of the right honourable gentleman's seat. At the close of the first day's polling, however, Mr. Stanley's committee were astounded to find Mr. Hunt in a considerable majority, the numbers being for Mr. Hunt, 1,204; for Mr. Stanley, 791. The second and third day's polling increased, although slightly, Mr. Hunt's majority, and the excitement of the contest had now risen to such a pitch as to have extended far beyond the boundaries of the borough. Day after day the town was crowded with large numbers of operatives and others from the different manufacturing districts of Lancashire, whose sympathies were enlisted on behalf of the ultra Radical candidate. The Huntites had monster processions every day, accompanied by numerous large banners, flags, and bands of music; these processions usually taking place in the evening, between the hours of seven and ten o'clock, when a number of burning tar barrels were introduced into the procession, illuminating the public thoroughfares in the darkness of the night. The

authorities appeared powerless to restrain the reckless
enthusiasm of the populace, and for the time the latter
might almost be said to have had possession of the town.
Mr. Hunt's speeches to the mob abounded in the most
violent and intemperate language towards Mr. Stanley
and the classes he represented, which had the effect of
still further increasing the great excitement that prevailed. Mr. Hunt's majority was considerably reduced
during the subsequent days of the polling, but still he
kept at the head of the poll, and his friends appeared determined, at all hazards, that he should be elected, for at
the polling booth they commenced a system of intimida-
tion, and resorted to other obstructive measures, which
prevented numbers of Mr. Stanley's supporters from
recording their votes. It was abundantly proved that
hundreds of non-residents voted for Mr. Hunt on the
occasion, and in one case it was ascertained beyond doubt
that a man from Blackburn voted for Mr. Hunt 13 times!
It would, perhaps, be idle to deny that, amidst the reckless disregard of order, and the saturnalia which prevailed, several fictitious votes were also given for Mr.
Stanley, but that he was defeated mainly by non-resi-
dent voters has never been questioned. After seven days'
voting the seat was given to Mr. Hunt, the numbers
being—for Mr. Hunt, 3,730, and for Mr. Stanley, 3,392;
the political connexion of the Stanley family with Preston, which had existed for so many years, being thus
suddenly and unexpectedly severed. Satisfied of the un-
due influences which had been used against him, and of
the illegal character of the voting, Mr. Stanley threatened to have a scrutiny of the votes at the close of the
poll, before the return was made, the returning officer at
that time having the power of deciding as to the validity
of votes so objected to. Arrangements were made for
this purpose, and Mr. Sergeant Mereweather came down
to conduct it on behalf of Mr. Stanley, but, after three
days' preparation, it was abandoned. The result was
deeply mortifying to Mr. Stanley himself, and not less to
the whole of the Knowsley family, who evinced their

sense of the slight by withdrawing all their patronage and influence from the town, which severely felt the separation. The then Earl of Derby, twelfth Earl, who, as well as the eleventh Earl and other members of the family, was born in Preston, keenly felt the blow, and in a short time after the close of the contest the windows of Patten House, in Church Street, the family mansion in Preston, were blocked up, and all the attendants withdrawn, giving to the otherwise noble building a desolate and dismal appearance; the races, also, which the family had warmly patronised, they no longer supported, which caused them to be discontinued, and generally the Stanleys withdrew themselves from all association with the town.

Two years after this memorable struggle—in 1832—the passing of the Reform Bill, under the auspices of Earl Grey's Government, was followed by a general election, with an entirely new constituency, when Peter Hesketh Fleetwood, Esq., and the Hon. Henry Thomas Stanley were elected, the former as a Conservative, and the latter as a Whig, Mr. Peter Hesketh Fleetwood polling 3,372 votes, and Mr. Stanley 3,273. The other candidates on this occasion were Mr. Henry Hunt, Captain Forbes, and Mr. Charles Crompton, afterwards Mr. Justice Crompton. Mr. Peter Hesketh Fleetwood was elected at the head of the poll at the two following elections, in 1835 and 1837 respectively, his colleague in 1835 being the Hon. H. T. Stanley, and in 1837 Mr. Robert Townley Parker. Col. Thompson, of corn law repeal celebrity, was one of the unsuccessful candidates at the election in 1835; and in 1837 Mr. Fergus O'Connor was nominated, but did not go to the poll. Between the years 1837 and 1841 Mr. Peter Hesketh Fleetwood was made a baronet, and at the election in the last named year he again came forward, but on this occasion in the Liberal interest, in conjunction with Sir George Strickland, Bart. The Conservative candidates were Mr. R. Townley Parker and Mr. Charles ¯wainson. The Liberal candidates were both elected, the numbers being, for Sir Hesketh Fleetwood, 1,655; Sir

George Strickland, 1,629 ; Mr. R. Townley Parker, 1,270;
Mr. Charles Swainson, 1,255. At the election in 1847
Sir Hesketh Fleetwood retired, having represented the
borough for nine years, and always elected at the head of
the poll. In 1847 Sir George Strickland and Mr. C.
Pascoe Grenfell, Liberals, were elected, the polling being
for Sir George Strickland, 1,404; Mr. Grenfell, 1,378;
and for Mr. R. Townley Parker, Conservative, 1,361. In
1852 Mr. R. Townley Parker, Conservative, and Sir
George Strickland, Liberal, were elected. At this election there were three Liberal candidates, and one Conservative candidate, the result of the poll being for Mr.
Parker, 1,335; Sir George Strickland, 1,253; Mr. Grenfell, 1,127; Mr. James German, 692. The next election
was in 1857, and Mr. Townley Parker having retired,
Mr. Grenfell, Liberal, and Mr. Richard Assheton Cross,
Conservative, were elected, the polling being for Mr.
Grenfell, 1,503; Mr. Cross, 1,433; and Sir George Strickland, Liberal, 1,094. Another election in 1859 resulted
in the election of Mr. R. Assheton Cross, Conservative,
and Mr. Grenfell, Liberal, the polling being for Mr. Cross,
1,542; Mr. Grenfell, 1,203; and Col. John Talbot Clifton,
Conservative, 1,168. In 1862 a bye-election took place
on the retirement of Mr. Cross, when Sir Thomas George
Fermor Hesketh, Conservative, was elected. The polling
on this occasion was, for Sir T. G. F. Hesketh, 1,527;
Mr. George Melly, Liberal, 1,014. At the election in
1865 Sir T. G. F. Hesketh and the Hon. F. A. Stanley,
Conservatives, were returned unopposed; and since this
period the representation of the borough has been exclusively in the hands of the Conservatives. On the occasion of the general election in 1868, following upon the
Reform Act passed during Mr. Disraeli's administration,
the candidates were Mr. Edward Hermon and Sir T. G.
F. Hesketh, Conservatives; and Mr. Joseph Francis Leese
and Lord Edward Howard, Liberals. The result of the
poll was, for Mr. Hermon, 5,803; Sir T. G. F. Hesketh,
5,700; Mr. Leese, 4,741 ; Lord Edward Howard, 4,663.
In 1872 a bye-election took place, consequent upon the

death of Sir T. G. F. Hesketh. The candidates were Mr. John Holker, Conservative; and Major German, Liberal; when Mr. Holker was elected, the polling being for Mr. Holker, 4,542; Major German, 3,824. On the dissolution of Parliament in 1874 by Mr. Gladstone, then Prime Minister, Mr. Hermon and Mr. Holker, Conservatives; and Mr. Thomas Mottershead, Liberal; were the candidates, when the Conservatives were both elected, the polling being for Mr. Hermon, 6,512; Mr. Holker, 5,211; Mr. Mottershead, 3,756. In the same year a bye-election took place on Mr. John Holker being appointed Solicitor-General, when he was re-elected unopposed. In the general election of 1880, following upon the dissolution of Parliament under the Earl of Beaconsfield's government, Mr. Hermon and Sir John Holker were the Conservative candidates; and Mr. George William Bahr was the candidate in the Liberal interest. The polling was for Mr. Hermon, 6,239; Sir John Holker, 5,641; Mr. G. W. Bahr, 5,355. In May, 1881, a bye-election took place caused by the death of Mr. Hermon. The candidates were Mr. William Farrer Ecroyd, Conservative; and Mr. Henry Yates Thompson, Liberal. The polling was, for Mr. Ecroyd, 6,004; Mr. Thompson, 4,340. In February, 1882, another bye election took place consequent on the elevation to the bench of Sir John Holker as one of the Lords Justices of Appeal. The candidates were the right hon. Henry Cecil Raikes, Conservative; and Mr. William Shaw Simpson, Liberal. The result of the poll was, for Mr. Raikes, 6,045; Mr. Simpson, 4,212.

TOPOGRAPHICAL
DESCRIPTION OF PRESTON.

HAVING endeavoured to sketch the various historical events with which, from the earliest periods, Preston has been associated, a brief topographical outline of the town, and its material conformation and progress, will not be uninteresting to the visitor and others, whilst it will enable them the better to appreciate the several physical and other features of the town which may come under their observation. According to several authorities Preston is believed to date so far back as the year 705, and Baines, in his History of Lancashire, inclines to the opinion that about this period the parish church of Preston was erected, and on the canonization of Archbishop Wilfrid was dedicated to that saint. Others again hold that Preston or "Priests' Town," had, in all probability, its origin immediately following upon the ruins of Ribchester, which, it is urged, was either destroyed by an earthquake, or by war. Leaving these several speculations for what they may be worth, and observing that the manufacturing and commercial emporium of the present was the aristociatic Lancashire centre of the past, we proceed to describe briefly its natural configuration, together with its progress and expansion during the present century, from the period when the introduction of the cotton manufacture gave it an entirely changed character.

CHARACTER OF ITS SITE.

Preston is situated upon high ground, which is a special feature in its favour as regards its drainage and sanitary conditions. There is, moreover, one peculiar and exceptional advantage which it possesses over the rest of the Lancashire manufacturing towns, and this consists in the fact that the river which flows beneath its banks prevents the extension of the town, and more especially on its south side, for those modern utilitarian purposes which, although they may add to the material prosperity of a community, are in many cases accompanied by a species of vandalism destructive of its natural beauties and surroundings. Preston, to a large extent, is protected from these incursions of manufacturing and commercial enterprise. The south boundary of the town stretches east and west along the cresting of lofty rising ground, beneath which is a beautifully laid out "park of slopes," descending gradually until it reaches the banks of the river Ribble, meandering at its feet. This charming resort, described in succeeding pages, was formed about fifteen years ago, a considerable portion of the land having been given for the purpose by the late Thomas Miller, Esq., of the well known firm of Horrockses, Miller, and Co. From this elevated site there is an extensive and pictures-que view of the valley of the Ribble, both in a south western and south eastern direction, but more especially the last named prospect, the immediate foreground embra-cing the winding course of the Ribble, whilst in the distance behind, the range of hills in the neighbourhood of Rivington rises prominently above the horizon, with the lofty summit of historical Hoghton Tower to the immediate east. The park and a portion of the river valley are intersected by two of the railways which cross over the Ribble on their entrance to the town, but the otherwise unsightly severance has been to a large extent minimised in its objectionable aspect by the artificial ornamentation of the railway embankments.

STREETS AND THOROUGHFARES.

Fishergate and Church Street, the two main and continuous thoroughfares, intersect the town, almost midway between its eastern and western boundary, and in former days there were few other streets in the ancient borough which could claim anything beyond very modest pretentions. Friargate, it is true, must be admitted as having long been an important artery, not only as a business thoroughfare, but as the chief approach to the district on the west, known as the Fylde. The Market Place and Cheapside also, with their quaint old structures of the mediæval period on the north and west sides, were no doubt objects of interest to strangers who in past times visited the town; whilst aristocratic Winckley Square as the chief home of the "quality," as the "upper ten" of Preston were wont to be designated, should not be ignored. With these exceptions, however, the prominent streets and thoroughfares in Preston were limited in number during the time when it was largely the residence of county and other high-class families, before its invasion about the commencement of the present century, by the impetus given to the cotton manufacture, following upon the discoveries of Arkwright, Wyatt, Hargreaves, and Crompton. Since the advent of the cotton manufacture the town has materially expanded, whilst it has at the same time been much modernised and architecturally improved, more especially as respects the main thoroughfares, in which several public and other new buildings have, within the last few years, been erected, many of them possessing fine architectural proportions. Some important new streets have also been opened out, both on the north and south sides of Fishergate and Church Street, one of the finest of them being Lancaster Road, on the north side of Church Street. This thoroughfare is upwards of 50 feet in width, and more than a mile in length, and the probability is that it will, at no distant day, be one of the chief business centres in the town. Several high-class houses and shops have already been erected in this new northern outlet by the Earl of Derby, who is the principal owner of property in the locality, and a long range of dilapidated property, on the west side of the street, is about to be removed in order to clear the site for still further new buildings. Another new business thoroughfare called Guild Hall Street, has likewise been opened out on the south side of Fishergate, a short distance to the west of the recently-erected town hall. The old North Road, some short distance eastward of the parish church, will be well remembered by those who knew the town antecedent to the introduction of the railway system, as the main coaching route to the north, but there is every reason to conclude that in the future, Lancaster Road will be the chief outlet from the town in that direction. This road gives the principal approach to the outlying district of Fulwood and Cadley, which, until the last few years was an essentially suburban locality. Building has, however, latterly been going forward here at a rapid rate, large blocks of residential property of a high class having been erected, occupied by a numerous and constantly increasing population. The construction and laying out of the Moor Park by the Corporation has in all probability given an impetus to building in the neighbourhood.

ARCHITECTURAL STREET CHANGES AND
TOWN IMPROVEMENTS.

Allusion has already been made to the changed

architectural character which has been given to the face of the several residences and other buildings in Fishergate. Within the last few years this thoroughfare may be said to have undergone an almost entire transformation, having been converted from a locality consisting very largely of private dwellings into a busy and active emporium of trade and commerce. This observation applies more especially to those portions situated between Winckley Street and Charles Street, the east side of the last-named street forming the western boundary of the spacious new Station of the London and North Western Railway Company. The houses on both sides of the street, from the point named, which were, until a comparatively recent period, the private residences of some of the oldest and best families in the town, and of retired tradesmen, consist now, for the most part, of shops, hotels, and other business premises.

Extensive street and other improvements of an important character are likewise about to be carried out by the Corporation, on the north and east sides of the Market Place, simultaneously with the erection of the Harris Free Library and Museum. By this improvement Church Street will be considerably widened from the Old Shambles, on the west side, to Lancaster Road on the east side, while two new streets, of 50 feet in width, each running from east to west, between Lancaster Road and the Market Place, will be formed, and two other streets of equal width, running northwards from the north side of the Market Place, are also to be constructed. These two new streets will extend to Earl Street, intersecting Lord Street in their course northwards, and running almost parallel with each other. That to the east will be in continuation of the widening of the Old Shambles from Church Street, the street on the west side being in continuation of Cheapside from its junction with Friargate, opposite the commencement of the new street, at the north west angle of the Market Place. In order to effect these improvements upwards of fifty houses, shops, and other property (many of them possessing much

historical interest in connection with the traditions of the
borough,) are at the present time in course of demolition,
preparatory to the intended works being carried out, the
cost to the Corporation, in the purchase of sites and compensation alone being estimated at £30,000.

EXPANSION OF THE TOWN AND
INCREASE OF POPULATION.

An important extension of the town is going forward
at its north-eastern extremity in the direction of Fulwood,
and likewise on the north-west side, stretching out
towards Ashton on the banks of the Ribble, where
what was not many years ago a rural neighbourhood
is rapidly being converted into a numerously populated
urban locality.   Extensive   tracts   of arable   and agricultural land have been laid out for building purposes,
new streets and roads of considerable length intersecting
each other at various points, and some hundreds of
houses have already been erected, several of them of
the villa class. To these may be added the extensive
lands on the high ground adjoining, commanding an
extensive view of the estuary of the Ribble, in the
direction of Lytham, which were recently left to the
representatives of Queen Anne's Bounty, by the late
Mr. Edmund Robert Harris. This estate, which is about
175 acres in extent, is intended to be laid out for building
upon. The town is likewise being largely extended in
the direction of Ribbleton, where a large and constantly
increasing population has sprung up within a comparatively recent period.

Between the year 1834, and the present time, upwards of 1000 acres of land, comprising various estates to
the north-east and north-west of the town, have in
succession been converted from agricultural to building
purposes. These several properties include, amongst
others, the Green Bank Estate, Ox Heys Estate, Moor
Hall Estate, Maudlands Estate, Peel Hall Estate, Free-

hold Park Estate, Fulwood; Hole House Estate, and
the Tulketh and Ashton Estates. The expansion of the
town in these several directions is still going forward, and
there is every prospect of Preston, at no distant day,
ranking amongst the most numerously populated commercial centres in the north of England.

The following statistics indicate the progress and
increase of the town. About the close of the eighteenth
and the commencement of the present century, its population was 6000. Between this period and the year 1809,
the cotton manufacture having been inaugurated in the
interval, the population had increased to 12000, having
thus doubled itself within less than a decade. Two years
afterwards, in 1811, the population had risen to 17,065.
In 1819, it had again further increased to 21,958; in
1821, to 24,627; in 1831, to 33,112; in 1836, to 36,000;
in 1841, to 50,073; in 1851, to 69,366; in 1861, to 82,944;
in 1871, to 85,408; whilst the last census returns in 1881,
showed its present population to be 96,524, including
the recently incorporated portions.

PRIMITIVE NOCTURNAL ILLUMINATION.

INTRODUCTION OF GAS LIGHTING.

At the commencement of the seventeenth century
the lighting of the town, during what may not inaptly
be termed its almost primitive condition, was of a curious
nature, for it is recorded that even oil lamps were not
then in use in the town, the consequence being that in
the evening the town was in darkness. This unpleasant
state of things appears, however, to have been remedied
to some extent, shortly after the time just named, by the
local authorities of the period, who passed a resolution to
the effect that "for the better going in the streets in the
winter evenings in the decrease of the moon, or when
clouds interpose, it has been thought necessary that some
lamps or convex lights should be provided." The record
of this tardy provision for the guidance and protection of

the evening wayfarer reads somewhat oddly; for it almost leads to the conclusion that the financial resources of the authorities must have been inconveniently limited, as we are informed that the Corporation furnished one lamp, whilst three others were provided by private gentlemen; and that "one was placed in the Market Place, another near the .Parish Church, the third at the top of Main Sprit Weind, and the fourth near the Butter Cross." It is further recorded that the "huge lantern, carried by the mayor," is still in the possession of the Corporation. Oil continued to be used for considerably upwards of a century, until gas was introduced for lighting purposes; and although many will be supposed to think, from the above narrative, that the authorities were somewhat indifferent to the comfort of the inhabitants, so far as regards nocturnal illumination, they appear to have made ample amends when gas came to the front, for Preston has the credit of being the first provincial town in England where gas was introduced for public consumption, and the old parish church was the first structure devoted to religious services that was lighted with gas, not even excepting the churches of the metropolis. This took place in the year 1816.

DEMOLITION OF THE TOWN HOUSE OF THE STANLEYS.

Several ancient landmarks and historical mansions associated with many old families connected with Preston have been swept away within the last half centnry, in order to make way for modern innovations in the interests of trade and commerce. Amongst the most prominent ot these is Patten House, in Church Street, the ancient town mansion of the Stanleys, which, at the time of its demolition in the year 1835, had been in possession of the family for nearly 200 years, and was for many years the residence of the Stanleys during the guilds, races, and other festal occasions, when it was the scene of much gaiety and hospitality. When the excavations were being made for the foundations of the houses and business premises, now covering the site upon which the mansion and grounds formerly stood, several human remains were discovered, which are believed to have been those of persons who lost their lives during some of the memorable engagements that took place at Preston at the period of the civil wars, in which the town played so prominent a part.

TRADE AND COMMERCE.

*U*NTIL about the middle of the seventeenth century Preston cannot be said to have possessed a staple trade of any description, maintaining to this period what seems to have been its normal character, as the home, to a large extent, of wealthy private families and the well-to-do classes of society. In the latter part of this century the woollen and the linen trades were carried on to a certain extent, for we find from the Corporation records that about this time several poor children were bound "prentice," one of them to Thomas Hodgson, of Preston, chapman, "to be instructed in the art or craft of weavinge Boone Lace, and in other arts which the said Thomas Hodgson now uses." Another entry records that in the year 1674 the Corporation ordered the establishment of "a workhouse and other offices, for the employment of the poor in the woollen manufacture." The linen trade, however, must have been carried on to a much larger extent than that of the woollen manufacture, which, there is reason to conclude, altogether disappeared from the town sometime about the commencement of the eighteenth century, whilst the linen trade, on the other hand, appears to have largely increased, as is shown by a petition presented to the House of Commons in 1704-5, by the Mayor, aldermen, and burgesses, in which they state that "the making of linen cloth hath, for many *ages* (?) been the settled trade of their neighbourhood, and is the sole dependence of *thousands** of families," Without criticising too nicely the manifest inaccuracies marked in italics, the presentation of this petition by the Corporation is a conclusive proof that, at the time named, the linen manufacture was the chief trade of the town, and that it continued relatively to flourish in the eighteenth century, many years before the cotton manufacture was introduced and eventually became the main staple trade of Preston.

The cotton manufacture, which has so enriched Lancashire, and rendered it the most numerously populated county in the United Kingdom, dates no farther back than the latter part of the eighteenth century, following upon the inventions of Arkwright, Hargreaves, and Wyatt; and Preston was one of the first towns in the county in which it was developed. Richard Arkwright, the barber, one of the earliest of the inventors, and afterwards a millionaire and a baronet, was, as is well known, a native of Preston, his place of business being a small shop on the north side of Lord Street, near Molyneaux Square. A few years ago this shop, with other adjoining structures, was taken down to clear the site for a new block of property called Stanley Buildings, which have since been erected by the Earl of Derby. It is worthy of record that Arkwright's first complete spinning machine, which he afterwards patented, and which contributed to the enormous fortune he amassed at the cotton mills which he erected at Cromford, in Derbyshire, was constructed in the house at the bottom of Stonygate, subsequently and for many years occupied by the Rev. Robert Harris, Head Master of the Preston Grammar School. This house is now known by the name of the "Arkwright's Arms," having been converted into a tavern shortly after the Grammar School was removed to the new building in Cross-street.

---

* At this time the entire population would not be more than from 2,000 to 3,000.

The pioneers of cotton spinning in Preston, after the several inventions of Arkwright and others had demonstrated that these inventions must necessarily lead to mighty results in the production of manufactures from this material, were Messrs. Collinson and Watson, who in the year 1777 erected a cotton mill in Moor Lane, the site of which is now occupied by the works of the Preston Gas Co., at the North end of the town, where it forms a junction with the main highway to Lancaster, a short distance southward of Gallows Hill, where several of the victims of the rebellion, already referred to, were executed. Messrs. Collinson and Watson were thus the fathers of the cotton manufacture in Preston. Its progress, however, was much retarded by what may be described as a suicidal opposition to Arkwright's inventions by many of the Lancashire cotton manufacturers of the time, but in the result this unwise antagonism was overcome, and Preston, in common with other Lancashire towns participated in the advantages which the discoveries of obscure scientific artisans had made manifest, although not without many of the latter having paid the proverbial penalty of inventors, by their discoveries being appropriated and themselves unrewarded. The great firm of Horrockes, Miller, & Co., has not only for years past been recognised as the leading cotton spinning and manufacturing establishment in Lancashire, but it has also a world-wide repute, its fame not being confined to our own country, but extending in almost every direction to foreign lands. Without any disparagement to other firms in different parts of Lancashire, it may indeed be affirmed that its celebrity is unique, and its original history and foundation will therefore be interesting to the reader. John Horrocks, the founder of the firm, was born at Edgeworth, near Bolton, in the year 1768, where his father rented a small quarry, carrying on, in conjunction with his two sons, John and Samuel, a business in the manufacture of millstones. Whilst so engaged in the millstone business at Edgeworth, the then youthful John Horrocks, who had scarcely attained his

majority, appears to have turned his attention to the
inventions of Watt, Arkwright, and others, in connexion
with the cotton trade, for it is recorded of him that in a
corner of his father's quarry, he fitted up a number of
small spinning machines, which he himself worked, producing from them yarns.   This enterprise of young
Horrocks seems to have been eminently successful, for he
sold his yarns at a profit, making weekly visits to Preston
for the purpose.   The fact that his yarns soon acquired
a high reputation, and commanded an exceptionally good
price, may be accepted as evidence that they were superior
in quality to others then in the market.   Cotton spinning
was at that time in its infancy, and that the produce of
young Horrocks's machines was limited in extent will be
well imagined when it is stated that a single horse was sufficient to carry on its back both the young spinner and his
yarns during his weekly visits between Edgeworth and
Preston.   It was in the year 1791, when he finally
removed from Edgeworth to Preston, where a considerable
number of the inhabitants followed the occupation of
hand loom weaving, and had the credit of being well
skilled in the art of making the finer descriptions of
cotton cloth.   It was with a view of taking advantage of
this, and becoming a manufacturer as well as a spinner,
that young Horrocks decided upon removing to Preston.
He was then only 23 years of age.   In the first instance
he rented a small warehouse in Turk's Head Court,
where he "put out" yarn and other necessary materials
to hand loom weavers, which they worked into cloth at
their own homes, afterwards returning it to Mr. Horrocks's
establishment in Turk's Head Court, and receiving payment for the weaving.   This was the general system
adopted in the cotton manufacturing districts of Lancashire, until the large establishments and weaving by
steam power superseded the primitive hand loom.   Mr.
Horrocks's success was so great in his new undertaking
at Preston that before the expiration of the first year he
was able to commence the erection of a large spinning
factory, which still remains, and is known as the "yard

factory," at the east end of the town. The success which attended this venture led to the erection of two other mills by Mr. Horrocks, in the years 1796 and 1797, one of them being known as the "Spitals' Moss Factory," and the other as the "Frenchwood Factory." The establishment at the East end of Church street, known as the "Yard Factory," has from time to time been very considerably enlarged, the several buildings for spinning and manufacturing purposes now covering an area of more than twelve acres in extent. Unprecedented success followed the erection of the above-named spinning mills and weaving sheds. New mills were in succession erected, and in little more than ten years from his first establishment in Preston, Mr. Horrocks was the owner of no less than seven factories in different parts of the town. These were followed by the erection of extensive weaving sheds in that part of the town not far from the "yard" works, and now known as "New Preston." In 1796, only five years after he had established himself in Preston, Mr. Horrocks's influence and business popularity had become so great that he was induced to offer himself as a candidate for the representation of the borough in parliament, but the Derby and aristocratic section being arrayed against him, he was not on that occasion successful, although only defeated by 14 votes. Six years afterwards, namely, in 1802, he again came forward, and as the population had in the meantime more than doubled itself, and his influence had become so great amongst the large numbers to whom he gave employment, he went into parliament unopposed under that notorious coalition arrangement elsewhere referred to. He died however in London two years afterwards, at the early age of 36, and was buried at Penwortham Church, in which parish he had erected a seat. It should be added that some years before his death he presented the organ now in the parish church, and which has since been rebuilt and enlarged. At the death of Mr. John Horrocks, Mr. Samuel Horrocks, his brother (who was for many years one of the parliamentary representatives for Preston), became the senior partner, and down to 1815, the title of the firm was "John Horrocks and Co.," when it was changed to "Horrockses, Miller, and Co." Mr. Miller, who had for some years been in the employment of the firm, having been admitted into partnership as one of the principals, and from that time to the present the firm has been known by the above named title, although by the mutations of time numerous changes in the proprietorship have taken place, and at this day the firm is Horrockses, Miller, and Co., in name only. A speciality as regards the successive partners in this establishment is worthy of record. On the deaths of Mr. Samuel Horrocks, sen., and Mr. Thomas Miller, sen., the partnership descended to their sons, Mr. Samuel Horrocks, jun., Mr. Thomas Miller, jun., and his brother Mr. Henry Miller. Mr. Horrocks, however, did not take an active part in the direction or management of the concern, which chiefly fell upon Mr. Thomas Miller, whose business capacity and general trade abilities were of a high order. In January, 1861, Mr. Edward Hermon, who had been the company's representative in London, was admitted into partnership. On the death of Mr. Horrocks, in the year 1846, Mr. Thomas Miller became the senior and principal partner. Mr. Henry Miller, sometime before his death, was understood to have withdrawn from the firm. In the year 1865, Mr. Thomas Miller died, having realised an enormous fortune, amounting, it has been stated, to something like a million sterling. Mr. Hermon was then left as the only surviving partner. In 1866, Mr. F. Styles of London, was admitted into partnership, and 1870, Mr. William Pollard, who had for many years been in the employment of the firm, was admitted, but retired in the year 1878, owing to failing health. In March and November, 1873, respectively, Mr. S. O. Hermon, of Manchester, and Mr. S. A. Hermon, of Preston (nephews of Mr. Edward Hermon), became partners. Mr. Edward Hermon, M.P., the senior partner, died in 1881, and the senior partner is now Mr. F. Styles, the junior partners being the two nephews of the late Mr. Hermon. The number of spindles in the several mills belonging to the firm is estimated at 170,000, requiring as a motive power for the machinery a number of steam engines of the aggregate horse power of 3,100, and giving employment to upwards of 3,000 workpeople. Horrockes' "long cloths" have a wide-world celebrity, and are to been seen in almost every retail drapery in the metropolis, and all the provincial towns.

The firm of Horrockses, Miller, & Co. is not, however, the only establishment of this character which has enriched its proprietors, and correspondingly increased the population and material prosperity of Preston, and its inhabitants. The respective firms of Swainson, Birley, & Co., the owners of one of the largest cotton factories in the town, well known as "Fishwick Mills" or "Big Factory," Calvert & Sons, Eccles Brothers, Robert Gardner & Co., John Humber, Hawkins & Sons, J. & A. Leigh, and several others must be included in the category. The total number of cotton mills in Preston at present is 46, giving employment to about 35,000 artisans and others.

STRIKES.

The high position to which Preston has attained by its cotton manufacture during the present century, has not, however, been reached without many trials and drawbacks. There is no sunshine without an occasionally overshadowing cloud, and the aphorism holds true when, in the retrospect, we view the periods of adversity through which both employers and employed have had to pass. Many causes have in turn contributed to these disastrous troubles, some of them being of a specially economic nature. Others have arisen out of the unfortunate differences between masters and men; whilst the terrible internecine war in the United States, during the years 1861-2, was perhaps the most crushing and distressing cause of all. The result of these several adverse periods was that whilst the labouring population had to endure bitter domestic suffering, the loss to the masters, shopkeepers, and the town gener-

ally, can only be estimated at untold thousands. Not
many years after the cotton manufacture began to flourish
in Preston, the employed became dissatisfied with the
wages which they were receiving, and labouring under
the impression that they were entitled to participate more
largely in the profits which the employers were enjoying;
the weavers made a demonstration in the year 1808,
assembling on the moor in large numbers, in order to
obtain an advance of wages. On this occasion disturbances and a breach of the peace were anticipated, for it is
recorded that it became necessary, as a precautionary
measure, to have the military within call, who "were
ready at a moment's notice." It appears that the weavers
failed to obtain an advance, as they also did ten years
later, when in 1818, a similar attempt was made, on
which occasion 1200 weavers paraded the streets of the
town. In the year 1831, Preston was the scene of one of
those unwise and suicidal resistances to the introduction
of improved machinery, which have on many repeated
occasions been manifested by the operative classes, under
the delusive impression that it must necessarily put an
end to manual labour, instead of, on the other hand, increasing the demand for it in the long run, which all
experience has proved to be the case. During this year
some new inventions in machinery connected with the
cotton manufacture, which were for the first time practically brought into use in several of the mills in Preston,
led to serious disturbances on the part of the operatives,
who threatened with destruction the establishments in
which this improved machinery had been introduced, the
Fishwick Mills, belonging to Swainson, Birleys, & Co.,
being one of the buildings singled out,and in the attack made
upon it considerable damage was done, but the chief sufferers were the attacking party themselves, whose efforts
to prevent the practical working of the newly introduced
machinery, were, of course, fruitless. One of the most
serious reverses which the trade underwent was in the
year 1836, when, in October of that year, there was a
strike of the spinners for an advance of wages. The em-

ployers consented to give them an advance of 10 per cent., but this was conditional on the operatives separating themselves from the trades' union. These terms were rejected by the men, the consequence being that for a period of three months the mills in the town were closed, during which about 9000 persons connected with the trade were thrown out of employment. For some weeks during the continuance of the strike the spinners and piecers employed by them, were to a certain extent supported from the trades' union funds, furnished from other towns, but the card-room hands, reelers, and power-loom weavers, who were also forcibly thrown out of employment by the action of the spinners, suffered the most severe privations. Pauperism rapidly increased, and whilst out-door relief was liberally given by the Overseers, the Workhouse became greatly overcrowded. Eventually, at the end of three months, the mills were finally re-opened, the spinners returning to their employment on the masters' terms, having been compelled to take this step in consequence of the funds of the trade union being exhausted. The total loss to the town by this strike and turn-out, was estimated at £108,000, of which sum £57,210 was lost to the operatives in wages; the loss to the masters was £45,000; and added to these sums was £5000, the estimated loss to shopkeepers.

Another of these trade convulsions took place in the month of August, 1842, when, throughout the whole of the cotton manufacturing districts in Lancashire, there was a demand for a higher rate of wages, and Preston did not escape the agitation. This demonstration on the part of the operatives was accompanied by rioting of a very alarming character, resulting in five persons being killed in Preston. One organisation of the disaffected operatives consisted of large mobs forcibly entering the different mills, and compelling the workmen to leave their employment. This movement was to a great extent successful, the liberated operatives swelling the numbers of the mob, and joining those who had induced them to leave their respective mills. On Friday, the 12th August, and up to

the morning of the following day, Saturday the 13th,
Preston might be said to have been in the hands of the
mob, but by eight o'clock on the morning of the last
named day a detachment of the military had arrived, and,
ioined by the police, charged the mob, who were then
assembled in large numbers, and as they refused to disperse,
the commanding officer gave the order to fire, when five
persons were killed, and three others were wounded.   A
few days afterwards further riots took place in the neigh-
bourhoods of Leyland, Farington, Penwortham, and
Walton, about thirty of the rioters being taken prisoners.

The most disastrous struggle, however, was that
which took place in the year 1853. It was for an advance
of ten per cent in the wages of the operatives, which had
been taken off in the years 1842-8, when trade was de-
pressed, and which the mill hands contended they now
ought to have restored, inasmuch as trade had revived
and the masters were making large profits, whilst it was
further alleged that provisions were very high. The employers were disposed to concede the demand under certain conditions, but the men insisted upon a uniform advance of ten per cent., taking the highest wages then
paid as their standard ; but as some of the employers
were paying a lower rate than others, this demand on the
part of the men was rejected, and the whole of the masters
came to a determination to close their mills rather than
submit to the demands of the men.   This determination
was carried out, the struggle commencing at the end of
August, and lasting until the 22nd of May, 1854, when
it was brought to a close, having extended over a period
of thirty-nine weeks, or about nine months, during which
time about 25,000 hands were thrown out of employment.
The wide spread distress and suffering which this deplor-
able dispute between the masters and men caused will be
easily imagined. The struggle ended by the workmen
being compelled to resume their employment on the
masters' terms. An exhaustive statistical statement as
to the enormous expenditure, and loss to both employers
and employed, as well as to the tradesmen in the town,

carriers, railway companies, and others, caused by the struggle, shows, among other items, that the sum of £64,000 was distributed in relief to the operatives and their families who had thus been thrown out of employment. These figures are taken from the last report of the operatives' committee, to whom was entrusted the distribution of the funds subscribed for the purpose by the operatives connected with the cotton trade in other towns. The loss of wages to the operatives is set down at £250,000. A similar report issued by the "Masters', Spinners', and Manufacturers' Defence Fund," gives the probable cost of the struggle to the masters. The capital sunk in their respective establishments in the town was stated to be £1,000,000. The loss to them during the continuance of the dispute was estimated at £165,000. This sum was made up by £50,000 being set down as the trading loss to the employers ; loss by depreciation, interest, and other contingencies, for 38 weeks, £67,000 ; unavoidable expenses in wages, fuel, and other items, during the continuance of the strike, £28,000 ; and loss in working machinery, with inferior description of hands, £20,000 ; the loss to tradesmen in the town, £11,250 ; the total loss, on the part of employers and employed during the continuance of the strike being £500,230, in addition to an estimated loss of £10,000 sustained by railway companies, carriers, and others.

THE AMERICAN CIVIL WAR.—PRIVATIONS OF THE COTTON OPERATIVES.—SPEECH OF THE EARL OF DERBY.

Some nine or ten years later, Preston, in common with the other manufacturing towns in the cotton districts, had again to pass through an exceptionally severe and prolonged period of adversity. This was not owing to any renewed disputes between masters and men, but was the result of that desolating and memorable civil war in America during the years 1862-3, which prevented the raw material from being imported from the United States, and thus brought all the cotton mills in Lancashire to a stand. The sufferings of the cotton operatives in Preston, in common with other towns in the country, were of the most harrowing description, and were not less eloquently than pathetically enlarged upon at Manchester, by the late Earl of Derby, on the occasion of a great county meeting held in that city, on the 2nd of December, 1862. The late Earl's close and intimate connection with Preston, invests his remarks, on that occasion, with a special interest.

" We are met together," said his lordship, " upon on occasion which must call forth the most painful, and which at the same time ought to excite—and I am sure will excite—the most kindly feelings of our human nature. We are met to consider the best means of palliating—would to God I could say removing—a great national calamity, the like whereof, in modern times, has never been witnessed in this favoured land; a calamity which it was impossible for those who are the greatest sufferers to foresee, or, if they had foreseen, to take any step to avoid ; a calamity which, though shared by the nation at large, falls more particularly, and with the heaviest weight, upon this hitherto prosperous and wealthy district ; a calamity which has converted this teeming hive of industry into a stagnant desert, comparatively of inactivity and idleness, and transformed that which has been the source of our greatest wealth into the deepest abyss of impoverishment ; a calamity which has impoverished the wealthy, which has brought brought distress upon those who have been somewhat above the world, by the exercise of frugal industry ; and a calamity which has reduced honest and struggling poverty to a state of absolute and humiliating destitution. It is to meet this calamity that we are met together, and to add our means and our assistance to those efforts which have been so nobly made throughout the country generally." His lordship then pointed out the great amount of distress and destitution which prevailed, by showing the enormous increase in the number of those who were receiving parochial relief in the manufacturing districts. in addition to those who were relieved by the several local committees in the various towns throughout the county ; and having further shown the very large excess in the amount of deposits withdrawn from the savings' banks, the noble Earl proceeded :—" We may figure to ourselves the amount of difficulty, sorrow, and privation, which that amount represents. . It represents the blighted hopes for life of many a family ; it represents the small sums set aside by honest, frugal, persevering industry, by years of toil and self-dependence, in the hope of it being, as it has been in many cases before, the foundations of colossal fortunes ; it represents the hopes for his family of many an industrious artisan ; and it is the first step in that downward progress which leads him to destitution and to pauperism. The first step is the withdrawal of the savings of honest industry from the savings' banks ; then comes the sacrifice of some little cherished article of furniture ; the cutting off of some little indulgence ; the sacrifice of that which makes in his home an additional appearance of comfort and happiness ; the sacrifice, one by one, of articles of furniture ; until at last the well-conducted, honest, frugal, saving artisan, finds himself on a level with the idle, the disssipated, and the impoverished, obliged to pawn the very clothes of his family, and only prevented by a noble independence from becoming the recipient of public or private charity, in the emphatic words of the dialect of his own county declaring, ' Nay, but we will clem first.' I cannot lose the opportunity of asking this great assembly, with what feelings this state of things should be contemplated by those in higher circumstances. In the first place, I will say with all reverence, that it is a subject for deep national humiliation. We have been accustomed for years to look with pride upon the enormous wealth of the manufacturing portion of the industry of this country ; we have seen, within the last twelve or fourteen years, the consumption of cotton in Europe extending from 50,000 to 90,000 bales per week ; we have seen the weight of cotton exported from this country amounting to no less than 983,000,000 lbs. in a single year ; and we have been accustomed to look down upon those less fortunate districts where wealth and fortune are built upon a less secure foundation—to consider the cotton manufactures as a security against the possibility of war between us and the cotton-producing districts, and to hold that in the cotton manufacture lies the great strength of the country, and of future national prosperity and peace. I am afraid we have looked at this too much in the spirit of the assyrian monarch of old, to whom the words were called forth, ' Thy Kingdom is departed from thee.' That which was his pride became his humiliation, and that which has been our pride has become our humiliation and punishment. That which we have considered the source of our wealth, and the sure foundation upon which we have built, has been itself the cause of our humiliation. The reed upon which we have leaned has gone through the hand that pressed upon it, and has pierced us to the heart."

PRESTON AND ITS RAILWAY HISTORY.

Railway communication has, within the last forty years, placed Preston in an exceedingly advantageous position as regards its trade and commerce. It was, indeed, one of the first towns in England into which the steam locomotive railway was introduced. When the pioneer passenger railway between Liverpool and Manchester was opened in 1830, a railway between Preston, Wigan, and Parkside, to connect Preston with the two great Lancashire towns at the last-named point, was first projected. Amongst the most enterprising and enthusiastic of the promoters of this undertaking was the late Mr. William Tomlinson, who laboured with unflagging energy to ensure the prosecution of the line ; but it was some years afterwards before the work was actually commenced, when an Act of Parliament having been obtained for the purpose, the construction of the line between Preston and Wigan, a distance of sixteen miles, was vigoronsly proceeded with, embracing the erection of the massive viaduct across the Ribble, Messrs. Mullen, Mc.Mahon, and Co. being the contractors. The short line of seven miles in length, between Wigan and Parkside, had already been completed and opened, some three or four years after the opening of the Liverpool and Manchester Railway. The line between Preston and Wigan, forming a junction with the Wigan and Parkside line, was opened on the 22nd of October, 1838, thus establishing railway communication between Preston and Liverpool and Manchester, *via* Parkside, the line 22½ miles in length, between Preston and Parkside, then being designated the North Union Railway. In the year 1841 another new railway was opened. This line, commenced by a junction with the North Union Railway at Euxton, passing through Chorley, and terminating by a junction with the Manchester and Bolton line, at the last-named town. The Manchester and Bolton line had been opened for traffic in May, 1838, and the opening of the line to Bolton, from the Euxton Station of the North Union Railway, placed Preston and Manchester in more direct communication by railway, the angular and circuitous route by Parkside being avoided, and the distance between the two towns very considerably reduced. The opening of the new route from Euxton to Bolton was followed by a prolonged competition for the traffic

between Preston and Manchester, by the owners of
the North Union line on the one hand, and the proprietors of the new Euxton and Bolton line on the other, the
last-named company having running powers over the
North Union Company's line between Preston and Euxton, with similar powers over the Bolton and Manchester
line. The competition between the two companies,
which continued for some time, was accompanied by reduced and abnormally low fares. Eventually, however,
terms of amalgamation were agreed upon, and the Bolton
section, from the junction at Euxton, became absorbed in
the North Union Company, the shares of the two undertakings being converted into £100 stock, when the
original or North Union proper holdings were registered
"North Union Stock A," and the Bolton and Euxton
shares "North Union Stock B," by which designation
they continue to be known up to the present time. This
stock is perhaps about the best and most secure railway
property in the country. and has a special history of its
own, no less interesting than unique. Sometime after
the union of the two above-named companies, negociations were opened with the view of bringing about an
amalgamation with the Liverpool and Manchester Company, which for many years past had been paying its
shareholders a dividend of ten per cent. per annum. The
terms of amalgamation offered to the North Union by
the directors of the Liverpool and Manchester Company
were seven per cent. dividend to the Stock A holders and
five per cent. to Stock B. At this time the North Union
line was paying a much lower dividend, and many shareholders were disposed to regard the offer of the Liverpool
and Manchester Company with much favour. When,
however, the meeting of North Union shareholders was
held at Preston, to consider the proposed terms of amalgamation, a very strong opposition to the proposal was
manifested by a large body of shareholders, notwithstanding that the North Union directors recommended
its acceptance. The Rev. John Shepherd Birley, who was
one of the leading opponents of the proposal, urged that,

although the North Union Company was at that time only paying a comparatively small rate of dividend, the shareholders would not be justified in accepting anything less than ten per cent., looking to the prospective value of the North Union line.   The meeting resulted in the rejection of the Liverpool and Manchester Company's proposals. The negotiations, however, were continued, and on a second meeting of North Union shareholders being called at Preston, to take into consideration the further proposals of the Liverpool and Manchester Company, it transpired that the directors of that company were disposed to concede the ten per cent., placing the stock of the North Union Company on the same level, as to value, with their own.   The Rev. J. Shepherd Birley and his friends were now, however, indisposed to sanction amalgamation on any terms.   It was pointed out with much force that the North Union line must eventually be the connecting link between London and the North, and that the two great trunk lines south of Preston, extending to the metropolis, would ultimately have possession of it. A lease of the line in perpetuity was therefore agreed upon by the shareholders as the most desirable course to adopt, and to these terms the Liverpool and Manchester Company at length consented, guaranteeing North Union Stock A a dividend of ten per cent., and Stock B a dividend of seven and a half per cent., the lease also containing a clause to the effect that the dividend was to be paid to the lessors by the Liverpool and Manchester directors before their own shareholders received anything. Some years afterwards the Liverpool and Manchester Company and the London and North-Western Company amalgamated, the London and North-Western taking over the Liverpool and Manchester Company with all its obligations to the North Union shareholders.   Since that time the dividends of the amalgamated companies have often fallen as low as four per cent., but the North Union Company's guaranteed dividends of ten and seven and a half per cent., respectively, remain intact, and the exceptionally high value of the stock is indicated by its price in the share market. The year 1840 saw three other local railways opened for traffic, all within a few months of each other; the Preston and Longridge line being opened on the 1st of May; the Preston and Lancaster line on the 25th of June; and the Preston and Wyre line to Fleetwood on the 15th of July. It should be added that since that time branch lines from the main line to Fleetwood have also been opened to Lytham and Blackpool, and likewise a further line between Preston, Lytham, and Blackpool direct. In 1845 the line between Preston and Blackburn was opened; and in the year 1849 a new direct line between Preston and Liverpool was completed and inaugurated. The line passes through Ormskirk and several other localities on the west coast of Lancashire. When the bill for the construction of this railway was under consideration before the Parliamentary Committee, it was strongly opposed in the interests of the North Union and Liverpool and Manchester Companies, the only route between Preston and Liverpool being then *via* Parkside. It was, however, proved before the Committee that the distances between the two towns would be very considerably reduced by the proposed line, its length being only about twenty-five miles, whereas the distance by the Parkside route was thirty-eight miles. The bill, consequently, received Parliamentary sanction. In the year 1855 a branch line from Burscough, on the Preston and Liverpool Railway, to Southport, was opened, thus giving Preston railway communication with this popular watering place. Another new railway between Preston and Southport is at present in course of construction. This line, which runs immediately along the coast of the Ribble in a south-westerly direction, is about fifteen miles in length, and will shorten the distance between Preston and Southport by several miles. It is expected to be completed and opened for traffic in the course of the present year. It will thus be seen that in connection with its trade, and passenger and merchandise traffic, Preston possesses the most ample railway facilities.

SHIPBUILDING AT PRESTON.

Shipbuilding on the banks of the Ribble has formed no inconsiderable portion of the commerce of Preston, more especially during the last three decades. Within that period several vessels of large tonnage have been built, Mr. Smith, Messrs. Ogle and Robinson, and other builders having, on repeated occasions, launched sailing vessels and steamers having a burthen of 1,000 tons each and upwards. The principal shipbuilders at present are Mr. Smith and Messrs. Allsup, the last-named firm having, for some time past, conducted an extensive business, and built and launched numerous vessels of large tonnage, including both steamships and sailing vessels, for the foreign as well as the coasting trade.

PRESTON AS A SEAPORT.—NAVIGATION OF THE RIBBLE.

The above statements relative to shipbuilding on the Ribble during many years past, will, in all probability, induce most persons to conclude that the several sailing and steam vessels of large tonnage, which have in succession been sent off the stocks at the different building yards, would have encouraged those more directly interested in the development of the Ribble, vigorously to proceed with the improvement of its navigation. Unfortunately, however, there appears to have been a marked absence of public spirit and enterprise, during several years past, on the part of the Ribble Navigation Company, although engineers of acknowledged eminence have at different periods shown that the deepening of the channel, so as to admit of vessels of large tonnage coming up to the quays, and making Preston a first-class port, is an under-taking easy of accomplishment. The improvement of the navigation of the Ribble, so as to increase its shipping facilities, is an important and vital element in view of the advancement and expansion of the trade and commerce of Preston, but there appears small hope of these much desired works being effected so long as their execution remains in present hands, and under the control of a corporate body which seems practically powerless. The partial improvements and their results, which have, indeed, already been made ought, in themselves, to be incentives to proceed, whereas they have apparently been followed by a lethargic inactivity, and a listless indifference to the prosecution of the work, which it is difficult to reconcile with the attributes of a robust business enterprise. It is only fair to admit that the manner in which the Ribble Navigation Company practically set to work, shortly after its incorporation in 1837, gave much promise, and was an earnest of an apparent determination to carry to a successful issue the various engineering operations which were indispensibly necessary for converting the Ribble into a high-class mercantile water-way. Acting upon the report which had been presented by Messrs. Stevenson and Sons, of Edinbugh, the works for the deepening of the channel between the quays at Preston and the Naze Point were commenced in the year 1839, the rock near the quays being excavated until a depth of nearly twenty feet of water was obtained, whilst the dredging operations in the channel below were simultaneously proceeded with. These works had not been in progress more than two years when a very great and sensible improvement was effected, amply sufficient to encourage the promoters of the work, and to stimulate them to continuous and persevering action. Subsequently, with the view of confining the channel, and thus securing an increased depth of water, a wall was constructed on the north side of the river extending to the Naze, whilst in 1843 quays were erected by the Corporation, independently of the works which had been executed by the Ribble Company. About this time the improvements which had been made in the navigation of the river began to show themselves financially, for at the close of 1842, only three years after the commencement of the works, the company's report stated that the tonnage for the half-year was "double in amount as compared with the corresponding half year," whilst according to the report at the meeting of the company in January, 1844, it was shown that the amount of customs duties had increased to £19,375, as against £6,309 in the year 1841, being upwards of two hundred per cent. of an increase in the space of two years. From this date the business of the port continued to increase, the report stating that during the year 1844 the value of the tonnage had gradually increased from £500 to nearly £2,000 a year, and that within the same period the amount received for customs was £23,303 13s. 7d. Year by year the shipping continued to be satisfactory, the tonnage dues at Preston, in 1845, amounting to £1,812 7s. 10d., and at the dock at Lytham, which was constructed in 1841, with the view to afford a safe harbour and anchorage for vessels until the tides permitted their approach to Preston, the dues for tonnage amounted to £154 4s. 9d., making a total of £4,963 12s. 7d.; whilst the customs for the same year amounted to £66,921 4s. 9d., being three times the amount of the previous year. During the years 1846, 1847, 1848, and 1849 there was a falling off in the imports and exports, with a decrease in the revenue from tonnage, this being to a large extent accounted for by the general stagnation of trade. In 1850, however, there was a considerable revival, the report of the company for this year stating that the increase of the tonnage over 1849 amounted in imports to 3,352 tons register, and in exports to 3,427 tons. Important practical testimony was made in 1851 of the beneficial results which, up to that period, had followed upon the company's works, for the report for that year states that "the pilots and mariners frequenting the river all concur in their testimony of the great improvement which is being effected in the navigation of the river." In 1852 the imports for the year were 39,716 tons, and the exports 24,888 tons. The engineer's report for this year contains some interesting particulars as to the discoveries made in the bed of the river during the dredging operations. The report states that forest trees of very large dimensions—in one or two instances containing one hundred cubic feet of timber in each tree—had been taken from the river's bed during the previous six months. Altogether upwards of one hundred of these trees were removed, containing from two thousand to three thousand cubic feet of timber. A great proportion of these forest trees were found near that part of the river named " Peg Hill," opposite to Ashton Marsh. In 1853 there was a further increase of tonnage over that of the previous year to the extent of 1,943 tons. Up to this year 914 acres of reclaimed land, consequent upon the improvements made in the river, had become available to the company. In the year 1854 the directors reported a still further increased revenue from tolls and dues, whilst in 1855 the revenue from this source had continued to expand, for the report states that the receipts of dues and tolls for the six months ending December, 1855, amounted to £1,030 11s. 10d., while for the corresponding six months ending December, 1854, they amounted to £780 3s. 9d. Of the land which had already been reclaimed, the directors state that up to February, 1855, 279 acres on the north side of the river had been sold for an aggregate sum of £7,031 17s. 9d., being at the rate of from £25 to £26 per acre. The land so reclaimed is situated on the banks of the river, in the parishes of Lea, Clifton, Freckleton, and Newton respectively, of which 49 acres in Lea were sold to Sir H. B. Hoghton for £1,275 19s.; 146 acres in Clifton to J. T. Clifton, Esq., for £3,656 5s., 48 acres in Freckleton to H. Pedder, Esq., for £1,191 17s. 6d.; and 36 acres in Newton to Messrs. Fisher and Loxham for £907 16s. 3d. The land reclaimed on the south side, in the parishes of Hutton, Hesketh, and Howick, up to this period, was 628 acres, of which 91 acres in Hutton were sold for £1,184, and 436 acres in Hesketh for £5,108; making the total amount realised by the sale of these lands £13,323 17s. 9d. The land reclaimed in the township of Howick, 101 acres in extent, was stated to be vested in the company absolutely, and retained by them. In their report dated February,

1856, the directors state that "the entire quantity of land which will ultimately be recoverable from the river will exceed 3,000 acres." The tolls and dues for the six months ending June 30th, 1856, amounted to £802 15s. 10d., as compared with £794 15s. 4d. for the corresponding six months in 1855. In their half-yearly report presented to the shareholders in August, 1855, the directors state that they had deemed it prudent, in the then state of the money market, to confine the works to mere repairs of the walls, and to delay the commencement of the important works on Hesketh and Longton marshes, but that they had now determined to proceed with them. During the two following years these works were forwarded. The report of 1859 stated that within the previous five years 624 acres of land had been further reclaimed, £9,000 having been obtained in the previous year for reclaimed land at Hesketh-with-Becconsal, sold to Sir T. G. Hesketh. Up to the end of 1859 the total sum obtained for the sale of reclaimed land was £25,819, whilst at the close of 1861 it had reached £29,178. The several reports of the company from 1860 to 1866 show that dredging and other works continued during these several years, and that the revenue from tonnage amounted to an average of from £1,800 to £2,000 a year. Within this period about 555 acres of land were reclaimed at Freckleton and Newton, this land having been secured by an embankment two miles in length, which was erected at a cost of £11,800. The new lighthouse at Lytham was also erected within this period, namely, in 1864. The total sum for land reclaimed and sold up to 1866 was £31,042. In this year the reclaimed land at Freckleton and Newton was let to the Preston Farming Company for 21 pears, at a rental of £3 per acre, thus producing an annual rental of upwards of £1,600. From the year 1866 little appears to have been done in the way of improving the river, whilst in subsequent years the revenue very considerably decreased, this decrease continuing up to the time when the company's report was issued in the year 1881. Since 1866 all works for the improvement of the river have practically been suspended. In that year Messrs. Bell and Miller, civil engineers, were requested by the Corporation, as the largest shareholders in the Ribble Navigation Company, to report upon the best means of improving the navigation of the river, and rendering it suitable for vessels of large tonnage. Their report, presented at the meeting of the company in February, 1867, was to the effect that there were no physical characteristics in the nature of the harbour or river to interpose any serious obstacles to improvement; but that, on the contrary, the conditions were highly favourable for the development of Preston into a port of a first-rate character, and fitted for the reception of almost any class of shipping. They then recommended that the river should be deepened to keep pace with the increasing size of vessels, and that as a first stage it should be made navigable for sailing ships up to 500 tons register, and steam ships of a corresponding large size; and that, after this had been attained, a continuous and gradual further deepening should be carried out according as the trade increased. The engineers further stated that the establishment of wet docks at Preston was a necessity, and without which no material increase in the trade of the port need be expected. They then suggested that the best mode of attaining this would be by impounding part of the river bed, and forming a new channel for the river. In concluding their report they remarked that they could not but be impressed by the many advantages which Preston possessed for the development of a great trade. The most important of these was the central position which the port held in Lancashire, and in being immediately connected with the great lines of railway ramifying to every part of the kingdom. A glance at the map would show that the port of Preston was nearer to many of the great seats of population and manufacturing industry than the port of Liverpool. Not only that, but Preston was in itself a place of large population and manufactures, and, therefore, formed at once a basis for the rapid development of a port. Further, a ready and convenient source of a great trade, if properly taken advantage of, was afforded by the vast coal-fields of Lancashire, a great portion of which were so near to Preston. The bulk of the Wigan coal-field was considerably nearer to Preston than either Liverpool, Garston, or Fleetwood, where the coal was chiefly shipped. The comparison of the Ribble with the Clyde formed an important and interesting feature in the report. On this point the engineers observed that from the great depth of water at high tide, which existed at a comparatively short distance from the harbour in the case of the Ribble, it was not necessary to carry the deepening operations one-half the distance that was required in the Clyde; and the great slope of the river bed confined the removal of material of the river bed chiefly to the wedge-shaped portion of the upper part of the channel. The actual quantity of material, therefore, even taking the bed of the river at its original level, and sup-posing it were lowered to admit of vessels getting up as large as those of the Clyde, was trifling compared with what it had been necessary to remove in that river. They added that the physical characteristics of the Ribble were much more favourable, in an economic point of view, for making a great improvement than were those of the Clyde. This report led to a special meeting of the company being held, for the purpose of considering the desirability of forming a Public Trust, under the name of the "Ribble Docks and Harbour Board," with the view of carrying out Messrs. Bell and Miller's recom-mendations. At this meeting it was resolved that the constitution of such a Board should be undertaken, with an application to Parliament for its incorporation, and powers to borrow money. In the meantime an applica-tion was made to the Public Works Loan Commissioners but this body stated that it was against the rule to make any advances before an Act of Parliament had actually been obtained constituting a Board for the construction of public works, adding that collateral security, in addition to that which the company at present could give for ad

vances, would in all probability be required. This reply
from the Public Works Loan Commissioners, made
known at the meeting of the company in February,
1868, was followed by the postponement of the proposed
application to Parliament for powers to form the "Ribble
Docks and Harbour Board," the consequence being that
Messrs. Bell and Miller's recommendations were not
adopted, and the suggested improvements in the navigation of the river and other works remained in abeyance.
In their report presented to the shareholders at the half-
yearly meeting in February, 1869, the directors stated
that up to that time 2,599 acres of land had been reclaimed. An unfavourable feature in the report, however,
was that the revenue from tonnage, and the imports and
exports, continued to decrease. This decrease still
continuing, the directors, in their report of August, 1869,
make the following remarks:—"No great increase will
take place in the revenue of the company, or of the quays
of the Corporation, until the scheme agreed upon in
1867 for the 'Ribble Dock and Harbour Board' is carried
out. They call the attention of the shareholders to the
absolute necessity of at once adopting some measures for
deepening the bed of the river, and making a dock, so as
to enable larger and more modern-built vessels to come
up to Preston." No further steps in this direction were
however taken, little work being done either in dredging
or confining the river by the construction of walls up to
the year 1879, when it appeared from the directors' report of that year that the sum which had been received
for the sale of reclaimed lands amounted to £33,395.
The report of February, 1881, stated that the directors
had entered into negociations with the Corporation for
the sale to them of the undertaking and property of the
company, the sum which the company asked for the entire property, including the Freckleton Farm, being
£72,650, The report of August, 1881, stated that the
Corporation declined to give £72,650 for the property,
but that negociations had recently been resumed between
the Corporation committee and the company. The re-

port likewise stated that the total amount which had
been received for the sale of reclaimed lands up to the
date of the issue of their report was £35,762. The last
report of the company—the eighty-eighth which has
been issued—was presented to the shareholders at their
half-yearly meeting in February of the present year; and
was again of an unsatisfactory character. It stated that
the revenue derived from tolls for the half-year ending
December 31st amounted to £450 19s. 3d., while that of
the corresponding half-year of 1880 amounted to £577
7s. 5d. It added that the negociations named in the last
report as having been resumed by the Corporation committee, for the purchase of the undertaking and property,
had ceased without any agreement. The engineer's report stated that the channel at the end of the south guide
wall continued to bear more away towards the south side
of the estuary, making it more difficult to navigate. The
directors in their report refer to the attempt which is now
being made to straighten the course of the channel below
the guide walls as far as Lytham Pier. Expressing the
hope that it may be successful, the directors observe that
should it not prove so, no cost of the experiment will fall
upon the company. An explanation of the process by
which the channel is expected to be straightened will not
be out of place, and here it may be observed that the
enterprising individual who has undertaken the task must
be confident of his labours resulting in success, inasmuch
as his arrangement with the Ribble Company involves
the principle of " no cure no pay." The apparatus by
which the work is proposed to be accomplished is unique
in its simplicity, and, assisted by the ebb and flow of the
tide, self-acting. The *Lytham Times*, in its issue of the
1st of February of the present year, has an interesting
description of the operations, from which it appears that
the contrivance consists of planks, chains, and anchors,
or other moorings, which may be carried to any length,
from twenty feet to twenty miles. The apparatus now
in operation is several hundred yards in length. A sluice
has been cut for some distance through the bank, in the

direction of Lytham, and it is within this that the apparatus is acting. In illustrating the manner of working the apparatus, it may be observed that if the current of the river was in all parts of it sufficiently strong to prevent the subsidence of small particles of sand no mud or sand banks could be formed, but at present they do form, and it is such banks that the apparatus is expected to remove, by dispersing it for the tidal current to carry away. The current over the bank on which the apparatus is placed is not sufficiently strong to move away the bank, but by concentrating the power, or a portion of the power, diffused through the whole width and depth of the current, and bringing it to bear upon a narrow line of operations, it is believed that sufficient force will be applied to wash away all sand and mud lying within the scope of its operation. The theory and working of the contrivance is that when the planks are in position, and acting, they may form a breastwork against the current, which, impeded in its course by the breastwork, will "back up," and, being continually pressed up from behind, will rush with great force through the interval between the bottom of the breastwork, and bottom of the sluice, carrying with it by force of scour a portion of the bank. The planks are moved with some little length of free chain, and when under water in a tide way they "wobble" about, and gradually displace the sand beneath them, which is carried away by the ebbing tide. Up to the early part of the present year the disturbing planks were moored by their ends, but that system of mooring has since been abandoned, although the principle of action remains the same. In the operations now going forward, stretching from nearly opposite the Freckleton farm to the old artillery battery, about half a mile from high water mark. is a mud bank choking up what once was a channel. The channel now runs round towards Hesketh Bank. From the upper end of the bank on the Warton side a sluice, about five feet wide and two feet deep, has been cut in almost a straight line to its lower end. In the sluice so cut planks crossed are moored from

their centres. The sluice is a mile and a quarter long,
and it has within the last few months been deepened by
men working with spades, with the hope of obtaining
more force of current through it. A screw steamer has
been on the spot to assist in loosening the mud on each
side of the sluice, and following upon that, the rising and
ebbing tides, working with the planks and chains, appear
to be having the effect of clearing away the sand and mud,
and cutting through and opening out the intended
straight channel in the direction of the Lytham Pier.
The loosened mud is, by force of scour, said to be carried
down to the outlet of the sluice during ebb, and there
deposited until the incoming tides catch it up, and, by
currents as they at present set, carry and pile up one part
of it near the front of the battery; whilst another current is said to be taking up the other part, and depositing
it in the present round-about channel. This process is
now going forward day by day, and those engaged in the
work have the greatest confidence that the narrow sluice,
under the operation of the self-acting submerged plank
and chain apparatus already described, will shortly become a navigable channel, which by its own force will
keep itself open. It is to be hoped that these sanguine
expectations will ultimately be realised, for, should the
works now in progress be brought to a successful issue,
an important step in advance will have been made in the
endeavour to secure a more direct navigable water-way
between Lytham and Preston. But, apart from these
experimental operations, much remains to be done in the
deepening of the river, between the points just named, up
to the quays on the Marsh, and, as there appears to be a
consentient opinion on the part of engineers of eminence
that the conversion of Preston into a high-class seaport
is easy of accomplishment, the sooner the undertaking of
the Ribble Navigation Company is transferred to some
such public board or trust as that of the Mersey, the more
likelihood will there be of this desirable end being attained, and of Preston taking its natural position as one
of the great shipping centres in the country.

PUBLIC BUILDINGS, PARKS, AND INSTITUTIONS.

A PERUSAL of the preceding pages will have given the visitor to Preston, some conception of its general character and extent, from which he will have learned that whilst its historical antecedents are not without interest, it possesses, at the present time, many modern features, both material and otherwise, with which he may make himself profitably acquainted. Assuming that in all probability the visitor will first enter the town on taking his leave of the great trunk line of railway which has brought him either from the north or the south, he will at once find himself on the platforms of one of the most extensive railway stations in the country.

THE LONDON AND NORTH WESTERN AND
LANCASHIRE AND YORKSHIRE STATION

at Preston, is said to be the longest structure of its kind in the United Kingdom, and in every other respect one of the most spacious and costly. The enormous amount of traffic passing through Preston, between London and Scotland, as also to and from Man-

chester, Liverpool, and other Lancashire and Yorkshire
towns, to the watering places of Lytham, Blackpool, Southport, and various other localities, rendered an exceptionally
large station absolutely necessary. This station which was
opened for traffic about two years since, occupied several
years in its construction, and is not yet completed, extensions on the west side being still in progress. These
extensions will admit of several additional lines of rails
being laid down, beyond the present net work of metals
stretching across the station to the width, with the platforms, of upwards of 350 feet. Exclusive of the metals
about to be added on the west side, there are at present
twelve lines of rails for the daily traffic arriving at and
departing from the station. On the north side the station
boundary extends to Fishergate, on the south side of
which thoroughfare it is approached by a spacious road
and carriage way, on a descending gradient, this carriage
way being about 400 feet in length, and 80 feet in width
The entire length of the station, from the approach in
Fishergate, to the southern boundary of the covered platforms, is about one-third of a mile in extent, whilst the
two central platforms are each 1,360 feet or more than a
quarter of a mile long, and 40 feet wide. They are technically designated the "island platforms," lines of rails
connected with the other platforms and station buildings
running entirely round them, on the east and west sides
In the centre of these island platforms, with access on
each side to both, there are three large blocks of buildings
separated by spacious open areas. Each block is 40 feet
in width. The north block is 120 feet long, and contains
in addition to four large and lofty waiting rooms, each 40
feet by 30 feet, the station master's offices and private
apartments. The central block is 170 feet in length, and
contains two spacious refreshment rooms 100 feet long
together with a fine dining saloon, 70 feet long, and
capable of dining 300 persons. Both the dining saloon
and the refreshment rooms are luxuriantly decorated and
furnished, and the floors are laid with ornamental encaustic tiles. In the basement, under the refreshment and

dining saloons there is a spacious kitchen, and an extensive suite of apartments connected with the *cuisine* department. The south block, 120 feet long, contains spacious general and other waiting rooms, duplicate booking and re-booking offices, telegraph office, transfer parcel office, and several other offices. All these are in addition to a large central block, at the approach to the station from Fishergate, containing the chief booking offices, parcel offices, cloak room, and several other offices. The Lancashire and Yorkshire section of the station is on the east side of that above described, and is connected with the London and North Western portion by a sub-way carried entirely across the station from east to west. The sub-way is approached at each end by an inclined plane, the walls being faced with white enamelled brick, whilst several opaque glass coverings in the ceiling give an abundance of light. The Lancashire and Yorkshire section of the station buildings has an entirely separate range of booking offices, waiting rooms, parcel offices, telegraph offices, and apartments, with two wide and long platforms, also two double lines of rails, and in addition to being connected with the London and North Western section by the sub-way, it is approached on the east side from Fishergate by a spacious carriage way. The entire station is covered in by an iron and glass roof, consisting of three wide bays, running the whole length of the station. The line on its way to the English northern counties, Scotland, and Lytham, Blackpool, and Fleetwood, passes under Fishergate by three underground openings or tunnels, but these having been found inadequate to the traffic, additional tunnels, with further lines of railway westward are contemplated, which will involve the purchase of some valuable property on both the north and south sides of Fishergate. The station has just been connected with

THE LONDON AND NORTH WESTERN AND

LANCASHIRE AND YORKSHIRE HOTEL

which has been built by the two companies, upon

an elevated piece of ground, on the south side of the station. The hotel overlooks the beautiful park immediately under it, and from its south frontage there is an extensive and picturesque view of the valley of the Ribble, and the country beyond, for several miles around, Hoghton Tower, and other prominent objects on the high ground, being conspicuous features in the distance. The hotel, which is built of red brick, and covered in with red Staffordshire tiles, is in the Elizabethan style of architecture. Its prominent architectural features consist of lofty surmounting gables, with a square tower and ornamental chimney shafts. The tower, while forming a special architectural feature, also acts in the ventilation of the whole of the building. The ventilation, heating, and sanitary arrangements have been carried out by the Sanitary Engineering Company, of Victoria Street, Westminster. The approach to the hotel, from the station platforms, is by a sub-way extending under the line of rails, and thence through a glass covered corridor, in open cutting, to the main entrance to the hotel. After clearing the rails the pathway gradually rises to the ground floor level. Passing below the carriage drive, it does not interfere either with it or the ornamental disposition of the ground. The side walls of the glass-covered corridor are panelled and faced with glazed bricks in neutral colours. They are surmounted with Longridge stone cope or gutter, and roofed in with light iron principals, covered with Rendle's patent glazing. Visitors reaching the hotel, either by road or rail enter through a glass-covered porch or vestibule. On the right hand side, and within the hotel doors, is situated the porters' office and luggage room, billiard room, and smoking room ; and on the left is the grand staircase. Passing along the corridor on the left hand leads to a number of private sitting rooms, public reading and writing rooms, public drawing room, and ladies' room, the last named room having a bow window in the angle. All these rooms, and likewise the spacious coffee room, overlook the Miller Park. On the right hand side of the corridor are four rooms, two of which, by the withdrawal of a moveable partition, are convertible into a large room for meetings, arbitrations, or other similar purposes; and the two adjoining rooms are then useable as ante-rooms.   Otherwise the four rooms may become either bed rooms or sitting rooms as desired. In communication with the coffee room are the coffee room bar, the serving room, waiters' room, plate room, and housekeeper or manager's private room or office. The serving room communicates with the kitchen premises and general stores (which are directly overhead) by hoist and back staircase.   Visitors may ascend the grand staircase, and have their luggage sent by the porters' lift, or, if they desire it, can be taken by hoist, direct to their floor.   In order to provide for the greater height necessary for the coffee room, the apartments over this portion and in the tower are kept at a higher level, and approached by a broad flight of steps from the main landing.   Mr. Mitchell, of Manchester, was the architect.   The cost of the hotel was about £40,000, exclusive of furnishing.

Leaving the railway station and finding himself in Fishergate, the visitor will notice, in that thoroughfare, several public buildings—many of them of modern erection —which, within a comparatively recent period, have materially added to the architectural ornamentation of that part of the town.   On the north side, a short distance to the west of the station approach, is a large block of buildings, now on the eve of completion, designated

THE COUNTY PUBLIC OFFICES.

This imposing structure covers an area of 32,000 superficial square feet, which was purchased by the county authorities, for the purposes of the building, at a cost of about £5,000.   The extensive block, which has been erected on the site is intended for the constabulary, and all other purposes connected with the county, Preston being the centre where all executive business connected with the County Palatine is transacted.   The buildings,

which have a frontage to Fishergate of 160 feet in length,
with a return frontage on the east side, in Pitt Street, of
200 feet, are 54 feet in height, and contain three floors
besides the basement. They are faced with red brick and
minerva stone, from the Welsh quarries near Wrexham.
The principal elevation is that in Fishergate. The several
floors contain ranges of three-light mullion windows, and
the frontage is surmounted by nine ornamental gables,
enriched by a free introduction of sculpture, which includes
the arms of the County Palatine on shields; the "red
rose of Lancashire," and the Prince of Wales's feathers.
There are three projecting entrances, massive cantilevers
supporting elaborately-carved canopies. The Pitt Street
frontage is in its main features uniform with the Fishergate elevation, with an entrance, principally for the
Magistrates, at the north end. The eastern portion of
the buildings contains the offices belonging to the Clerk
of the Peace's department, the treasurer, and auditor,
together with a spacious apartment for the meetings of
the Magistrates of the county; another large apartment
for the storage of the county records, the Magistrates'
dining room, and other apartments; whilst the western
portion of the buildings is set apart for the business
connected with the county constabulary. This last named
part of the building is already completed and occupied,
and the other portion is expected to be finished during
the present year. Within the building there is an
open area from the basement to the top, faced with
white enamelled bricks. The basement contains kitchen,
stores, and several apartments for the sergeants and other
members of the constabulary force. On the ground floor
a corridor, six feet in width, and extending the entire
depth of the building, from the Fishergate frontage, gives
access to the various offices. The floor of the corridor is
laid with polished concrete marble, manufactured in Ger-
many, and the walls are faced with a dado in white and
grey enamelled tiles. The offices of the Clerk of the
Peace, the Deputy Clerk of the Peace, and the several
clerks' offices, are on this floor, as also the record room,

the Magistrates' dining room, and stationery room. . A spacious stone staircase, approached from the Pitt Street entrance, leads to the court room, on the first floor, in which the annual meeting and other meetings of the Magistrates of the county will be held. The dimensions of this room are 63 feet by 45 feet, and its height from the floor to the apex of an ornamental lantern light, is also 45 feet. The lantern light is glazed with embossed coloured glass. Its dimensions are 44 feet by 16 feet. The offices of the county auditor, the treasurer, the bridge-master, and those of their respective subordinates, are also on this floor, along which there are corridors uniform with those on the ground floor, and similarly paved with polished concrete marble. An octagonal staircase, in Hopton Wood stone, from the Derbyshire quarries, having Dalbeattie polished granite columns at the foot, leads to the several offices in the upper part of the building. The second floor contains what are designated spare rooms. All the record rooms, which will contain documents of great value, are fire-proof. Mr. Little, of Manchester, is the architect of the building, and Mr. John Walmsley, of Preston, the contractor. The sculpture is by Mr. Miles, who executed similar work at the Town Hall. The estimated cost of the entire building is £50,000.

THE BAPTIST CHAPEL.

On the north side of Fishergate, some distance eastward of the building just described, is a handsome Baptist Chapel, which stands out as a prominent architectural feature in the thoroughfare. This building, which was erected in the year 1857, from the designs of Mr. James Hibbert, architect, is in the Byzantine style of architecture, and built of Longridge stone. It is ornamented by a lofty tower, and has seating accommodation for between six and seven hundred persons. Beneath the chapel there are spacious schools. On the opposite side is

THE THEATRE ROYAL,

which was built in 1802, by a company of shareholders, the immediate object at the time, being to provide a suitable building for theatrical representations in anticipation of the Guild, which was to be celebrated in that year. Up to that time Preston could not boast of any structure for high class dramatic representations. The only establishment of such character which had for many years before existed, was a small unpretending building in Woodcock's Court, which stood upon a site afterwards occupied by a malt kiln. The present edifice is a spacious and well formed structure, with accommodation for an audience of from 1,500 to 2,000 persons. The building, as originally erected, had a portico entrance, with a large open area in front, but within the last few years this area has been built upon, two shops, with offices over them, having been erected, together with a spacious entrance to the theatre in the centre, the entire *facade* which is in the Italian style of architecture, being surmounted by an ornamental pediment, 'enriched by sculpture, and contributing to the architectural improvement of the thoroughfare. Mr. James Hibbert furnished the designs.

ST. JOSEPH'S ORPHANAGE.—
ST. JOSEPH'S INSTITUTION FOR THE SICK POOR.

These are two distinct charitable institutions, although physically connected with each other by a covered corridor. They were both erected by Mrs. Holland, a lady belonging to one of the oldest Roman Catholic families in the town, who has been a liberal benefactress to the churches and charitable institutions connected with the Roman Catholic religion. The St. Joseph's Orphanage, which was erected in the year 1872, is situated at the extreme south end of Theatre Street, and has a north frontage facing Fishergate, about 80 feet in length, the elevation being upwards of 50 feet in height. The structure is

built in the mixed Gothic style of architecture, being faced
with red brick and stone dressings. The elevation at the
east and west ends is surmounted by lofty gables, and as
these portions of the frontage project several feet beyond
the central part of the building they may be described as
wings. Close adjoining the eastern gable is a tower, terminating with a spire in two courses, the spire being faced
with tiles. The height of the tower and spire is about
120 feet. A central gable, several feet lower than those
at the east and west sides, encloses two gothic windows.
The building has a high-pitched roof, covered with tiles.
The entrance is under the tower, and on a stone slab above
the arched door way is the following inscription:—" St.
Joseph's Orphanage, erected and endowed by Mrs. Maria
Holland, 1872." The north frontage is similar in design
to that on the south side, and when seen from the East
Cliff, forms a prominent architectural feature. The cost
of the building was upwards of £7,000.

The Institution for the sick poor has its main frontage in Mount Street, the inscription over the entrance
being as follows:—" St. Joseph's Institution for the Sick
Poor, Erected by Mrs. Maria Holland, A.D. 1877." It
has a frontage to Mount Street 50 feet in length, and is
carried to an extreme height of 70 feet, the north portion
of the frontage, above the entrance, projecting several feet
beyond the southern face of the elevation, which is set
back some distance from the street line, the fore court
being enclosed by a high wall. The north end of the
frontage terminates with a gable, enclosing a three-light
gothic window. The building contains three lofty floors
above the basement, the windows of each floor having
ventilators above the principal frame work. In addition
to the three floors there are pediment dormers in the high-
pitched roof. The cost of this building was also £7,000.
The contractor was Mr. John Walmsley, of Theatre Street.

ST. WILFRID'S ROMAN CATHOLIC CHURCH.

As he journeys eastward along Fishergate, the visitor will be amply repaid by turning into Chapel Street, on the south side, and spending a short time in the inspection of the above edifice, which now presents one of the finest ecclesiastical interiors the town can boast of. Externally he will not see much in the structure to excite his admiration, for the building is of an exceptionally plain character, having no pretensions to architectural ornamentation. It may, however, be stated that although it is the most ancient Roman Catholic place of worship in Preston, the main walls are of a very substantial character, and are about to be entirely refaced in terra-cotta, from designs which have already been approved, and when this work is completed the Chapel Street, as well as the north and south frontages of the building, will present a handsome and attractive appearance.

About five years ago the interior underwent a complete re-construction, the main walls only remaining, and the church now presents a noble and imposing appearance, having been restored in the Italian style of architecture. The roof, which is semi-circular, or what is technically termed waggon-headed in form, is supported by ten fine Corinthian columns in Shap granite, having black Belgian bases. They are 30 feet in height, with richly carved stone capitals, which are ultimately intended to be gilt, the whole being surmounted by an entablature of elegant design, and terminating with a bold apsis at the altar end. The roof is well lighted by windows groined in the waggon head, and a pleasing effect is given by two tints of cathedral glass. The windows in the Chapel Street elevation are encased in terra-cotta mouldings, and a massive circular window at the north or organ gallery end of the building, containing a free introduction of stained glass, serves to throw a mellow light throughout the interior, and gives an imposing appearance to the noble sanctuary and altar. The organ gallery contains a fine new instrument, built by Messrs. Hill & Co., of London, at a cost of £1,000. It is the gift of Mrs. Holland, whose father built the present edifice whén it was re-erected in the early part of the present century.   The organ is so placed as not to interfere with the large circular stained glass window at the north end.

The pilasters of the side walls correspond to the columns supporting the roof.   An extra aisle is added to the building on the east or gospel side, terminating with two chapels, one dedicated to St. Joseph, and the other to the Blessed Virgin.   The designs for these, and also for the high altar, which is a magnificent structure, were furnished by the Rev. Fath·r J. Scoles, one of the priests of St. Mary's Chapel. The whole of the centre altar is of highly polished Italian marbles of varied colours ; and the altar steps and other parts have rich inlays of malachite, porphory, gallo antiguo, and other precious marbles.   This altar is the magnificent gift of Mrs. Edward Sidgreaves. The work was executed by Mr. Sherratt, of Preston.

The sanctuary is paved with marble, and the communion rails are of marble and alabaster, with metal panels of rich design. The gates of the sanctuary are also of metal, exquisitely worked, and in design harmonising with the rails.   They are the gift of Mrs. J. Pyke.   The pulpit, which is of marble, with gilt metal panels, is placed on the epistle side of the altar, and is intended as a memorial of the late Father Cobb, who laboured for many years at St. Wilfrid's.   The large picture of the Crucifixion, after Guido, near the high altar, has added to it three additional figures, the work of Mr. Bouvier, artist, of London.

The altar on the gospel side of the church is of stone, alabaster, and marble, and is dedicated to the Sacred Heart.   In connection with it is a statue of the Sacred Heart, in alabaster, carved by Mr. Ruddock, of London. On the epistle side another altar is erected, and dedicated to the Holy Ghost.   This is surmounted by a picture of the Descent of the Holy Ghost, painted by Mr. Bouvier. The side altars are the special designs of Mr. Nicholl, architect, of London, and form important adjuncts to the effectiveness of the general design. This portion of the work was carried out by Mr. Anstey, of London. The centre arch pilasters are very massive, and are formed of beautiful rose vif marble. A handsome carved doorway leads to the sacristies, and within the wood work over the door in the church is a niche, in which a clock has been placed. The clock is the gift of Mr. Dickinson, jeweller, of Friargate. The centre sanctuary is lit by a sun light, and the main portion of the church by sixteen gaselier lights between the columns.

The church is seated with new benches of pitch-pine and mahogany, which are richly varnished and upholstered. The tabernacle of the high altar is very imposing, the door being of highly wrought gilt metal work supplied from Munich. Over the altar dome is the inscription, in plain gilt letters, " In nomine Jesu omnie genu flectatur." In the side lady altar is placed a beautiful statue of Our Lady ; and a picture representing the Flight into Egypt, painted by Father Scoles. The sacristies are also objects worthy of notice. The wood work is massive, yet appropriate, and every arrangement is made to meet the special requirements of this portion of the church service.

The designs and plans for the re-construction of the interior of the edifice were furnished by Mr. Nicholl, of London, and Father Scoles ; and Mr. John Walmsley, builder, of Theatre Street, Preston, was the general contractor, Mr. Walmsley's contract alone, being upwards of £10,000. The entire cost of the several works, including the marbles, paintings, statuary, and organ, is said to have been upwards of £20,000.

THE SAVINGS' BANK.

This building was erected a few years ago, on the site in Fishergate formerly occupied by the old Dispensary. The structure is in the Greek and Italian style of architecture, the Greek characteristics being predominant. The elevation, in Longridge stone, is 45 feet in length, and 60 feet in height, the building containing three storeys. The banking room, which occupies nearly the whole of the ground floor, is considered to be more admirably adapted to its purpose than that of any similar building in the town. Mr. James Hibbert was the architect.

THE NEW EXCHANGE AND MUSIC HALL.

Turning out of Fishergate, on the north side into Lune Street, the visitor will notice, near the bottom of that street, the Corn Exchange buildings. The Corn Exchange was completed and opened in 1824, and, with the several rooms connected with it, has for many years past been utilised for public meetings and entertainments. The building has just been entirely reconstructed internally the external walls only remaining, whilst the height has been very considerably increased, and westward the structure has been extended by the erection of an entirely new block, containing a range of several apartments in connexion with the general purposes to which it is in future to be applied. The structure is now 230 feet in length and 95 feet in width, and covers a ground area of about 22,000 superficial feet. The principal entrance to the interior of the building is on the east side, leading into a vestibule, 12 feet in width, with pay offices on each side. Through the vestibule a spacious entrance hall, 34 feet by 28 feet, is reached, having on each side several retiring rooms and lavatories. From this entrance hall the large hall on the ground floor is approached. It is 147 feet in length, by 63 feet in width, having a promenade on the north and south sides, 16 feet in width each, which can be either added to or partitioned off from the main body of the hall, at any time, by means of revolving shutters. The full width of the hall and promenades will thus be 95 feet. When used for meetings, concerts, or other similar purposes, it is estimated to seat an audience of 1,500 persons, for whom seven exits are provided. At the

west end of the hall is an orchestra, 44 feet in width, by
36 feet in depth, designed with special regard to orchestral performances, and having accommodation for 300
performers.   At the rear of the orchestra is a spacious
organ chamber, for which a powerful organ has been
erected by Mr. Wilkinson, of Kendal, at the cost of
£3,000.   The organ is the munificent gift of Mr. John
Dewhurst, coal merchant, of Preston.   The front of the
organ chamber is an important feature in the work, having
ornamental pilasters, with elaborate capitals and spandrils,
and enriched plaster work, modelled from special designs
of the architect.   In the new portion of the building, at
the west end, behind the orchestra, there are ladies' and
gentlemen's retiring and waiting rooms, on the ground
and first floors, with kitchens, heating apparatus, and
storage rooms in the basement.   The entrance for the
band and principals, on musical occasions, is from
the waiting rooms on the ground floor; whilst the
entrance for the chorus is on each side of the organ
chamber, from the waiting room on the first floor.   Above
the promenades, galleries are carried along the north and
south sides, and also at the east end opposite the orchestra,
the last named gallery being circular on plan.   Behind
this gallery there is a balcony or promenade, eight feet
in width.   The galleries and balcony are estimated to
hold an audience of 1,500 persons, and have four separate
entrances and exits.   The front of the gallery has a
handsome brass railing, with wrought iron scroll work.
The iron columns are 14 feet apart, with ornamental
enriched capitals, from which spring circular arches.
Above these runs an enriched pilaster frieze and cornice,
surmounted by a cove to the under side of the ceiling,
the latter being perforated by a series of circular lights.
The hall is heated by hot water pipes, and lighted
by three sun burners in the ceiling, each having a large
extracting shaft, for carrying off the vitiated air.   The
first floor over the principal entrance, at the east end,
contains a spacious assembly room, 102 feet in length,
and 45 feet in width.   The architect is Mr. Sykes (of the

firm of Messrs. Garlick, Park, and Sykes), of Preston, and the contractor Mr. Robert Saul, also of Preston. The estimated cost of the reconstructed building, exclusive of the organ and fittings, is about £12,000.

THE WESLEYAN CHAPEL, LUNE STREET.

One of the oldest Wesleyan Chapels in Preston is on the west side of Lune Street. For many years it was a plain brick edifice, but of large dimensions, extending in depth to Fox Street. It was rebuilt within the last few years, and has now a bold and handsome elevation to Lune Street, having a frontage of 50 feet in length, and upwards of 40 feet in height. It is faced with stone from the Longridge quarries, the central portion of the frontage being its chief feature. This consists of a deeply recessed and lofty arch, carried up to within a few feet from the apex of the elevation, and receding upwards of twelve feet from the street line, forming an area beneath, from which there are entrances to the Chapel on the north and south sides. The arch is surmounted by a pediment, with bold overhanging cornice. In addition to the entrances under the arch there are also two other entrances to the edifice from the extreme north and south sides of the frontage.

THE UNION BANK OF PRESTON.

Immediately adjoining the Wesleyan Chapel above described, is the Union Bank of Preston, which was recently erected on the site formerly occupied by the old Savings' Bank buildings. The elevation in stone, is classic in style, a surmounting pediment being supported by panelled piers, enclosing Greek columns. The borough arms are immediately over the entrance.

THE PRESTON BANKING COMPANY'S BUILDINGS.

Returning up Lune Street into Fishergate, the handsome block of buildings erected for the Preston Banking Company will be noticed on the south side. The buildings were erected and opened for business in the year 1856, the company, which was originally established in 1844, having in the meantime conducted their operations in more unpretending premises in the immediate locality. The site of the buildings forms a portion of what was known as " The Terrace," formerly occupied chiefly by the old families and " Quality," before Preston was changed from what may be termed an aristocratic to a commercial and trading community. The bank buildings, which are in the Italian style of architecture, with an elaborately-carved and decorated *facade*, are built of stone from the Longridge quarries in the neighbourhood. They contain three lofty floors, the elevation, to the main cornice, being 50 feet in height. The first floor portion of the elevation is rusticated in character, the doors and windows having arched heads, with sculptured figure heads for key stones. The spandrils of the arches are filled in with groups of fruit and flowers, hanging from tigers' mouths in the string course. The principal feature in the first storey above the ground floor is a Corinthian Colonnade, each window being ornamented by a handsome cornice, pediment in form. The upper floor windows have moulded architraves, the surmounting cornice of the elevation, with carved string course being massive in character. The ground floor portion of the building is entirely set apart for banking purposes, the upper storeys forming the manager's residence.   Mr. J. H. Park was the architect of the building.

THE LANCASTER BANKING COMPANY'S BUILDINGS.

A short distance eastward, on the same side of Fish-

ergate as the Preston Banking Company's premises, are
the Lancaster Banking Company's buildings. When this
company first opened a branch in Preston, now almost
half a century since—namely in 1833—the business was
for some years conducted in one of the buildings on the
north side of Fishergate, rented for the purpose. Subsequently the business of the bank was removed to more
convenient premises on the south side of this thoroughfare, and in 1856, the business having largely increased,
entirely new bank buildings were erected by the company,
a spacious site having been secured by the purchase and
demolition of houses and shops near Butler's Court.
Upon this site handsome new bank buildings were erected,
from the designs of Mr. J. H. Park, architect. The buildings, which are in stone, have an ornamental elevation
fronting Fishergate, containing the banking offices on the
ground floor, the two upper floors containing the residential apartments of the manager of the bank.   Some time
after the erection of the new premises, an extension of
the banking offices became necessary, and an annexe was
added on the east side, by which the area of the banking
house was very considerably enlarged, and which now
has a frontage to Fishergate about 60 feet in length. Not
many yards eastward are

THE REFORM CLUB BUILDINGS,

a structure containing three floors, the principal portion
of the elevation, from the ground line to the cornice,
being made up of spacious glass windows to each floor,
with pilasters and columns carried up in stone. The
building contains, on the ground floor the Registration
office, the Luncheon room, and at the rear a spacious
billiard room, in which there are two tables. On the first
floor is the reading and news room, whilst on the floor
above, which has a lofty and open timbered ceiling, is
another billiard room, furnished with two tables.

THE POST OFFICE AND INLAND REVENUE BUILDINGS.

Nearly opposite the Reform Club, on the north side
of Fishergate, are the Post Office buildings, erected by the
Government a few years ago. Previous to the erection
of the new building the post office accommodation was
altogether inadequate to the increasing requirements of
the town. The building, which extends to a depth of
120 feet northwards, has a frontage to Fishergate, of 40
feet in length, and is about 50 feet in height. It is plain
in design, having few pretensions to architectural effect,
but nevertheless of a substantial character. The ground
floor portion of the elevation is faced with rusticated
stone, and ornamented with stone columns, carried up to
a frieze, stretching across the frontage above the ground
floor windows. The entrance to the general office is at
the west end of the frontage. This apartment, which
occupies the entire width of the structure, with the exception of the lobby or corridor on the west side leading
to the upper floors, is about 80 feet in depth, and contains
the various offices connected with the several postal, telegraph, and other departments. At the extreme rear of
the building are the sorters' offices, and several other
spacious apartments, including the offices in which the
mails are made up for despatch ; also the letter carriers
offices and other rooms. This portion of the building is
approached by a road way on the east side. The upper
floors consist of the offices connected with the Inland
Revenue department of the Government.

THE GAS COMPANY'S OFFICES.

Immediately to the east of the Post Office building
are the offices of the Gas Company, which take rank
amongst the most ornamental public buildings in the
town. They have an elevation on the north side of Fishergate, 38 feet in length, and 48 feet in height to the
parapet, with a tower at the east end 100 feet in height

and at the west end a turret 69 feet high. The building is carried to an extreme depth of about 100 feet. It is faced with stone from the Longridge quarries, and is in the decorated style of gothic architecture. The ground floor portion of the elevation has three elaborately carved tracery windows, flanked on each side with polished Shap granite shafts, and surmounted by carved capitals. The entrance to the building is on the east side of the elevation, the gothic doorway having polished grey Aberdeen shafts on each side. The first floor has a range of four richly decorated gothic windows, surmounted by ornamentally-carved pediments or hoods. The second floor has three double gothic windows, divided in the centre by polished Shap granite columns. At the west angle of the elevation there is a small oriel window and octagonal tower, surmounted by the turret already referred to; whilst the specially prominent feature of the frontage is the tower at the east end. Above the entrance on the east side is a carved representation of the borough arms, and on the west side a similar representation of the arms of the palatinate. There are likewise carved circular panels between the arches of the ground floor windows. The return elevation on the west side, to the extent of about 60 feet in length, is uniform in design with the Fishergate frontage, but much plainer in detail and decorative character. The entrance to the building leads into a handsome gothic corridor, eight feet in width, and about 60 feet in length. The general offices on the ground floor are approached from the west side of the corridor. They are 54 feet in length, and 24 feet in width, and comprise a lofty and noble apartment, very artistically and richly decorated. The east and west walls are faced at intervals with Shap polished granite pilasters, having carved and moulded capitals. The ceiling is divided into panels, formed of stained and polished pitch pine, the whole being massive, and richly and ornamentally carved. That part of the floor area for the use of the public, in front of the counter, is paved with Godwin's encaustic tiles, in varied colours and patterns, specially designed and manufactured for the purpose. A chief feature of this portion of the work consists of square floor panels, having emblems of the borough arms at each angle, with a central allegorical female figure, representative of Science in the laboratory experimenting upon the gas retort. The staircase leading to the board room on the first floor, and the other offices and apartments in the upper portions of the building, is 12 feet in width, the stone steps being upwards of four feet wide, with an ornamental balustrade in iron work. It is very lofty, extending to the top of the building, where it is enclosed by a coved ceiling in pitch pine, with very elaborate carving in fruit and flowers; whilst in the centre is an ornamental lantern light in stained glass. From the staircase landing, a gothic arched corridor, uniform with that on the ground floor, leads to the board room, an elegantly decorated apartment, 34 feet long, and 24 feet wide. It has a coved and panelled ceiling, in stained and polished pitch pine, supported by brackets of the same material springing from polished granite shafts. A carved and panelled dado, also in pitch pine, and about four feet in height, is carried round the apartment, the mural spaces between the windows, together with the window frames and doors, being similarly decorated with the same material. The central portion of the floor is laid with pitch pine, surrounded by a panelled border, about three feet in width, in oak and ebony. At each end of the room there is a large fire place, harmonising with the general character of the apartment. The jambs consist of double polished granite columns, upon which rests a pyramidical stone mantel, the hearth stone being laid with encaustic tiles of varied colours. The building was erected from the designs of Messrs. Garlick, Park, and Sykes.

THE CONSERVATIVE CLUB.

The most prominent building in the recently formed Guildhall Street, leading from the south side of Fishergate, is the Conservative Club, on the east side of the first-named thoroughfare.   This building, which was erected from the designs of Messrs. Garlick, Park, and Sykes, is in the decorated gothic style of architecture. The foundation stone was laid on the 6th of January, 1877, by the late Edward Hermon, Esq., M.P. for Preston.   It has an elevation to Guildhall Street, 57 feet in length, and extends to a depth of nearly 70 feet.   It is upwards of 60 feet in height, the elevation being surmounted by two bold and lofty gables, on the north and south sides, together with a small central gable.   The interior of the building is approached by a deeply-recessed gothic entrance, 12 feet in width.   Immediately above this gothic entrance is an ornamental balcony in stone, in the centre of which are the arms of the club, elaborately carved.   The building contains three lofty floors, each floor having spacious mullion windows, 12 feet in width, and in six divisions.   The windows of the upper floor, immediately beneath the surmounting gables, are gothic in character, and deeply recessed.   In the upper portions of the ground and first floor windows stained glass is introduced, in which appear the arms and shields of several well known conservatives connected with the town and county.   The materials of the elevation consist of brick piers, carried up between the windows, whilst at the north and south angles of the frontage, black and white diaper work is introduced above each floor windows, and also within the surmounting gables.   The vestibule or entrance hall, 15 feet by 20 feet, is paved with encaustic tiles.   The news room, on the right hand side of the vestibule, is a handsome and lofty apartment, 60 feet in length, and 20 feet in width.   The dining room is on the opposite or north side of the vestibule.   A broad staircase leads to the two upper floors, the first floor containing committee rooms, card rooms, and offices.   The whole of the upper floor is fitted up as a spacious billiard room, and contains three full-sized tables.   This apartment is very lofty, having an open roof and ceiling, upwards of 20 feet in height from the floor level.

THE "GUARDIAN" OFFICE BUILDINGS.

Amongst the several public buildings in Fishergate the offices of the *Preston Guardian*, erected a few years ago, by Mr. G. Toulmin, the proprietor, claim a notice. These buildings are situated on the north side of Fishergate, a short distance west of the town hall. They are in the Italian style of architecture, and have a bold and handsome *facade*, in Longridge stone, elaborately carved. The elevation is about 27 feet in length, and upwards of 50 feet in height, and consists of the ground and two upper floors. There are two arched entrances to the building, that at the west side leading to the business offices of the *Guardian*, on the ground floor, and that at the east side being the approach to the upper floors, which are let as offices. The lower storey is divided by rustic quoined pilasters. Above the ground floor windows is an ornamental parapet, on which rests a balcony and balustrade carried across the elevation. The first floor has a range of five windows, the central portion being surmounted by an ornamental carved pediment, resting on four carved cantilevers. Above these again is another balcony. The second floor has a range of five arched windows, and the elevation is finally surmounted by a richly carved projecting cornice and baluster parapet, in the centre of which there is a carved canopy, forming a niche, in which is a boldly treated piece of sculpture representing the head and bust of Caxton. This head and bust were copied from the frontispiece to Johnson's *Typographia*. The sculptor was Mr. Miles, who executed the sculpture work at the town hall. The block of stone from which the head and bust of the pioneer of printing was carved, weighed nearly two tons. Mr. T. H. Myres was the architect of the building.

THE TOWN HALL.

The new Town Hall, the foundation stone of which

was laid during the guild week, in 1862, by Robert Townley Parker, Esq., the guild mayor; and opened in September, 1867, with considerable ceremony, by his royal
highness the Duke of Cambridge, is admitted to be one
of the most splendid municipal structures in the country.
It was erected from the designs of the late Sir Gilbert
Scott, and is regarded as amongst the finest of that great
architect's productions.

Before entering upon a description of this noble
building it will be interesting to make some reference to
the ancient public halls which preceded it. The records in
the corporation archives bear out the popular belief that
there were several town hall buildings in Preston, before
the two which immediately preceded the grand structure of
which we shall shortly have to speak. There seems to be
little, if any doubt, that a town hall, which stood in the year
1323 was destroyed when the Scots under Robert Bruce,
during one of their incursions in the reign of Edward the
Third, burnt a great part of the town, the public hall,
which was in all probability a wooden structure, suffering
amongst the rest, and it is believed that on this occasion
several guild records were lost. The town hall which
was erected in its place must have stood for several centuries, and in it many of the scenes enacted during the
civil wars and other eventful periods, took place. This
building fell in the year 1780, under rather romantic circumstances. A race ball had been held in it on the previous Thursday evening, the company not leaving until
about three o'clock on the Friday morning following,
shortly after which the fire broke out, and the structure
was destroyed. The new town hall which succeeded it
was finished and opened in 1783, and this building was
used for general municipal purposes until the year 1862,
when it was taken down, and the erection of the present
structure was commenced. It was, however, almost ten
years after the subject of rebuilding the edifice was first
mooted, before the erection of the structure commenced,
it having been originally decided in 1853 that a new
building was necessary. A marked diversity of opinion

amongst the municipal authorities led to the delay.
Whilst the majority were in favor of the present site,
there were others who warmly supported the proposal to
erect the new building a little more to the eastward, with
its principal frontage between the Old Shambles and
Lancaster Road, the elevation being set back several
yards from the general street line so as to secure a spacious
area and carriage approach in front of the building. The
site of the old structure upon which the building now
stands, was, however, ultimately agreed upon, but it must
be added that there appears now to be a consentient
opinion amongst the inhabitants that in the site of the
costly structure an irremediable error of judgment was
committed, and a feeling of regret that the site between
the Old Shambles and Lancaster Road was not adopted.
Whether the unfortunate mistake may be ascribed to
the want of firmness and independence on the part of
the majority of the council at the time, it is not for
the writer to determine; but if it is traceable to a too
yielding deference to individual crochets, or to the indis-
creet hero worship of the period, the undignified servility
which it betrays is much to be lamented. With these
speculations, however, the author is not mainly concerned,
nor do they affect the material grandeur of the palatial
building which has to be described.

The new Town Hall is a magnificient example of
that gothic revival of which Sir Gilbert Scott was so
much enamoured, and which forms a distinguishing
feature in almost all the buildings this great architect
erected. The building is bounded on the north by the
Market Place, on the south by Fishergate, on the east
by what are known as the Strait Shambles, but which
will shortly disappear when certain town improvements
are carried out, and on the west by Cheapside. The
principal frontage is that to Fishergate, which is 92 feet
in length. The height of this elevation up to the parapet at the base of the arch is 58 feet, and from the
parapet to the ridge of the roof, is an additional 28 feet,
the extreme height of the frontage being thus 86 feet from

the ground line. One of the most prominent architectural features of this portion of the building is an
elaborately groined arcade, having four gothic arches
springing from polished Aberdeen granite columns,
resting on massive stone bases, very richly carved. All
the arches have label terminations representing different
English monarchs, including Henry the First, Richard
the First, King John, Edward the First, Henry the
Eighth, Queen Elizabeth, Charles the First, and Charles
the Second. Above the arcade is a massive stone balcony,
supported by artistically carved corbels, with a frontage
of richly executed wrought iron work. The first floor of
the elevation has five two-light gothic windows, one of
which opens from the tower. All the windows are
divided by broad stone transoms, filled in with ornamental foliage. These several transoms are faced with
allegorical representations of Fortitude, Prudence, Justice,
Temperance, and Faith. All the windows have trefoil
heads, and the tympanum is filled in with a six-foil light,
surmounting the trefoils. Moulded arches spring from
the windows, all of which are deeply recessed. Between
the windows are niches with deeply-canopied heads, in
which statuary is intended to be introduced. The
frontage terminates with a massive cornice, supported
upon corbels, and surmounted by a balustrade of polished
granite shafts, and carved capitals. At the termination
of the angular buttresses are three heraldic lions, bearing
shields, with a handsome wind vane attached to each.
The roof, which is covered in with Westmoreland slate, is
pierced with four dormors covered with lead, the gables
being richly crocketted, and terminating with finials.

The tower is at the south west angle of the building,
and, when approached from Fishergate, forms a conspicuous object amongst the other architectural structures in
the locality. Its extreme height from the street level to
the apex of the spire, including the vane, is 198 feet. It
may not inaptly be described as a beacon, inasmuch as it
can be distinctly seen on the river by mariners when
approaching from Lytham, and for several miles around.

The angles of the tower are composed of clustered shafts
rising up to the parapet line; and above the parapet, on
the north, south, and west sides, is a three light lancet
window, divided by stone mullions, and faced by granite
shafts and stone bosses, with carved capitals, the tympanum being filled in with rich diaper work, and each
window having a very beautiful moulded pointed arch.
Above these is a four-light lancet window divided by
massive mullions, and faced with polished granite shafts.
The first-range of these windows light the chamber for
the bell chimes, and the last range the chamber for the
hour bell.   The clustered angles of the tower are terminated by a heavy cornice directly under the dials of the
clock, which are four in number, and may be seen from
a long distance.   The clock was made by Mr. Potts, of
Leeds, from the design of Sir Edmund Beckett, better
known as Mr. Edmund Beckett Denison, Q.C., a recognised authority in horology.   It is on the same principle
as the great clock of the houses of parliament.   It has
Sir Edmund Beckett's gravity escapement, and a compensated $1\frac{1}{2}$ seconds pendulum, with his maintaining
power for keeping it going whilst winding.   It strikes
quarters of St. Mary's, Cambridge, which were also
copied at Westminster, and which are regarded as exceptionally musical.   They are on four bells, of the notes D,
C, B flat, and F, the great hour bell being the B flat below,
weighing 4 tons 16 cwt., 6 feet 3 inches in diameter, and
struck with a hammer of 2 cwt.   With the exception of
" Big Ben " at Westminster, and "Great Paul" at St.
Paul's Cathedral, there are no bells in the kingdom more
powerful in effect, although there are a few larger bells,
but these are struck by clocks and hammers too feeble for
them.   This is altogether the largest clock in England
with the exception of that at Westminster.   It is all made
of iron except the small wheels in the escapement, which
are steel and brass.   The hammers are raised by large cams
faced with steel.   The pendulum weighs 2 cwt., and its
compensation is effected by means of zinc and iron tubes
as in the Westminster and other large clocks.   The dials

are 9 feet 6 inches in diameter, of glass, in iron frames, for illumination. The bells are by Mr. Taylor, of Loughborough, and were made from Sir Edmund Beckett's pattern and specification. The great bell has the " mushroom top." of the Westminster bells, to enable it to be turned round to strike on any fresh place when worn in another. The clock goes about 8 days without winding, but the striking parts are made to wind every day, in order to avoid the enormous weights which such heavy bells and hammers would require if wound only once a week. Above the clock chamber the spire rises from between four pinnacles, one at each angle, between each pinnacle being a gablet surmounted by a carved cornice. On each gablet there is a representation of the arms of the borough, and surmounting both pinnacles and gablets are carved finials. Surrounding the base of each pinnacle the angular shafts are terminated by a series of grotesque figures. The spire is composed of timber. In shape it is octagonal, and springs from a square tower. About midway, at each angle, are richly gabled and crocketted spire lights, surmounted by finials. As far as the foot of the spire lights the spire is covered with Westminster slate, and at the summit of the slating is a heavy cornice covered with lead, and filled in with rich lead foliage. At the intersection of the gable of each of the spire lights are lead gargoyles. The spire terminates with a very handsome wrought iron vane, and attached to it is a lightning conductor which runs down to the west side of the building.

The west frontage is 137 feet long. In the centre is a handsome and massive porch, which forms the principal entrance to the building. It is approached by a series of stone steps, and the porch is surmounted by a spacious balcony, having a polished granite balustrade, and carved capitals, with an elaborate cornice and arcaded corbelling below. The entrance is formed into a triple archway, the outside buttresses being of massive design. The two inner double columns are in polished granite, resting upon stone bases, and are surmounted by richly carved capitals. From these spring the moulded arches supporting the balcony. There are also entrances from the sides of the porch, and the arches there correspond with those already described. In the spandrils of the arches are carved representations of the Royal arms, the arms of the Prince of Wales, the arms of the Borough of Preston, and the arms of the County of Lancaster. Between the porch and the tower are six two-light trefoil headed windows, the tympanum of each being pierced by a quatrefoil; and between the three upper windows are two angular buttresses terminating at the gable of the roof of the great hall, with heraldic figures bearing various shields. Above the three upper windows is a continuation of the parapet, with polished granite balustrade; and still higher is a large circular window filled in with richly moulded tracery. Beyond this is a handsome canopied niche intended for statuary. The northern angle of the gable is terminated by an elaborately arcaded pinnacle. Above the porch is a double two-light window, with granite shafts, the tympanum being ornamented with allegorical sculpture; and on the north side of the porch are three square-headed two-light windows, opening from the basement floor, each being divided by a granite shaft. Above these, opening from the first floor, are windows of the same design, but larger in size; and over these, lighting the second floor, are three two-light windows, with pointed arches, the tympanums containing sculptured allegorical representations. The parapet on this side is broken by four two-light dormer windows, the tympanums of which are pierced by a quatrefoil. At the angle of the north-west front is an octagonal turret, with handsome canopied niches, the pinnacle being arcaded, and the gables terminating with finials. In one of the centre transoms is a representation of Conscience.

The north frontage, which overlooks the old market place, is 74 feet long. In the centre is a spacious porch, which is approached on the east and west sides by flights of stone steps. The archway rests on massive polished granite pillars, with elaborately-carved capitals. The arch is pointed and deeply moulded, and at the angle, some distance above the capitals, are the arms of Edmund Birley, Esq., who was Mayor when the building was opened in 1867, and who now again fills a similar position as the Guild Mayor. There are also the arms of the late Robert Townley Parker, Esq., who as Guild Mayor, laid the foundation stone of the building during the celebration of the Guild in 1862. In immediate proximity are the arms of the Earl of Derby, and also those of the late alderman Thomas Miller. Above these run an arcaded corbelling, supporting a cornice, and beyond this rises a stone balustrade, filled with granite shafts, running the whole length of the north side. Over the balustrade are five square-headed two-light windows, with allegorical representations in the tympanums; and surmounting the whole is a continuation of the parapet, which is broken by three two-light dormer windows, terminating with carved finials. At each corner the junction is intersected by octagonal turrets and pinacles, uniform with those at the west frontage.

In the east frontage the main characteristics of the other three elevations are maintained, but there is no entrance to the building in this *facade*. The exigencies of the site on this side of the building neccessitated the narrowing of the building from south to north, but this was carried out with much skill on the part of the architect. An octagonal structure, in the form of an apse, conceals to a great extent the irregularity which would otherwise have been apparent. In the transoms of the four windows are representations of Hope, Charity, Humility, and Truth. Bas reliefs form a special feature in the several frontages. On the north side there is an emblematical representation of Agriculture; on the east side a similar representation of Commerce; and on the west side, Manufacture. The building is surrounded by 14 ornamental lamps, designed by the architect.

The interior arrangements and decorations of the building are of an exceptionally artistic and costly character. It has been already stated that the principal entrance

is on the west side. In this frontage there are three doorways corresponding with the pointed arches already described. The entrance is approached by a flight of six
steps from the exterior, there being a second series of steps
beyond the door-way. Dwarf walls with gabled coping
and floriated capitals divide the principal entrance into
three compartments, and at the termination of each wall
is a very ornamental gas standard, containing five clustered lights. At this point an attractive feature of the
building is the ceiling, which is magnificently decorated.
It is geometrical in character, the designs being carried
out in blue, white, and gold, and lined with lavender.
By a second flight of steps the entrance hall is reached.
This is on a level with the ground floor, and is approached
by a triple archway of massive design. The central arch
is supported by polished granite columns. On the left is
a small ticket office, with an arcaded two-light window,
filled in with an ornamental brass grille ; and on the right
side is a flight of steps descending to the Merchants' Exchange Hall. The ceiling here is composed of highly
decorated cast iron girders, which support the stone landing above. The floor is paved with tiles, 12 inches square,
consisting of Hoptonwood and red Mansfield stone, alternately laid. A third flight of steps constitutes the grand
staircase, having on each side a wrought iron balustrade,
with wainscot hand rail, very artistically decorated, in the
form of oak wreaths, in blue, red, and gold. This part
of the wall, to the height of four feet, is ornamented with
an encaustic-tiled dado. The corridors and passages leading to the grand staircase are all decorated with drapery,
chiefly on light vellum ground. The ceiling over the
lobby of the principal entrance is in pale ashen blue
vellum tint, white, and gold. The glass over the chief
entrance is of geometrical character. In the middle of
the passage, at right angles with the principal corridor,
is a door, the panels and tympanum of which are filled
with embossed glass of design, corresponding with the
general decorations. In the tympanum are represented
the Borough Arms, surrounded by an emblematical repre-

sentation of the "Red Rose of Lancaster." The grand
staircase turns to the right and left, and after passing up
a fourth flight of steps the landing approaching the great
or "Guild Hall" is reached. On the wall to the west,
which divides the staircase from the main portion of the
building, there is a well executed painting, allegorical of
Industry, and on each side of it similar allegorical representations of Manufactures and Commerce. Immediately
below the central figure is the word "Industria;" and
surmounting the three is the following passage from
Scripture:—"Thou shalt remember the Lord thy God,
for it is He that giveth thee power to get wealth." Beneath the allegorical representations are full length painted
figures of several eminent inventors, engineers, and others,
each showing a device by which he was enabled to benefit
the world. They include Arkwright, Watt, Stephenson,
Caxton, Columbus, Raleigh, Linnæus, Dalton, Wheat-
stone, and Sir Robert Peel. On the east side there are
two two-light windows, filled in with richly ornamented
glass of geometrical character, the prevailing ground
being white, with borders rich in design and colour.
Crowned and coronetted shields are introduced representing John of Gaunt, Henry the Fourth, Henry the Fifth,
and Henry the Sixth. Passing up from the landing an
octagonal staircase leads to the corridor approach to the
Guild Hall. The roof extending from the division wall
to the staircase is semicircular in form, and is composed
of pitch pine divided into panels, with carved bosses at
the intersection of the ribs.

After ascending the staircase and passing along the
corridor the great Guild Hall is reached. This apartment
is 82 feet 6 inches in length by 54 feet in width. The
height from the floor to the cornice is 33 feet, and from the
cornice to the apex of the roof 15 feet, the extreme height
of the hall being thus 48 feet. On the south side is a
spacious gallery, approached by a corridor running along
the east side. The gallery is 69 feet long, and 15 feet
wide. It is estimated that the body of the hall and the
gallery will seat an audience of 1,100 persons, this being

exclusive of the platform and orchestral space at the west
side of the hall. There are eleven lofty two-light windows
in the hall, in addition to two circular windows at the
east and west gables. The open roof, in varnished timber,
is elegantly decorated in varied colours and gold, the
panels having pale azure blue panel borders, with gold
stars, and red and white ornamentation. The mural
decorations of the hall are also very artistic. The ground
is in vellum, on which is ornamentation of rich design
and execution. A handsome dado is carried round the
apartment, very elaborately decorated on a maroon
ground. The circular window within the east gable contains seven compartments, in the central compartment
the arms of the County Palatine being introduced. In the
other compartments are the arms of Preston, Liverpool,
Manchester, Clitheroe, Wigan, and Lancaster. The west
circular window has also seven compartments, in the central compartment being introduced a representation of
the arms of the United Kingdom ; and surrounding it are
separate shields of England, Ireland, and Scotland, alter-
nated with those of the sovereigns of the House of Lancaster, Henry the Fourth, Henry the Fifth, and Henry
the Sixth. The other windows are all formed of stained
glass, each window having alternately a badge representing the arms of the borough of Preston, and the "Red Rose
of Lancaster." In the circles above the large windows are
the arms of Blackburn, Bolton, Burnley, Rochdale, Stock-
port, Oldham, Salford, and Warrington. In a circle quatre
on the west side are representations of the heads of Henry
the Fourth, Henry the Fifth, and Henry the Sixth. Beneath the spring of the roof there is a frieze in the coloured decorations, representing portraits of celebrities in
Literature, Science, Art, and Discovery. These portraits
are 36 in number, including distinguished men in Music,
Science, Philosophy, Extension of British Empire, Mar-
itime, and Inland Discovery, War, Art, Literature, Poetry,
and Anatomy. Amongst others they embrace the portraits of Purcell, Mozart, Handel, Beethoven, Mendels-
sohn, Faraday, Newton, Bacon, Herschell, Clive, Cook,

Sir J. Franklin, Dr. Livingstone, Nelson, Wellington, M. Angelo, Raphael, Titian, Reynolds, Flaxman, Wren, Gibbon, Goldsmith, Dr. Johnson, Addison, Maculay, Chaucer, Shakspere, Milton, Scott, Byron, Burns, Hunter, Harvey, and Cuvier. The gallery is divided from the main portion of the roof by an arcade of four bays, supported upon ornamented fluted iron double columns, the capitals being filled in with rich foliage in wrought iron. The front of the gallery is open, and its ceiling is supported by five pairs of moulded, stained, and varnished principals. The ceiling of the main part of the hall is composed of six pairs of principals, and is divided into 120 panels, the chief principals being pierced with quatrefoils, springing from handsomely carved stone corbels. The roof is supported on the south side by fluted iron columns, each flute and the capitals being filled in with foliage corresponding with that in the gallery. The retiring rooms for ladies and gentlemen are immediately adjacent to the Guild Hall. Adjoining these on the right is one for committees of the council. The lobby running between this room and the landing is richly vaulted. On the left, at the north end of the edifice, is the Mayor's Parlour, which is elegantly decorated, and on the stone fire place are carved the arms of Edmund Birley, Esq., (mayor when the hall was opened); the arms of Robert Townley Parker, Esq., Guild mayor in 1862; and the arms of the Borough.

At the north eastern angle, and nearly facing the Mayor's Parlour, is the Council Chamber, an apartment 35 feet long, 25 feet wide, and 16 feet 6 inches high. It is lighted by five two-light windows. A pitch pine dado runs along the sides of the chamber, the ceiling being composed of the same material, and in panels. The artistic mural decorations are on a green ground. A carved wooden cornice runs round the ceiling, and immediately under it, on the right side, are shields containing the arms of all the known guild mayors of the Borough from the year 1328 to 1862 inclusive. Between each shield are three red roses representing the historic rose of Lancaster. On the left side is a similar number of vacant shields, presumably intended for the arms of future Preston celebrities. The chimney piece consists of carved red Mansfield stone, supported by Rouge Royal marble pillar jambs, and surmounted by a mantel and shelf in Irish green marble. In the centre of the carved work are the Borough Arms, and under the twisted pillar jambs are corbel angels.

A short distance to the south of the council chamber is a large committee room, 26 feet by 21 feet, having two two-light square-headed windows. The ceiling of this room is very effectively decorated, in what are known as linen fold panels. It has a handsome stone chimney piece, containing on each side a representation of the Borough Arms.

The vestibule, immediately opposite the entrance to the Guild Hall, is one of the most attractive parts of the interior. The floor is composed of inlaid marble, of varied colours. Over the door way leading into the Guild Hall is a sculptured allegorical representation of Music; over the gentlemen's retiring room a representation of Painting; over the ladies' retiring room, of Sculpture; and over the committee room, of Architecture. Over the door of the council chamber the Borough Arms are sculptured. The upper part of the walls in the south vestibule has a striking picture in twelve divisions, of a Guild procession in the time of Henry the Eighth. Beneath the picture is the following extract :—" Moreover we have granted, and by these for ourselves, our heirs and successors, we have conferred to the aforesaid mayor, bailiffs, and burgesses of the said borough of Preston, and their successors, that the said mayor, bailiffs, burgesses, and their successors shall have a Gild Merchant in the aforesaid borough, with all the liberties and free customs appertaining to such Gild as they have heretofore enjoyed. Charter, Elizabeth, granted 1565." The glass filling the skylight above the vestibule is devoted to the heraldic bearings of the entire list of mayors of Preston since the passing of the municipal reform act. The north vestibule contains pictures of a similar character to those depicting the Guild procession in the south vestibule. They represent Peace and War in a series of incidents, namely:—Peace at sea by ships engaged in trade, a fishing incident, a merchant inspecting merchandise on a quay; with the scriptural text "Thou wast replenished and made very glorious in the midst of the seas."—Ezk. 27 c., 25 v.—War at sea, by ships of war engaged, firing from a fort, flags of truce carried in a boat; with the text—"Thou hast girded me with strength into the battle; Thou hast subdued under me those that rose up against me."—Psalm 18, v. 39.—Peace on land represented by persons in the act of ploughing, reaping, and sowing; with the text—"He maketh peace in thy borders, and filleth thee with the finest of wheat."—Psalm 147, v. 14.—War on land, represented by the keys of a town being delivered up: a general battle, and carrying the wounded; with the text—"The Lord our God be with us, as he was with our fathers; let Him not leave us nor forsake us."—1st Kings, 8 c., v. 57. The glass of the skylight above the north vestibule is filled with the royal heraldry of England.

The offices of the town clerk and his subordinates are under the mayor's parlour, and those of the borough treasurer and his clerks are under the council chamber.

The ground floor portion of the structure, approached under the arcade, in the south or Fishergate frontage, contains a noble apartment, 84 feet by 39 feet, designated the Merchants' Exchange, but which is at present used as the Free Library. The height from the floor to the capital of the columns by which the ceiling is supported and the room adorned, is 12 feet, and the total height is 19 feet 6 inches. The ceiling, which is vaulted and groined in stone, is supported by eight polished granite pillars, with carved capitals in Penswick stone, the vaulting being in Longridge stone, richly moulded ribs having carved stone bosses at the point of intersection. The cells of these are filled in with Dinnett's patent plastic. The responds to the granite pillars are 16 in number, and are formed of Devonshire marble. There are three large two-light windows at each end, and four three-light windows on the south side, overlooking the arcade. There are very elaborately-carved chimney pieces at each end of the room, containing in the centre the Borough Arms, supported by angels bearing shields, and also by pillars of Rouge royal marble. The carving on the capitals of the pillars consists of foliage, with animals and other figures interspersed. Amongst the specimens of flowers, fruit, and other natural foliage represented are the geranium, hop, gooseberry, hawthorn, shamrock, fern, maple, lily, water lily, dock leaf, and Indian palm. Over the entrance, on the inside, the Borough Arms are carved. The mural decorations consist of diaper work on vellum tint, with a coloured dado of floriated patterns. The ceiling is adorned with round bosses.

The building is warmed throughout with hot water circulating in the various rooms and vestibules through 3,500 feet of iron pipes. All the fire stoves or grates throughout the building were specially designed so as to harmonise in their general character and details, with the architectural style of the building. The sides of that in the council chamber are inlaid with tiles, and the bars are supported on fluted pillars of electro bronze, relieved with rosettes of polished brass. All the hearths are laid with Minton's encaustic tiles, and the fenders harmonise with the grates.

Messrs. Cooper and Tullis, of Preston, were the general contractors, but a large number of tradesmen in Preston and other towns were associated with the carrying out of the different portions of the work. The sculpture and carving was executed by Messrs. Yarmer and Brindley, of London ; and the decorators were Messrs. Clayton and Bell, of London. The whole of the furniture was supplied by Messrs. Bell and Coupland, of Preston. The cost of the building was upwards of £90,000.

INDUSTRIAL INSTITUTE FOR THE BLIND.

In the year 1874, a new building designated the Preston Industrial Institute for the Blind, was formally opened by the mayor. The building is situated at the bottom of Glover Street, approached from Church Street, nearly opposite the Town Hall. The structure consists of two floors and a basement. The ground floor portion of the frontage is faced with Longridge stone, the upper portion being of red brick. The sale shop on the ground floor is 30 feet square. In the rear are rooms for cane seating, a large brush room, 40 feet by 28 feet, with "pair" room, and apparatus, occupying one end. The remaining portion of the frontage is the residence for the saleswoman. The cellars under the whole of the buildings are lofty and well ventilated. They are used as work rooms and store rooms, the largest being 52 feet by 28 feet, for skip making. The first floor is approached by two staircases, one for the house portion, and the other for the public in case of meetings, or for educational purposes for the blind. Each staircase leads to a large committee room, and the secretary's office, and these rooms are so constructed that by removing a sliding partition one large room for public entertainments can be formed. Adjoining these rooms are lavatories, cloak and ante rooms. The total cost of the building was £3,000, the whole of which was raised at a bazaar held in April, 1872, when the sum of £3,444 was realised. Mr. T. Harrison Myres was the architect, and Mr. John Walmsley the contractor.

THE PARISH CHURCH.

The present Parish Church, dedicated to St. John the Evangelist, which was erected upon the site of the former old edifice, in Church Street, in the year 1855, is architecturally, a very handsome ecclesiastical structure. There are few places in the united kingdom which

possessed a parish church at so early a period as Preston.
The first church erected on the site can be traced so far
back as the tenth century. It is recorded that in the
year 957, the parish church, dedicated to St. Wilfrid,
was built and opened. It is believed to have been re-
built about the year 1580, when it was first dedicated to
St. John. In something less than two hundred years afterwards, namely in 1770, it was again rebuilt, the body of the
church having given way. Further structural alterations
took place during the early part of the present century,
when, in the year 1814, the tower was taken down
and rebuilt. In 1817, the chancel was re-erected, by
Sir Henry Hoghton, Bart. Between the years 1849
and 1850, a strong desire was evinced for the entire
rebuilding of the church, which had for some time past
shown evidences of dilapidation, and the re-erection of
the edifice having been determined upon, the old structure was entirely taken down, with the exception of the
lower portion of the tower, immediately after which the
erection of the present edifice was proceeded with, from
designs furnished by Mr. Shellard, of Manchester. The
style of architecture is that known as the decorated
English. The building consists of a nave, and two side
aisles, together with a spacious chancel. The structure
from west to east, is of great length, the nave and chancel
being together about 190 feet long. It is ornamented by
a handsome tower and spire, 205 feet in height. There
are elaborately sculptured crocketted turrets at the summit of each angle of the tower, with similar turrets at
the projecting gothic entrance at the west end, and likewise along the face of the elevation, above the clerestory
and chancel windows. The richly stained glass windows
form a strikingly artistic feature in the interior decorations
of the church, the whole of them, both on the north and
south sides of the main body of the church, the clerestory,
and the chancel, being of this character. All these
several windows are gifts from gentlemen whose families
have for many years past been connected with the
town and neighbourhood. The great east window is

the gift of Sir Henry Hoghton, Bart., in whose family
the patronage of the living was for many years vested
before it passed into the hands of the Trustees of Hulme's
Charity. And here it may be stated that the Hulme
Trustees make it a condition precedent to the appoint-
ment of all future vicars of Preston, that they shall have
graduated at Brazenose College, Oxford. The late vicar,
the Rev. John Owen Parr, was the first of the appoint-
ments made under this stipulation, which was also carried
out when the present vicar, the Rev. J. H. Rawdon,
succeeded him, in the year 1877. The east window
which was designed by Sir Henry Hoghton himself, and
executed by Mr. Wailes, of Newcastle, represents the
crucifixion, and passages from the Saviour's passion.
There are no less than seven other of these beautiful
and costly windows on the north and south sides of the
chancel. The eastern window of the side chancel aisle,
which represents the four evangelists, with parables from
each, underneath, in medallions, was presented by John
Bairstow, Esq. The next window, the first on the south,
representing the calling of St. John, was given by John
Horrocks, Esq. The adjoining window representing Christ
blessing little children, was presented by R. Newsham,
Esq. The next on the south side, which represents the
Transfiguration, was the gift of Charles Jacson, Esq.
The whole of these windows, as well as the great east
window, were executed by Mr. Wailes. On the north
side of the chancel, the first window from the east, which
represents the figures of Faith, Hope, and Charity, was
presented by E. C. Lowndes, Esq., and is a memorial
window. It was the work of Mr. Lamb, of London.
The next in order on the north side, was presented by
Thomas German, Esq. The principal portion of it forms
what was the east window of the old church. The
executant was Mr. Ballantine of Edinburgh. The adjoining window was presented by Mr. John Gorst, and
was designed and executed by Mr. Lamb. It contains the
figures of St. Stephen, St. Peter, and St. John the
Baptist. All the windows in the nave and clerestory

were presented by the late recorder, Thomas Batty
Addison, Esq., and his brother, John Addison, Esq.
They contain medallions representing subjects from
scripture, armorial shields of sovereigns who have visited
Preston; Guild mayors; ecclesiastical functionaries connected with Preston; and several families in the town
and neighbourhood. The window in the baptistry
was the gift of Thomas Miller, Esq. The font in
the baptistry was presented by Mrs. W. A. Hulton,
Miss Gorst, and Miss Barbara Gorst. A brass plate on
the north-west side of the nave contains the following
inscription recording the rebuilding of the church :—
"This parish church of St. John the Evangelist, Preston,
was rebuilt by public subscription in the year of our
Lord, MDCCCLV, John Owen Parr, M.A., vicar; William
Birley, and Miles Myres, Esquires, churchwardens;
Edwin Hugh Shellard, Esquire, architect." The organ,
which has from time to time been enlarged and rebuilt,
has now 36 sounding stops, and is of great power. It is
now fifty years since Mr. J. J. Greaves, the venerable
organist, was appointed, and in commemoration of the
jubilee, he was, in December last, presented with a testimonial in money, amounting to £100, when the vicar,
the Rev. J. H. Rawdon, presided. The churchwardens
and the members of the choir, also took part in the
proceedings.

Proceeding eastward, to the termination of Church
Street, the House of Correction, or

COUNTY PRISON,

forms a prominent object. It is now nearly a century
since it was erected, having been first opened in 1789.
It is stated that in its construction the designs and plans
of John Howard, the well known prison philanthropist,
were adopted. Unlike the generality of buildings of a
similar character, the prison stands, so to speak, within
its own grounds, the governor's house forming a central

and prominent feature in the general elevation, with a spacious area of land in front. The prison has on several occasions been enlarged. In the year 1817 eighteen new cells were added. Two years after this date, namely in June, 1819, two celebrities in connection with the history and management of prisons, paid a visit to the establishment. The visitors were Mrs. Fry, and her brother, Mr. John Gurney, of Norwich; and in October of the following year, 1820, Mrs. Fry made a second visit. Mr. Gurney appears to have been favourably impressed with what he saw at the gaol at Preston, for in his published records of these prison inspections he observes:—"About one thousand persons are computed to pass through this House of Correction in the course of the year, and many of them learn in it those habits of industry, and that knowledge of a trade, by which they are enabled to respectably maintain their families when they leave it. We have, in the course of our journey, visited no prison which appeared to us to be so much a house of reformation as the bridewell at Preston." In the year 1832, three "martello towers" were erected upon the walls, in order to prevent the prison from attacks which had been threatened by mobs of operatives, who at the time were doing great damage by breaking new machinery which had been introduced in connexion with the cotton manufacture. Up to the year 1834, the governor's house was in a court yard within the main entrance to the prison. In that year the central structure which now forms the governor's residence, was erected, the architect being Mr. John Dewhurst. The building is of stone in the castellated style, with octagonal towers at the north and south angles. In the year 1842 further enlargements were carried out. They consisted of a new females' ward, containing thirty-three cells, six day rooms, a residence for matron and female warders, washhouses, laundry, and other offices. In the same year the first block of sixty cells, under the new regulation for separate confinement, was erected; and in 1847 the second block containing ninety-nine cells, was added. In the year 1876 the martello towers were removed, and a new block of buildings was erected a short distance to the south east of the governor's house, and between that building and the court house. The new block referred to was built for the purpose of forming a new carriage entrance to the interior of the prison, under a lofty archway in the centre of the block. On each side of the archway are residences for some of the prison officials. The entrance was formerly through a door way on the north side of the governor's house, which was approached through the grounds, along a carriage way at the bottom of Church Street. The entrance to the prison grounds and the prison itself, at this point, is now closed, and a new carriage road and entrance formed in Stanley Street.

On the south side of the prison is

THE COURT HOUSE,

which was erected in the year 1829. The business of quarter sessions has been held in this building since its completion, the sessions for the trial of prisoners having previously been held in a room inside the prison, attached to the former residence of the governor. The annual and other meetings of the magistrates, in transacting the business of the county, have also been hitherto held in this building, but in future the magistrates will hold all their meetings in the new County offices in Fishergate. The court house was erected from the designs of Mr. Rickman, architect. It is a stone building, which was originally surmounted by a circular dome, giving light to the court. In 1849 this dome was superseded by another dome, rectangular in form. There are two court rooms, besides the magistrates' private room, grand and petty jury rooms, barristers' robing room, attorneys' and witnesses' rooms, and several other rooms and offices. The second court was added a few years ago, in consequence of the great increase of business.

THE MILITIA STORES.

Preston is the head quarters of the third regiment of Lancashire Militia, and new offices and stores having been found necessary, a spacious new building for the purpose was erected at the south side of the court house, in the year 1854. The building, which is of brick, is quadrangular in form, having square towers at each angle. All the clothing, arms, and accoutrements of the regiment are deposited in this building, which also contains the commanding officer's apartments, and those of the adjutant, the staff, and the regimental tradesmen, together with stables and cells.

THE PRESTON AND COUNTY OF LANCASTER
ROYAL INFIRMARY.

The above structure, standing within its own grounds of several acres in extent, is situated at the north-east end of the town, the site being a portion of what was formerly known as an open waste, immediately adjoining or forming a part of Preston moor.   The central portion of the building was erected about half a century ago, as the House of Recovery.   The present building is of comparatively modern erection, having been built in 1867, from the designs of Mr. James Hibbert, architect.   The building, is quadrangular in form, consisting of the central portion and east and west wings, the old House of Recovery, forming, as already stated, the central section of the quadrangle.   At present the west wing only has been erected.   The building is a handsome structure, containing two lofty floors in addition to the basement.   It is built of red brick, with Longridge stone dressings, and surmounted at the several angles by ornamental towers, having elaborately moulded iron castings.

In the erection of the structure the pavilion principle has been adopted, the west wing for the reception of the sick in the several wards being separated, for sanitary reasons, from the central or old building, by a corridor 45 feet in length, and 12 feet in height, from the floor to the ceiling, the floors of the upper and lower wards being uniform in all their arrangements. The pavilions comprise on each floor, wards for 24 beds, the entire length of the upper and lower wards being 109 feet, and their width 26 feet. There is also another ward 36 feet long, and 26 feet wide, containing eight beds, for casualty or other cases that it may be considered desirable to keep apart; and two smaller wards for special cases. At the extreme end of the wards there are nurses' rooms, ward sculleries, lavatories, and general conveniences. The wards on the ground floor portion of the building are appropriated to males, and the upper floor to females. The floor space per bed averages 110 square feet, and the cubic space nearly 1900 feet. The baths, lavatories, and closets are separated from the wards by well ventilated intercepting lobbies. The ventilation of the wards is effected by tri partite sash windows, the two lower sheets hung to the transoms. The wards are warmed by fire grates in the two bed space, affording room for resort to patients who are able to leave their beds. The ceilings internally are plastered with the lime of the district, which is of a much harder and less absorbent nature than the chalk lime of the south. All the windows are glazed with plate glass. In connexion with the building there is a spacious and convenient administrative block, whilst the cooking and storage arrangements in the basement are of the most admirable description. The laundry block and other necessary outbuildings are equally spacious and well arranged.

In the year 1874 an important addition was made to the buildings by the liberality of the late Mr. Edmund Robert Harris. This addition consists of an entirely distinct and separate block comprising the infectious wards. The building, which was also designed by Mr. Hibbert, and erected under his personal superintendence, consists of three separate pavilions, one storey in height, each pavilion being connected by covered ways. The central pavilion contains the wards for cases of enteric fever, with 15 beds; the western pavilion the wards for scarlet or typhus fever, with 8 beds; and the eastern pavilion the wards for small pox, with 8 beds; in all 32 beds. The height of the pavilions, from the ground floor to the top of the cornice, is 19 feet 6 inches, and the distance between them, along the corridors, 40 feet. Every ward has its separate bath and lavatory, water closet, and sink, the water closets and sinks being built externally to the main building, and cut off by a lobby, separately lighted and ventilated by cross windows, from the wards. There are day rooms for convalescents, male and female, of the various classes; and sleeping rooms are provided for the nurses and attendants of the different pavilions, when off duty. A separate kitchen is provided for each pavilion. An inscription under the cornice of the elevation of the building, designates them the "Harris Infectious Wards."

The total cost of the whole of the Infirmary buildings up to the present time is £22,000, of which sum £15,000 have been expended on the main buildings, and £7,000 on the Harris Wards. The estimated cost of completing the design by the erection of the east wing, is £10,000.

Returning westward along Church Street, and turning into the new thoroughfare called Lancaster Road, on the north side, the visitor will notice several new buildings which have already been erected on the east side. A clearance is about to be made of the dilapidated old structures on the west side, including the butchers' and other ancient shops known as the Shambles.

On a portion of the site, extending westward to the Market Place,

THE FREE LIBRARY, MUSEUM, AND ART GALLERY

is about to be erected, at a cost of £60,000, being part of the fund bequeathed to the trustees for that and other similar purposes, by the late Mr. Edmund Robert Harris. The corporation have agreed to provide the site for the

building, at an estimated cost, it is stated, of £25,000.
The building will be of large dimensions, occupying a
ground area of about 26,000 superficial feet, and will have
four distinct frontages, being completely isolated from the
neighbouring buildings. The principal frontage, on the
east side of the Market Place, will be 130 feet in length.
This will be the west front, and form a fitting architectural
companion to the north elevation of the late Sir Gilbert
Scott's noble gothic production, the Town Hall. There
will likewise be a frontage on the east side, of similar
length, facing Lancaster Road. The north and south
frontages will each be 160 feet in length, facing the two
proposed new streets of 50 feet in width, which are about
to be constructed by the corporation, under their comprehensive street improvement undertaking. The building
will include lending and reference libraries, a reading and
news room, together with the museum and art galleries.
When completed the cost of the care and maintenance of
the building will be defrayed by the corporation. Pending
the erection of the new building the large room on the
ground floor of the Town Hall, intended as the Exchange
Rooms, will continue to be occupied as the Free Library.

THE BOROUGH POLICE STATION AND
MAGISTRATES' COURT.

Up to the year 1856, the borough police station
buildings were in Avenham Street, and the magistrates
sat in the old town hall for the disposal of police charges.
and other magisterial business. In that year the police
station buildings were purchased by Messrs. Horrocks,
Jacson, & Co., for the enlargement of their cotton spinning
establishment; and new police buildings were consequently
required. The site fixed upon for the erection of these
new buildings was in Lancaster Road, on the west side, a
short distance northwards of Lord Street. Mr. J. H.
Park was appointed architect by the corporation, with
instructions to prepare designs and plans for a police

station in combination with a magistrates' court and offices. The building, which is of stone and in the Italian style, contains two main frontages, one to the east in Lancaster Road, 50 feet long, and the other in Earl Street, facing the north, 104 feet in length. It is two storeys in height. The ground floor portion of the structure contains the private offices of the superintendent of police, together with the book-keeper's office, general police offices, store room, lavatory, and four cells. The magistrates' clerk's room is also on this floor. The upper floor contains the court room, an apartment 40 feet long, and 32 feet wide; also the magistrates' private room, a jury room, and attorney's room. There are likewise three cells on this floor, in addition to the four cells on the ground floor. The floors of the building are all fire-proof. The cost of the structure was upwards of £3000.

THE COVERED MARKET.

A few years ago a spacious covered market was erected on the large open space known as Chadwick's Orchard, on the north side of Earl Street, Lancaster Road. The market is 355 feet in length, and 101 feet in width, and occupies an aggregate area of 35,855 feet. The market was originally intended to have shops carried round its several sides, but this was strongly objected to by large numbers of the inhabitants, on the ground that the project was unfair to the tradesmen of the town, whose business it was alleged, it would seriously affect. This part of the undertaking was therefore abandoned by the corporation, and the market now consists of an open covered structure only, having a handsome roof resting on iron columns and girders. During certain days in the week it serves the purpose of a hay and straw market, when farmers in large numbers, from different districts in the country around, expose this kind of agricultural produce for sale. On Saturdays it is used as a meat, vegetable, fruit, and general market, when it is much frequented by the inhabitants and others, and a considerable amount of business is transacted. It is now also utilised, together with the several thoroughfares immediately around it, for holding the great annual horse fair in the first full week of the new year. The scene of this well known fair was formerly in Church Street, extending from about the Town Hall, on the west side. to some distance eastward of the Parish Church. The transactions as regards the most valuable animals brought to the fair, were, however, carried on in and about the stables belonging to the principal hotels in the neighbourhood, and this feature of the fair remains under the altered arrangement.

Not far from this locality on the west side of Lancaster Road, are

THE BATHS AND WASH-HOUSES,

in Saul Street, which were erected and opened, in the year 1851, at the cost of the corporation. The baths have a frontage to Saul Street of 80 feet in length, and extend 110 feet in depth, thus occupying a ground area of 8800 superficial feet. There are 63 private baths, 16 being first class baths for men, 8 first class baths for women; and 31 second class baths for men, and 8 second class baths for women. In addition to the private baths there is also a swimming bath 34 feet by 24 feet, which being supplied with both hot and cold water, is generally kept in a tepid state. The establishment also includes vapour and shower baths, and is thus on a more than usually comprehensive scale. That portion of the building devoted to wash-house purposes is spacious, and very conveniently fitted, having every necessary appliance for washing and drying clothes. The cost of the land and buildings was £11,200. The designs were furnished by Mr. P. P. Baly, architect, and engineer, of London.

WINCKLEY SQUARE AND ITS SURROUNDINGS.

This fashionable part of Preston, is situated on the south side of Fishergate, from which it is approached either along Chapel Street or Winckley Street. Its nomenclature is traceable to the fact that a former townsman named Winckley, an alderman of the borough, was the principal owner of the land now forming the square.   It has for many years past been deservedly regarded as one of the most ornamental and picturesque squares of which any town can boast.   It has long been the residence of several of the most wealthy families in the town, and its beautifully laid out central gardens, with their profusion of trees in full and ample foliage, impart to it, more especially in the summer season, a suburban rather than an urban character, even in the midst of its town-life surroundings.   It is a noteworthy fact, however, that within the last few years the disciples of Esculapius have largely taken possession of this retired and favourite quarter of the town, for although there are not more than about forty residences in the square, many of them partaking of the detatched mansion type, almost one half are at present occupied by professors of the healing art, and during the present year a block of three high class and costly new residences has been erected on the south side, by Mr. John Walmsley, all of which are occupied by the professional followers of St. Luke.   A prominent feature within the gardens, on the east side of the square, opposite Cross Street, is the

STATUE OF THE LATE SIR ROBERT PEEL,

which was erected in 1852, shortly after the lamented baronet died, from the effects of a fall from his horse, in Piccadilly.   The statue was chiselled from one large block of lime stone.   It is of colossal size, and with the pedestal, is 18 feet in height from the ground line.   It is admitted to be a truthful likeness of the deceased statesman.   On the pedestal is the following inscription :—

"SIR
ROBERT PEEL,
BARONET.
_____

ERECTED
BY PUBLIC SUBSCRIPTION,
1852."

Mr. Thomas Duckett, of Preston, was the sculptor.

THE WINCKLEY CLUB HOUSE,

on the east side of the square, nearly opposite to the statue of Sir Robert Peel, but a little to the north of it, is one of the most conspicuous buildings in the square. It forms part of a group of public buildings which were erected in the year 1844, the other portion of the group forming the Literary and Philosophical Institution, but which now no longer exists, having some time since being merged into a museum in connexion with Dr. Shepherd's Library. The buildings are of stone, the most prominent feature of the Winckley Club frontage of the structure consisting of a square tower, 50 feet in height, and a lofty surmounting gable, containing a projecting oriel window. The Winckley Square frontage has a free introduction of sculpture, consisting of carved heads and allegorical figures, this portion of the work having been executed by Mr. T. Duckett. This part of the structure, which belongs to 80 shareholders, contains a large and handsome news-room on the ground floor, artistically decorated and fitted, with two billiard rooms on the upper floor. The care taker's and servants' apartments are in the basement below. The adjoining portion of the block, originally built as the Literary and Plilosophical Institution, but now known as

DR. SHEPHERD'S LIBRARY AND MUSEUM,

is at the angle of Winckley Square and Cross Street, having an elevation to each. The Winckley Square portion of the frontage has two square towers at the north and south angles, surmounted by open octagonal lanterns. The central space between the towers contains a bold projecting gothic window, surmounted by a gable. The Cross Street portion of the frontage is 160 feet in length, the style of architecture being of a mixed character. The building contains two floors above the basement, the principal apartment on the ground floor, now forming the library and reading room, being 50 feet in length, by 24 feet in width. There are also smaller rooms on the same floor. Above the library and reading room there is another room of similar dimensions, now occupied as a museum. The building also contains a spacious lecture theatre, 41 feet by 36 feet, which is capable of containing an audience of 300 persons. "Dr. Shepherd's Library" was the gift of Richard Shepherd, an eminent physician in Preston, who died in the year 1761, and who bequeathed his valuable library to the mayor and aldermen of the borough for public use. In addition to the library itself Dr. Shepherd also left the corporation a sum of £1,000, the interest of which was from time to time to be expended in the purchase of additional books for the library, and this having been carried out for considerably more than a century past, the library is now one of the finest and most extensive in the country. Half a century ago it contained about 4,000 volumes. In 1852, this number had been increased to 5,800 volumes. Five years afterwards, namely in 1856, a further increase had taken place, bringing up the number of volumes to 7,000, and the continued rate of increase is indicated by the fact that it is now said to contain 10,000 volumes. For many years the home of the library was in the upper part of a plain and unpretending building in Shepherd Street, adjoining the old grammar school; but a little more than thirty years ago the necessity of its removal to a more eligible and convenient site became manifest, not only from the expansion of the town and the increase of its population, but also owing to the circumstance that the locality in which the library was then situated was daily becoming one of the least attractive parts of the town, and altogether unsuited as the depository of such priceless literary treasures. The corporation therefore decided upon providing a large building, and one more worthy of the library and the town. In the first instance it was contemplated to erect a new building in conjunction with the new grammar school in Cross Street, but the site was eventually found to be too limited in its dimensions for both the library and school, and an entirely new and distinct structure for the purposes of the library was determined upon by the corporation. A site in Cross Street, opposite to the grammar school, was selected, and Mr. Charles Barry, M. C. B. A. (son of the late Sir Charles Barry, architect of the houses of parliament), was commissioned to prepare designs and plans for the projected new building. These plans were prepared accordingly, but the corporation took no further steps for the erection of the building. It 1851, however, one of the large rooms in the Avenham Institution was placed at the disposal of the corporation, and the books were removed from Shepherd Street to the Avenham establishment, where they remained until the year 1868, when the library was transferred to the establishment in which it is now provided in Cross Street, under the terms, already referred to, which were made with the Literary and Philosophical Society.

THE GRAMMAR SCHOOL.

The New Grammar School, which was erected in the year 1842, on the old school buildings in Shepherd Street being vacated, forms the remaining portion of the block, constituting its eastern boundary. It has a frontage to Cross Street about 100 feet in length, extending to

Guild Hall Street, with a return frontage to the last named street, 70 feet long, adjacent to this frontage there being a spacious play ground. The building is in the Tudor style of architecture. At the west end of the Cross Street frontage there is a bold and prominent gable, enclosing a lofty and handsome tracery window. Immediately to the west of this gable a flight of steps leads to an entrance into one of the large class rooms, which is on a higher level than the principal class room, approached from the main entrance. Eastward from the gable the elevation contains ranges of mullion windows. At the eastern boundary of the frontage the elevation has two octagonal towers between the arched and recessed entrance, above which is a three-light mullion window, surmounted by a gable. Over the entrance there is a considerable amount of carving and sculpture, including ornamental panels, foliage, and scroll work, the Borough Arms being a conspicuous feature. Immediately over the doorway is the following design and inscription:—

The principal class room is used for prayer in the morning, before the commencement of the day's studies. At the north end of this room there are some well executed frescoes. Besides the two large class rooms already named there are also similar rooms in the basement portion of the building.

THE INSTITUTION FOR THE DIFFUSION OF KNOWLEDGE.

About the period when the late Lord Brougham was

foremost in establishing mechanics' institutions in different parts of the country, a number of gentlemen in Preston, interested in the advancement of that popular education, in which Lord Brougham and those associated with him were engaged, conceived the idea of establishing some such institution in the town, and in the year 1828, a literary and scientific organisation was formed under the name of " The Institution for the diffusion of useful Knowledge," the objects aimed at being on the same lines as those which were being pursued in other towns by the establishments then more generally designated " Mechanics' Institutions." The institution commenced its operations at a building in Cannon Street, the large numbers of operatives and others who enrolled themselves as members, during the first year of its existence, giving encouraging promises of success. At the end of the first year, the institution found itself with about 800 members on its books, which, taking into account the then comparatively small population of the town, was considerably more than might reasonably have been expected. At the same period the institution was in possession of 1500 volumes of standard works, mostly of a scientific character, for during the first nine years of its existence, novels and romances, and dramatic literature, including even the works of Shakspere, were rigidly excluded from the shelves of the institution. In 1837, however, a concession was made to a generally expressed wish for the admission of works embracing a wider field, and the creations of the " Wizard of the North," and others of his school, found a place in the institution, side by side with the researches and productions of a deeper philosophy, and of science and art. A museum in connexion with the institution was also formed during the first year of its existence, numbering about 800 specimens in natural history. As years rolled on the institution ceased to be one of a merely educational character for the class known as " mechanics," who gave it little more than a nominal support. It was, however, increasingly patronised by what may be described as the middle and well to do lower classes, and became in course of years a recognised and well established literary institution, possessing a constantly increasing library of the best standard and other works, and embracing amongst its features lectures upon various subjects by distinguished professors.   About the year 1840, the accommodation of the premises in Cannon Street was found to be altogether inadequate for carrying on the work of the institution, and a new building was projected.   By the aid of an exhibition of works of art, private subscriptions, to which the corporation subscribed £250, and a bazaar held in the Corn Exchange, which yielded the sum of £1800, a sufficient sum to defray the cost of a new building was raised.   The site fixed upon was immediately opposite Avenham Walk, near the junction of Ribblesdale Place and Avenham Lane.   The foundation stone of the building was laid in June, 1846, by the late Thomas German, Esq., then mayor of the borough ; and was completed in 1849, the opening ceremony taking place in October of that year.   The building, which is of stone, from the Longridge quarries, is a combination of Greek and modern Italian architecture, having a commanding frontage to Avenham Walk, about 60 feet in length, and 40 feet in height.   It extends to a depth of 120 feet, the entire building covering a ground area of about 7,200 feet.   In the centre of the elevation there is a bold projecting portico, supported, on the east and west sides, by massive piers enclosing Corinthian columns, having carved capitals.   At the east and west angles of the *facade* there are double pilasters.   The building is approached by a flight of thirteen steps, sixteen feet in width, in front of the elevation, leading up to the terrace, and five more leading up to the floor level of the entrance under the portico, and thence into the vestibule, and reading room and library.   On each side of the steps there is a stone balustrade, and a terrace or balcony on the east and west sides of the portico.   The building contains a spacious basement, and two floors above.   The basement has a range of several class rooms and other offices.   The lecture room or theatre is also in the basement, and including the gallery it will hold six hundred persons. The ground or first floor contains the reading room and library, together with committee room and ante-rooms. The upper floor, which is reached by a spacious stone staircase, contains two large exhibition rooms lighted from the roof, together with two smaller apartments. The building, which was erected at a cost of about £6,400, was designed by Mr. Welch.

The library now contains 11,000 volumes, but under a change which is about to take place in the nature and character of the institution the probability is that this valuable collection will shortly be transferred to either one or both of the two other public libraries in the town. The trustees under the will of the late Mr. Edmund Robert Harris, who some few years since bequeathed the whole of his personal estate, (amounting, it is understood, to about £250,000), to be expended in the establishment of educational and charitable institutions in Preston, have appropriated the sum of £40,000 for the foundation and endowment of an institution for promoting the systematic study of Art, Science, and Literature, and for the advancement of Technical Education. Under a scheme, which has been agreed upon, the Avenham Institution will merge into an educational establishment to be called "The Harris Institute," and, for the purposes of the scheme, the land and buildings now the property of the old Institution, together with such of the books and other property of the Institution as may be required, are vested in seven gentlemen to be known as the "Harris Institute Trustees." A council has been appointed, to whom the trustees are to pay the income arising from the Endowment Fund. It is also provided that on the application of the council the trustees are to be at liberty to expend out of the Endowment Fund any sum, not exceeding in the whole £5,000 in repairs of buildings used for the purposes of the scheme or in the erection, extension, or adaptation of buildings on the site, or any other site, or in the purchase of books plant, or appliances. The council consists of fifteen co-optative members, and six representative members three to be appointed by the corporation of Preston, out of their own body; and the other three to be elected by the donors and subscribers at every annual meeting. The subjects to be taught to the students in the Institute include mathematics, pure and applied mechanics, machine and building construction, chemistry, physics; freehand, model, perspective, and landscape drawing; modelling, painting, mechanical drawing, and its application to machine and building construction; botany, geology, cotton spinning and weaving; pattern designing, and its practical application to textile and other trades; and such other subjects in art, science, literature, and technical and industrial education as the council may from time to time think necessary. The entrance and other fees of students are to be regulated by the council, who are also to have power to require any student, before entering upon the work of any study, to pass such a satisfactory examination, or to produce evidence of having passed such an examination, as shall show that he has acquired the knowledge necessary for the proper and intelligent study of the art, science, or subject which he proposes to pursue. The council are likewise from time to time to determine what number of masters, teachers, or lecturers shall be employed. By way of exhibitions, tenable at the institute itself, the council may grant exemptions from the payment of tuition fees, or may make pecuniary grants for such periods and on such conditions as they may think fit, and shall each year throw open to competition, by boys or girls under the age of 18 years, attending elementary schools or evening schools in connexion therewith, within seven miles of the Preston Town Hall, at least 50 of such exhibitions. The council will also be empowered to establish studentships or scholarships, to be awarded on competitive examination, open to all pupils who have been in the Institute for not less than two years immediately preceding the examination, and tenable at any college or place of higher education. The council are finally to have power to affiliate the Harris Institute to any university or public body having similar objects. It will thus be seen that both as regards technical education and several of the most important branches in connexion with what is known as higher education, Preston will shortly possess an institution ranking amongst the most valuable in the country. It is expected that the Institute will be in full operation during the present year.

AVENHAM WALK.

From the portico entrance to the building just described there is a commanding view of Avenham Walk, one of the most picturesque and charming resorts of which the town can boast. It likewise has a special historical interest of its own, having existed as a place of recreation for the inhabitants since about the middle of the seventeenth century ; for we gather from the corporation archives that in the year 1696 the municipal authorities entered into negociations with Mr. Alderman Lemon for the purchase of the land forming the promenade, and in the following year, 1697, it was conveyed to the corporation. In the deed of conveyance it is described as " all that little close or parcel of land lying and being in or upon Aenam *alias* Avenham, commonly called or known by the name of Aenam Walk, or Little Avenham, containing by estimation about half an acre of land." After its purchase by the corporation for the modest sum of £15, it was planted with lime trees, and a gravelled walk was formed, with seats for the use of the inhabitants. It is further stated that in the year 1707, and again in 1736-7, the walk being out of order, it was repaired, the records of the period noting that " the ladies, who took great advantage of the walk, subscribed £10 towards repairing it, and this sum was supplemented by £10 voted by the corporation." About this time the land to the east now called Bushell Place, was leased to the corporation by Madam Bushell, widow of Dr. Bushell, who founded Goosnargh Hospital. This lease, however, was only during the lifetime of Mrs. Bushell, and at present for that portion of the walk which is between the lime trees in the centre, and the lime trees in Bushell Place, the corporation pay an annual rental of fifteen shillings to the trustees of Dr. Bushell. In the year 1844 the walk was extended on the west side, and a retaining wall built in front of the Colonnade. In the same year the reversionary interest of six acres of land, in the occupation of Mr. Charles Jackson, was purchased, and in 1845 the south side of the walk was widened, and the two lower terraces, extending in the direction of Frenchwood, and the valley of the Ribble on the south, were formed. The lime trees on the walk are said to be about 190 years old, having, it is stated, stood since they were first planted in 1697. The municipal authorities would, however, do well to pay some attention to their nursing and preservation, inasmuch as several of them exhibit symptoms of dilapidation and decay. There are few towns possessing such a beautiful prospect, almost at their doors, as that which Avenham Walk commands, both in a south, east, and west direction.

AVENHAM PARK.

This artistically laid out Park, with its pretty walks, its wooded foliage, and velvet carpetted greensward, is in immediate contiguity to Avenham Walk, from the eastern terraces of which it is approached, as well as from several other points in the town, in a westerly direction. From time to time plots of land in the locality were purchased in order to secure the necessary area for its construction. In the year 1848, the land between the old tramway and Avenham walk, and between the Colonade and the tramway engine house, was purchased from Mrs. Cross, other adjoining property being purchased in succession, including a considerable area of land stretching westward, from Jackson's gardens to the East Lancashire Railway. In the previous year the taking down of old hedge rows and the filling up of ditches, on the land which had already been acquired, was proceeded with, in anticipation of the commencement of laying out the park. In the year 1860, the formation of the park from Jackson's gardens, in the direction of the East Lancashire Railway, was entered upon, but it was not until 1862 that the laying out of the park was commenced in earnest, and in 1864 the services of Mr. Milner, of London, the well known landscape gardener, were engaged, and to Mr. Milner is due the credit—assisted, it must be admitted, by their natural conformation—of those beautiful grounds which the inhabitants of Preston now enjoy, and which command the admiration of strangers and visitors. The special peculiarity of this park, and its neighbour on the immediate west, Miller Park, is that their northern boundary forms a crescent on a high level, the grounds gradually falling down to the margin of the meandering Ribble beneath. The upper portion of the park is laid out in slopes and terraced walks, with winding walks and trees, shrubs, and flower beds, on the lower level; a large portion of the central area, consisting of several acres being set apart as a recreation ground, where, in favourable weather, and more especially on holiday occasions thousands of juveniles, as well as "children of a larger growth," may be seen revelling in their gambols. At the west boundary of the park, immediately below the East Lancashire Railway, which intersects the two parks there is a small lake, surrounded by artistically arranged rockwork, the crevices of the rockery being filled in with ferns, plants, and flowers. A speciality of the park consists of numerous fine and full grown trees, included amongst the several purchases of land, and which were utilised in the laying out and construction of the park. The upper terrace walk, 24 feet in width, passes under the East Lancashire Railway, by an ornamental bridge opening out, at the west side, upon the

MILLER PARK,

which was also laid out by Mr. Milner, and is very

artistic in design and execution. It takes its name from the late Mr. Alderman Miller, who in the year 1864, purchased the land which now forms part of the park, shortly afterwards presenting it to the Corporation, accompanied by his desire that it should be laid out for the recreation and benefit of the inhabitants. This park consists of terraced and winding walks, uniform in the main with its immediate neighbour, but its numerous flower beds, shrubs, and plants, impart to it a more garden-like character. In the lower parts of the grounds below the terraces, is an ornamental playing fountain. The park is bounded on the west by the London and North Western Railway embankment, which is planted with trees and shrubs, whilst immediately beneath it is a rockery and waterfall. Nearly opposite the fountain, on the upper terrace of the park is a

STATUE OF THE LATE EARL OF DERBY,

which was unveiled in the year 1873, at a cost of £2,500, provided by a county subscription. The plinth is in red Aberdeen granite, and the pedestal in grey polished granite. The statue is in white Sicilian marble, and of collossal dimensions, being 9 feet in height. The Earl is represented as standing in ordinary dress, having in his hand a roll of paper, and in the act of addressing the House of Lords. The statue, which was sculptured by Noble, is a striking likeness of the late Earl. With the pedestal upon which it stands it is 24 feet in height, and forms a prominent and attractive object when viewed from the footpath on the banks of the Ribble. On the south face of the pedestal is the following inscription :— " Edward Geoffrey Stanley, 14th Earl of Derby, K. G. Born 29th March, 1799 ; Died 23rd October, 1869."

THE MOOR PARK,

at the north end of the town, approached by the main high road to Lancaster, and also at the north-east end of

the town along Deepdale Road, and the Fulwood route
to the Barracks, is in point of area, one of the finest
public parks in the country. It is altogether about 400
acres in extent, thus containing an area about equal to
Hyde Park, in London, and somewhat in excess of Sefton
Park, at the south end of Liverpool, which was laid out
a few years ago. Originally it was an open space, known
as Preston Moor, over which the old freemen of Preston
had rights of pastorage and other privileges.   These
privileges were, however, taken away some years before
the passing of the Municipal Reform Act, when the old
corporation enclosed it, but not without an effort being
made on the part of the freemen to retain the privileges
which they had for some centuries possessed. There was
considerable agitation on the subject at the time, leading
to legal proceedings being taken against the corporation
to prevent them from making the enclosure, but ultimately the freemen failed to sustain their claims, and the
enclosure accordingly took place in the year 1834. For
considerably more than half a century before the period
of the enclosure horse races were annually held on the
moor, under the patronage of the corporation, but in the
year 1786, when political antagonism between the corporation and the Derby family was running very high, a
race course was formed on Fulwood Moor adjoining, by
the Derby family and their political supporters, and races
were held there until the year 1833, when they were
finally given up, three years after the late Earl of Derby
was defeated for Preston by Mr. Henry Hunt. The races
on Preston Moor were discontinued very shortly after
the construction of the rival course at Fulwood.
     Sometime after the corporation enclosed the moor a
broad avenue and carriage drive was constructed across it
from east to west, with plantations on each side, and an
entrance lodge at the west end, but it is only within the
last few years that it has been ornamentally laid-out as a
park, and with its broad meandering walks and drives,
plantations, and lakes, it is now a great centre of attraction for recreation purposes, and more especially in the

summer months, is frequented by large numbers of the inhabitants. The landscape gardener has done his work most artistically in the construction of charming flower beds, shrubberies, and rock work, whilst the artistically thrown up moulds, encircling the winding lake, with its central islands, is one of those triumphs of art, assisted by nature, which are amongst the most pleasing features of Æsthetic skill and refined taste. The Serpentine Road, which is of considerable length, leads to the lake, and is one of the most frequented walks and drives in the park. A large area in the central portion of the park is available for sports and pastimes of a varied character, and during certain portions of the year is also utilised for the grazing of cattle. Approached from the north side of the broad avenue, running east and west, is a spacious bowling green, and a short distance to the west of the bowling green an area of several acres in extent is set apart as a cricket ground.

THE CHURCHES AND CHAPELS.

---

*T*HE multiplication of the places of worship in a community may be regarded as a tolerably correct index of its expansion, and viewed from this standpoint, it will be seen that the increase in the number of inhabitants of Preston within the last half century has been considerable. Up to the year 1726 the parish church was the only edifice connected with the Church of England which the town possessed. In that year a chapel-of-ease to the parent church, was erected on a site a short distance north of Fishergate. The building was designated St. George's Chapel, and the approach to it from Fishergate, taking its name from the chapel itself, was called Chapel Walk, its nomenclature remaining unchanged up to the present day. In 1814 the erection of Trinity Church was commenced, and completed and opened in the following year. This was followed in 1824, by the erection of St. Peter's Church, in the Fylde Road. In 1825, St. Paul's Church, Park Road, was built and opened. Eleven years elapsed before another church was erected. In the year 1836, Christ Church, Bow Lane, was built and opened. The erection of St. Mary's Church, close to the prison, at

the east end of the town, commenced shortly after Christ
Church, the foundation stone having been laid in 1836,
and the church opened in 1838. St. Thomas's Church,
in Lancaster Road, was commenced in 1837, and consecrated in 1841. St. James's Church, in Avenham Lane,
was first built and opened as a dissenting chapel, in 1837,
but in 1841, it was purchased and consecrated as a
Church of England Church. It was entirely rebuilt in
1870. The first stone of All Saints, Elizabeth Street,
was laid in October, 1846, and the church was opened in
the following year. In 1859, St. Luke's Church, in
Ribbbleton Lane, was consecrated. This was followed by
the erection and opening of St. Mark's Church, near the
Maudlands, in 1863. To this succeeded St. Saviour's
Church, in Leeming Street, which was built and opened
in 1868. The erection of Emmanuel Church, in Brook
Street, Adelphi Street, followed, the edifice being consecrated and opened in 1870. In 1870 the Bairstow
Memorial Church, at the bottom of Fishergate, was
erected; and at the present time St. Matthew's Church,
in New Hall Lane, is in course of erection. These constitute the whole of the places of worship in connexion
with the Church of England, with the exception of St.
Barnabas' School Chapel, which is a chapel-of-ease to St.
Paul's.

The Roman Catholics have, from the earliest periods
of its history, formed a considerable proportion of the
population of Preston, and they have at present no less
than seven large places of worship connected with their
order, two of the most costly, which rank with the finest
architectural buildings in the town, having been erected
within the last few years. The oldest of them is St.
Mary's, in Friargate. St. Wilfrid's, erected in 1793; St.
Ignatius's, built in 1833; St. Augustine's, the first stone
of which was laid in 1838; St. Walburge's, Maudlands,
built in 1850-54; the church of the English Martyrs,
built and opened in the year 1867; and St. Joseph's
Church, Ribbleton Lane, which was erected and opened
in 1874. Another new Roman Catholic Church is about

to be erected at Fulwood, on a site between the Preston workhouse and the barracks, which has been given by Mr. Weld Blundell.

There are upwards of twenty chapels connected with the various dissenting bodies in the town, the principal of which are the Wesleyan Chapels in Lune Street, North Road, and Marsh Lane; the Independent Chapels in Cannon Street, Grimshaw Street, and Lancaster Road; the Protestant Wesleyan Methodists' Chapel in Chadwick's Orchard; the Baptists' Chapels in Fishergate and Pole Street; and the New Jerusalem Church, in Avenham Road.

ST. GEORGE'S CHURCH, CHAPEL WALKS,

originally a chapel of ease to the Parish Church, as already stated, is now an independent district church. When first erected it was a plain brick building. In the year 1844 it was externally re-constructed, the several frontages being faced with stone. In the year 1848 a new chancel was erected, and in 1849 a new pulpit and reading desk were constructed. All these several works were executed at the cost of the late T. M. Lowndes, Esq., in memory of whom a mural monument has been erected in the church, at the cost of E. C. Lowndes, Esq., brother of the former. The Rev. Robert Harris, formerly head master of the grammar school, was incumbent of this church for the long period of 64 years, and preached his last sermon there on Christmas Day, 1861, in the 98th year of his age. It is stated that there is a probability of the church being shortly rebuilt.

TRINITY CHURCH

is situated on a site known as Patten Field, Snow Hill, approached from Union Street, Friargate. The first stone was laid by Sir Henry Hoghton, Bart., in the year 1814, and in the following year the church was completed and consecrated. The edifice is in the decorated style of mediæval architecture, and has a square tower at the west end. It contains nave and side aisles, with north, south, and west galleries. The east end window over the chancel, is filled with stained glass, executed by Mr. W. R. Egginton, of Birmingham. In the year 1842 the old organ, which stood in a gallery above the west end gallery, was removed, the gallery in which it was placed being taken down at the same time, and a powerful new organ was erected by Messrs. Gray & Davison, of London, which occupies a large space in the west end gallery. On the occasion of the opening of this organ the Rev. Dr. Hook, then vicar of Leeds, preached the sermons, Dr. S. S. Wesley, (who at the time was organist at the Leeds Parish Church), accompanying him to Preston, in order to preside at the organ on its opening.

ST. PETER'S CHURCH, FYLDE ROAD.

Mr. Justice Park, who was then recorder of Preston, laid the foundation stone of St. Peter's Church during the Guild week in 1822. The recorder's son, Mr. James Allen Park, gave the land on which the church was built. The style of architecture of the church is that known as the perpendicular or florid gothic. The church is built of stone, from the Longridge quarries, and from the designs of Mr. Rickman, of Birmingham. The cost of the church was £7,000, furnished by the commissioners for building churches. The church, as originally erected, was surmounted by turrets or spirelets, but in 1852 a tower and spire were erected out of funds bequeathed for the purpose by the late Thomas German, Esq. The architect of this portion of the edifice was Mr. Joseph Mitchell, of Sheffield.

ST. PAUL'S CHURCH, PARK ROAD.

The erection of this church, which quickly followed
the building of St. Peter's, was likewise due to a grant
made by the commissioners for building churches.   The
foundation stone was laid in October, 1823, by the Rev.
R. Carus Wilson, then Vicar of Preston, the land having
been given by Samuel Pole Shawe, Esq.   The church,
built of stone, is in the early English style of architecture,
having two spirelets at the east and west ends respectively.
It was erected from designs furnished by Messrs. Rickman
and Hutchinson, and cost upwards of £6,500.   In 1844
a large and powerful organ was erected in the church.
It was the gift of the late Thomas and Henry Miller,
Esquires.

CHRIST CHURCH, JORDAN STREET.

This church, which is in the Norman style of
architecture, and built of lime stone, was first opened for
service in March, 1837, when the Rev. R. Carus Wilson,
the vicar, who had taken great interest in its erection,
preached.   It had previously been consecrated in October,
1836, by the Bishop of Chester, John Bird Sumner
(afterwards Archbishop of Canterbury).   The church
externally, has a heavy and unprepossessing appearance,
with slight pretensions to architectural effect or beauty.
At the south end there are two octagonal towers.   Mr.
John Latham was the architect.   In 1852 the church was
enlarged.   In November, 1880, a memorial baptistry
was erected in the church, in memory of Mrs. Cedric
Houghton.   A step of red granite raises the baptistry
above the south aisle.   Figured tiles form the pavement,
and cover the wall.   Two massive steps of polished grey
granite lead up to the font, which stands on a St.
Andrew's Cross of red granite.   In design the font par-
takes of the early English, retaining some features of
the Norman, thus harmonising with the architecture

of the church. The bowl of the font and the base of the pillars are of white statuary marble, the central pillar being of red and the corner ones of green serpentine. On each side is a bench of English oak, enriched by pillars and arches. On the wall is a black marble slab, bearing a plate of polished brass, on which, in red and black letters is the following inscription:— "To the glory of God, and in loving remembrance of Gertrude (Ransome), wife of Cedric Houghton, who entered into rest on Easter Eve, 1880, aged 34 years; this baptistry is erected by her husband 'Until the day break and the shadows flee away.'" The baptistry was designed by Mr. T. Harrison Myres, architect.

ST. MARY'S CHURCH, OFF NEW HALL LANE.

The erection and opening of St. Mary's Church followed quickly upon that of Christ Church. The foundation stone was laid in 1836, and in 1838, two years afterwards, the church was opened for service. Like Christ Church, it is in the Norman style of architecture, and has a diminishing tower, surmounted by a central and two side turrets. The site was the gift of Mr. John Smith. Mr. John Latham was the architect. Some years after its erection the church was enlarged by the erection of an additional transept, Mr. Shellard, of Manchester, being the architect.

ST. THOMAS'S CHURCH, LANCASTER ROAD.

The foundation stone of this church, which is also in the Norman style of architecture, from the designs of Mr. John Latham, was laid in the year 1837. It was erected out of the funds derivable from a legacy of £50,000, bequeathed by Miss Catherine Elizabeth Hyndman, for church building purposes. It has a tower and spire, rising to a height of about 100 feet. The tower is

stunted and unsightly in appearance. It would have
added much to the architectural attractiveness of the
structure had the spire been carried to a greater height,
and tapered more gradually.

ST. JAMES'S CHURCH, AVENHAM LANE.

This church, which is now one of the finest ecclesiastical structures in the town, was originally a dissenting
chapel, being a plain brick building, erected in the year
1837. It subsequently became connected with the Church
of England (having been purchased by the vicar, the Rev.
R. Carus Wilson), and was consecrated in 1841. It was afterwards structurally improved, the external walls having
stone buttresses added to them, but in the year 1870 the
entire re-building of the edifice was resolved upon, the
designs being entrusted to Mr. James Hibbert. The
edifice is in the style of architecture known as the
geometrical gothic, and the materials Longridge stone.
The extreme length of the church is 139 feet, the nave
being 99 feet long, and the chancel 40 feet. The nave is
25 feet in width clear, and one of the aisles is 12 feet wide,
and the other 19 feet. The most striking feature of the
church externally, is the tower at the north west angle.
It is 24 feet square at the base, and is carried up to a
height of 100 feet. The upper, or decorated portion of
the tower, was erected at a cost of £2,000, contributed by
Richard Newsham, Esq., as a memorial of his late wife.
The effect of the design of this part of the edifice is that
of a tomb raised in the air. The angles of the tower are
surmounted by kneeling angels and other symbolical
figures. The principal entrance to the church is by a
deeply recessed gothic archway, under the tower, ten feet
in width. All the windows in the church are traceried,
varied in design according to their position. The nave
of the church is arcaded by four polished granite columns,
from which spring gothic arches. The height of the
church is 50 feet to the ridge of the nave. Amongst the

interesting internal features of the church are its massive open roof, its stained glass windows, and the reredos. The stained glass consists of a triplet of three lights in the centre of the church, by Harvey, of Birmingham. This window is a memorial of the late Mr. Alderman Spencer, who was twice mayor of Preston. A second triplet to the right of the centre, is now in the hands of Mr. Hardman, of Birmingham, as a memorial of the late Edward Hermon, Esq., formerly M.P. for Preston. Another memorial window, also by Mr. Hardman, in the west aisle, has been erected by his friends, to the memory of the late Mr. W. Fisher, manager of the Preston branch of the Lancaster Bank, and for a considerable time honorary organist of the church. The subject of the reredos is the Last Supper, which in the figure work follows very closely the well known example of Leonardo Da Vinci. It is executed in polished alabaster, as a memorial of the late Rev. John Wilson, formerly vicar of the church.

ALL SAINTS' CHURCH, ELIZABETH STREET.

The erection of this Church arose out of one of those intestine differences and jealousies which periodically occur in the religious as well as in the secular world. The Rev. William Walling, who had for some time been the incumbent of St. James's Church, resigned the incumbency in consequence of some disagreement between himself and the authorities of the Church. This was much regretted, more especially by the humbler members of the congregation, with whom he was extremely popular; and in order to prevent his leaving the town an effort was made to erect another Church specially for the rev. gentlemen. Funds for this purpose were readily forthcoming, the working classes, in large numbers, being amongst the contributors, and the foundation stone of the edifice was laid in October, 1846. The building, which is of brick, with stone dressings, is in the Ionic order of Grecian architecture, the designs being furnished by Mr. John Latham. Internally it is very spacious, having seating room for a congregation of about 1,500 persons.

ST. SAVIOUR'S CHURCH, LEEMING STREET.

This Church was erected in the year 1868 on a site which was for many years occupied by a Baptist Chapel, of which the Rev. William Giles, father of the Rev. John Eustice Giles, was the minister. The Church is peculiar for novelty of plan and distinctive design of architectural detail. It consists of a broad nave and north aisle, the latter sufficiently wide and lofty to receive a spacious gallery, without extending up to the arcade dividing the two. The principal entrance under the tower is boldly treated, and in the simplicity of the arch-molds the architect has deviated from the ancient type. It is surmounted by a well-executed medallion of the head of Christ. The west windows of the nave and aisle have tracery of an early character. Stone crosses support the east and west gables of the nave, and over the aisle gable is a crown of thorns, in wrought iron work. At the east end of the Church is a large memorial window, the gift of Edward Swainson, Esq., executed by Czell, of Paris, the subjects being figures of Christ and the four evangelists. On the south side of the chancel there is a memorial window, dedicated to the memory of the wife of the first and present vicar of St. Saviour's, the Rev. W. D. Thompson. The window is a two-light one. The subject of the dexter light is the "Resurrection," and that of the sinister light the "Ascension." In the base of the former are the sleeping guards; beyond them is a kneeling angel, who moves from the mouth of the se-pulchre, the stone, on which is carved the inscription, "Humani Generis Redemptor;" and above, the figure of our Lord, with the banner of triumph, rises from the sepulchre. The upper part of the sinister light is occupied

by the figure of our Lord ascending into the open heaven;
below are grouped the Apostles, prominent among whom
are the youthful features of St. John, and the kneeling
figure of St. Peter. Both subjects are set under canopies,
the heads of the lights being filled with pomegranate
foliage and fruit, in rich colour. At the foot of each light
run the respective inscriptions, " The third day he rose
again from the dead," "He ascended into heaven." The
tracery, which is a rose of eight foils, contains the subject
of the " Nativity of Our Lord," the blessed Virgin and
St. Joseph kneeling in adoration of the child ; the foils
are occupied by the heads of seraphim, with flaming
wings. On the sills of the window are two handsome
memorial brasses, on which appears the following inscription :—" This window is dedicated by the congregation
and a few friends to the revered memory of Jane, wife of
William Dent Thompson, first vicar of this parish. Her
life afforded a rare example of sound judgment, earnest
piety, and practical benevolence. To her husband she
proved a 'helpmeet for him,' to the poor a mother, to
the parishioners a loyal friend and wise adviser. Born
December 24th, 1834; died September 27th, 1881." The
window was unveiled on Sunday, July 9th, 1882, when
there were four services in commemoration of the event,
commencing with the holy communion at half-past eight
o'clock in the morning. At the morning and evening
services the pulpit was occupied by the Rev. J. M. Dan-
son, M.A., vicar of St. Andrew's, Aberdeen, and diocesan
inspector of schools, an old friend of the vicar and the
late Mrs. Thompson. At the close of an eloquent
discourse, after morning prayer, he made a touching reference to the special object of the day's services, dwelling
upon the many virtues of the deceased lady, with whom
he had been intimately acquainted. At the afternoon
service the preacher was the Rev. J. H. Rawdon, M.A.,
vicar of Preston, who bore personal testimony to the
worth of the deceased, to whose memory the window was
dedicated. The Rev. A. B. Beaven, M.A., head master
of the Preston grammar school, assisted at the evening

service. The window was designed and executed by
Messrs. Shrigley and Hunt, John O'Gaunt's Gate, Lancaster; and 28, John Street, Bedford Row, London. In
the western gable is a four-light window, by Hardman,
representing "The Good Samaritan." It is the gift of
Richard Newsham, Esq., in memory of the late J. Bairstow, Esq. At the west end there are likewise three
memorial windows, executed by Hardman, of Birmingham. The subjects are respectively "Christ blessing
little children," "The harvest of the world, and the
putting in of the sickle," and the "Agony in Gethsemane."
They are the gift of the widow and family of the late Mr.
John Smith, father of the late Mrs. Thompson, James
Hibbert, Esq. (the architect), and W. B. Roper, Esq.
The chancel is paved with Godwin's tiles, in a marked
arrangement of design, and rich depth of tone. The
pulpit, which is of oak, with polished stone substructure,
and steps, is the gift of Mrs. Newsham. Significance
is given to it by the prominent application of the mono-
gram and symbol of the Saviour, upon an aureole. In
the centre, on each side of the octagon, is an emblem
of the Trinity, and of Eternity. The roof ridge of
the chancel and nave is continuous, but the point of
separation is marked by greater richness and size of the
principals, the carved rafters of which are decorated with
various devices of symbolic character. At the apex is a
conspicuous emblem of the Holy Ghost as a descending
dove. The wall principals at the east end are similarly
decorated. The roof principals over the sacrarium are
decorated with conventional representations of the vine
and the passion flower. The two corbels to the chancel
principals represent angels. The corbels to the sacrarium
and wall principals are decorated with various emblems.
Among the carved terminations to the hood mouldings
of the arcade are symbols of the "Bread of Life," and the
"Harp of Judah." The gallery ceilings are divided into
bays by the supporting timbers, decoratively treated, and
each bay is further ornamented with coloured stencil
bordering. The space below the west gallery is near the

principal entrance, and being partially screened off from the open nave, forms a quasi narthex or vestibule. Here is a very handsome Baptismal Font, the gift of the late Sir T. G. Fermor Hesketh, M.P., in polished red granite and Cornish serpentine, placed upon a platform of encaustic tiles. The communion plate, the gift of Richard Newsham, Esq., designed by Mr. Butterfield, is of very elegant form and workmanship, consisting of flagon, two chalices, and paten, enclosed in a massive oak cabinet, which also contains a pair of richly chased gilt metal alms plates. The designs for the Church were prepared by Mr. James Hibbert, architect, under whose personal superintendence the building was erected.

ST. LUKE'S CHURCH, RIBBLETON LANE.

This Church is one of the most recently erected edifices in the town, in connexion with the established church. It was built in the year 1859, in St. Luke's Square, in consequence of the very large increase of the population of that locality, which had taken place during the previous few years. It is a stone building, in the gothic style of architecture, and consists of nave, aisles, transepts, chancel, and organ chamber. The nave is of considerable height, with an open roof several feet above the clerestory windows. The Church stands east and west, the chancel being at the east end, and the principal entrance at the west end. The tower and spire, about 120 feet in height, are at the south-west end of the Church. There is seating room for between 600 and 700 persons. Mr. Shellard was the architect.

ST. MARK'S CHURCH, MAUDLANDS.

This edifice, which was erected in 1863, is situated on high ground, at the north-west side of the town, near the Maudlands, and in the immediate locality which over-

looks the Marsh. It is a gothic structure and cruciform
in shape. It is built of stone from the Longridge quarries. The principal entrance is at the west end, under an
arcade of three arches. At the north-east end there is a
handsome and lofty tower, surmounted by pinnacles at
each angle. The tower contains a peal of six fine toned
bells, by Mears, of London. The spacious transepts form
an integral part of the architectural character of the
edifice, and the chancel is in the form of an apse. As
regards the internal portion of the Church there is an
absence of the arcading which obtains generally in ecclesiastical structures, dividing the nave from the aisles.
The open timber roof is carried the entire width of the
Church, the principals and timber arches which support
it resting on lofty iron columns nearly the full height of
the Church. The internal walls are faced with red brick.
The organ chamber is on the south side of the chancel.
There are galleries over the transepts, and at the west
end a lofty screen is carried across the entire width of the
Church, supporting a small gallery in the centre. The
open benches, choir stalls, and reading desk, are of pitch
pine, and the pulpit of oak.

EMMANUEL CHURCH.

This church, which is situated in Brook Street,
Adelphi Street, at the north end of the town, was erected
in 1869, and opened in the early part of 1870. It is built
of brick, interspersed with strings and bands of coloured
and moulded bricks, with stone dressings. The style of
architecture is geometrical gothic. The plan is cruciform,
and the ground floor accommodates 632 persons;
in the west gallery 150; and in each transept gallery 92.
There are four entrances to the church, one being under
the tower, which is at the south west corner; also the
double doorways at the west end, and one to each transept.
The west entrance is approached by a porch, projecting
about seven feet, which is surmounted by an ornamental

carved stone cornice, and a neat balcony with trefoil and
quatrefoil perforations. The vestry is on the north side
of the chancel, and the organ chamber on the south side,
having arches opening into the nave and chancel.   The
tower of the church, at the south west corner, which is a
prominent feature in the design, and is 100 feet in height,
being 12 feet square inside, with ample space for six bells.
The top is surrounded with a dwarf brick arcade walling,
springing from a richly-carved stone string, encircling the
tower, filled in with light iron railing.   The whole is
covered with a stone cornice.   At the four corners are
octagonal pinnacles of brick, terminating in massive stone
weatherings and *fleur de lis*.   The chancel window is a
five-light, with two quatrefoils and a large circle above,
containing three trefoils.   The west window is a four-light,
with tracery above.   The roofs throughout are open
timber, of pitch pine. The pulpit is of Caen stone, resting
upon five columns, and is octagonal in form.   The font is
also of Caen stone.   The pulpit, font, and prayer desk,
were presented by Thomas Tomlinson, Esq., who also
gave the site of the edifice and schools adjoining.   The
lectern was presented by the late M. Myres, Esq.   It is
of novel design, in iron and brass.   The open benches
throughout are of pitch pine.   The floor within the
communion rails is laid with Minton's encaustic tiles.
The architects were Messrs. Myres, Veevers, and Myres;
and Mr. J. Bamber, the contractor.

THE BAIRSTOW MEMORIAL CHURCH, BROADGATE.

In the year 1870, shortly before the consecration and
opening of Emmanuel Church, a plain and small edifice
was erected at the bottom of Fishergate Hill, in Bird
Street.   It is designated the Bairstow Memorial Church,
and was built conjointly by Mr. R. Newsham, Mr. J. F.
Higgins, and Mr. W. B. Roper, (to each of whom Mr.
Bairstow, in his will, bequeathed large legacies,) in
memory of the late J. Bairstow, Esq., an old and highly

respected townsman, and formerly one of the partners in the well known firm of Horrockses, Miller, & Co. The church is built of brick, with an entrance porch at the west end, surmounted by a bell turret. Internally the church presents no appearance of ecclesiastical structural arrangement, being, on the other hand, severely plain and unpretending. There are no ordinary seats or benches, moveable chairs being arranged on the floor area of the edifice for the seating of about 240 persons which the church will accommodate. There is an organ at the south east corner; and a reading desk on the opposite side, standing upon a small platform, suffices for the pulpit. At the west end of the church, under the doorway, there is a marble tablet to the memory of Mr. Bairstow. The cost of the structure, which serves as a chapel of ease to Christ Church, was £1,000.

ST. MATTHEW'S CHURCH, NEW HALL LANE.

This church, situated in what is known as New Preston, at the south east end of the town, is at present in course of construction. It is in the geometric style of gothic architecture, and when completed will consist of a nave 25 feet wide, and 96 feet long; east and west aisles, 16 feet wide each; east and west transepts, 20 feet wide, and 18 feet deep; chancel 25 feet wide, and 42 feet long; and organ chamber, 16 feet square. The design includes a tower over the organ chamber, the dimensions of which will be 24 feet square, and 100 feet in height. The internal arcade consists of six bays. The height of the nave, from the ground floor to the ridge is 58 feet. The roofs are open timber, and of massive construction. The church will seat 1,000 persons when finished, the estimated cost being £10,000. A portion only of the church is at present being built, and does not include the chancel, organ gallery, tower, vestry, and transepts. The last bay of the nave, which is wider than the rest, will be fitted as a temporary chancel. The portion of the church now being erected will provide nearly 700 sittings, at a cost of about £6,000. Mr. James Hibbert is the architect.

CHRIST CHURCH, FULWOOD.

The rapid increase in the population of Fulwood, which although in the parish of Lancaster, from which it is some twenty miles distant, is in reality an immediate suburb, if not actually a part of, Preston, some years ago rendered necessary the erection of a new church in that locality, and in the year 1865, Christ Church was built and opened. It is built of stone from the Roddlesworth quarries, with Longridge stone for dressings. The edifice comprises a main building 70 feet long, and 36 feet wide, and consists of a nave, side aisles, chancel, choir, vestry, and organ chamber. The chancel and choir are 23 feet by 18 feet, the full length of the building thus being 93 feet. The height of the main building, from the ground to the roof, is 46 feet. The spire, which stands on the north side of the church, is 100 feet in height: the principal entrance to the church is under it; there being a porch entrance on the opposite or south side. The church accommodates a congregation of 450 persons, 140 of the seats, all of which are open benches, being free. The edifice is in the early decorated style of gothic architecture, Mr. T. H. Myres being the architect.

The Roman Catholic churches were erected in the following order:—

ST. MARY'S CHURCH, FRIARGATE.

The first building used by the Roman Catholics in Preston, for public worship, after the Reformation, is said to have been erected in Chapel Yard, Friargate, in the year 1605. In the year 1761, St. Mary's Chapel was erected on part of the site formerly occupied by the Convent of Grey Friars, on Friargate Brow.   When St. Wilfrid's Church in Chapel Street, was erected thirty-two years afterwards, namely, in the year 1793, St. Mary's was closed, and for many years it was used as a warehouse for the storage of cotton.   The Roman Catholic population, however, having increased, and requiring more accommodation than St. Wilfrid's afforded, St. Mary's was, in 1815, again fitted, and re-opened for the services of the church.   In the year 1856, it was entirely re-built and very much enlarged.

ST. WILFRID'S CHURCH, CHAPEL STREET.

[This edifice is fully described in page 102.]

ST. IGNATIUS CHURCH, ST. IGNATIUS SQUARE.

In May, 1833, the foundation of this church, which is situated some distance to the east of Park and North Roads, was laid with considerable ceremony.   The building, which is of stone, with a handsome tower and spire 120 feet in height, is in the perpendicular style of architecture, and cruciform in shape.   Its dimensions are 120 feet in length, the nave being 50 feet wide.   Internally the church is elaborately decorated, a prominent feature being the altar table, which is artistically carved, figures of the apostles being introduced.   There are several stained glass windows in the church, which have been provided at a large outlay, and are the gifts of the late J. F. Anderton, Esq., of Haighton House, and other friends. Mr. Anderton was also the donor of the altar table, with the carving above named.   Attached to the church is a residence for the clergy, and the entire cost of the church and clergy house, was upwards of £8,000, exclusive of the stained glass windows and altar table.   Mr. J. J. Scholes, of London, was the architect.   Some years since an additional sacristy was added to the building.

ST. AUGUSTINE'S CHURCH, ST. AUGUSTINE'S PLACE.

The erection of St. Augustine's Church was commenced in November, 1838. The land for this church was given by the Right Rev. Dr. Briggs, the then Roman Catholic Bishop of the district. The building is cruciform in character, a special feature at the entrance being a Roman Ionic portico. The interior decorations are very artistic, the high altar being adorned with an oil painting of large size, painted by Mr. Taylor Bulwer, after the original by Paolo Veronesse. Mr. Tuach was the architect.

ST. WALBURGE'S CHURCH, MAUDLANDS.

St. Walburge's is the largest and finest church in Preston of which the Roman Catholics can boast, and as a specimen of gothic architecture is, perhaps, unequalled by any other ecclesiastical building in the town. A unique feature of the edifice is its massiveness and great height, with a noble tower and spire, carried to an unusually lofty altitude. The structure is likewise identified with interesting local historical associations, having been erected upon the site on which, at a period considerably antecedent to the Reformation, stood the hospital dedicated to St. Mary Magdalene. The foundation stone of the structure was laid in the year 1850, but it was not until August, 1854, that the edifice was opened for service. The materials used in the building of the church consist of stone of various kinds, the body of the church being of grey flag, with white grit dressings; whilst the tower and spire are of lime stone. The church is 165 feet long, and 55 feet wide. The principal elevation, which is on the west side, is divided into three portions by two buttresses, on each side of the main entrance, rising to a height of 69 feet, and surmounted by conical turrets. There are also similar buttresses at each angle of the elevation, with entrances on the north and south sides of the two central buttresses respectively. Immediately above the central entrance is an arcade consisting of five lancet-headed lights. Rising above these the elevation is surmounted by a lofty gable, the entire height of the elevation, to the apex of a richly sculptured cross, being 91 feet. Within the gable, immediately above the arcade, is a large decorated circular window, 22 feet in diameter, filled in with geometric tracery. The north and south elevations have each a range of seven buttresses, uniform with those at the west frontage, with the exception of the terminating turrets. The roof is 83 feet from the parapet, and is surmounted by ornamental ridge tiles. The tower and spire are at the east end, on the south side of the church. The spacious dimensions of this portion of the splendid structure is indicated by the base of the tower, which is 40 feet square. The tower itself is 115 feet in height, and capable of containing a peal of 12 bells. The lofty and gracefully tapering spire above the tower is 85 feet in height to the apex of a surmounting cross, the entire height, from the ground line of the tower and spire, being 301 feet. With the exception of that at Salisbury Cathedral, and one in Lincolnshire, this tower and spire are believed to be the loftiest in the country. They may not inappropriately be designated as architectural gems. They stand out like a prominent beacon visible at various points in and around the town, amidst the tall cotton mill chimneys by which they are surrounded, and their beautiful architectural symmetry and grandeur command universal admiration. They can be seen at several miles distance from the town, and are distinctly observable from Southport and other places in that locality, as well as from districts on the north and east sides of the town.

The interior of the structure is no less ornamental and magnificent than its architectural exterior. In the absence of arcading the vast area of the splendid interior is at once exposed to view as the spectator enters the edifice, the effect being grand and imposing. The whole of the windows are of stained glass, those at the east end and on the north and south sides of the chancel and altars, which are carried entirely across the church, being

very lofty, and containing, amongst other artistic representations, full length figures of numerous saints of the
church. The central east window, above the high altar,
is about 35 feet in height, the upper portion containing a
splendidly executed representation of the Crucifixion,
surrounded by numerous groups of scriptural characters.
Each of the two-light windows to the north and south of
the central east window just described, are also filled in
with full length figures, six in each window. In addition
to these windows there are likewise two lofty windows
within the chancel, on the north and south sides, containing, amongst others, full length figures of St.
Catharine, St. Cecilia, St. Philomene, St. Walburgh, St.
Monica, St. Carola, St. Thomas, St. Elizabeth, St. James,
and St. Henricus. The chancel and altars are approached
from the body of the church by a flight of ten steps, and
the floor is laid with encaustic tiles of varied colours. On
the north and south sides of the central or high altar
there are full length statuary figures of our Lady and St.
Ignatius, standing on polished granite columns, with
stone bases, the figures being surmounted by ornamental
canopies. In front of the north and south altars there
are similar figures of St. Joseph, St. David, St. Abraham,
St. Patrick, and St. Margaret. Within panels facing the
marble altar on the south side is a carved group of figures
representing Moses, and others. The pulpit, which is of
Caen stone, projects out of the wall on the north side of
the church, and is of oriel construction, and angular in
shape, faced on the east and west fronts by a range of
three gothic arches, and on the south front by one gothic
arch. Above the pulpit is a spacious overhanging canopy.
The pulpit is approached by a flight of steps along a
recess in the wall, enclosed by a gothic arched balustrade
and hand rail. On the north and south sides are moulded
and coloured figure groups representative of the several
stations of the Cross, surmounted by gothic arches. The
organ gallery is at the west end of the church, supported
on six iron columns, from which spring gothic arches.
Resting on each of the 16 flying buttresses or brackets on

the north and south sides of the church, from which spring the principals of the open timber roof, are full length statuary figures of the Saints and Fathers of the church. Mr. Hansom, of London, was the architect of the building.

Occupying a large space of ground on the north side of the church, upwards of an acre in extent, is the clergy house and ornamentally laid out grounds, together with two blocks of large school buildings.

THE CHURCH OF THE ENGLISH MARTYRS,

GARSTANG ROAD.

The above-named Church is another of those elaborate and ornate structures which the Roman Catholic portion of the community·have within the last few years raised up in the town. Apart from its architectural and decorative attractiveness, it possesses an exceptional historical interest. The site upon which the Church stands is a portion of what was formerly known as the "Gallows Hill," where a number of the partisans of the House of Stuart were executed in January, 1716, for endeavouring to place the Chevalier de St. George on the English throne. The rebel army was beaten at Preston by the King's troops, which resulted in several members of well known Preston families being put to death on the site on which the Church now stands. In preceding pages, under the head of "Historical Records," the names of those who were executed are given.

The designs for the Church were furnished by the well known architect, Mr. Edward Pugin, for the Rev. James Taylor, first priest of the mission, and the foundation stone was laid on Whit-Monday, 1866, by the Right Rev. Dr. Goss, Roman Catholic Bishop of the diocese. The Church is gothic in character, and is built of Yorkshire stone. Externally the west end is the grandest architectural feature of the edifice. A bold and massive gable rises majestically between two gracefully proportioned and elaborately-carved turrets, the height of the gable being 80 feet from the ground line. From the apex of the gable springs a lofty central turret, the lower portion of which has niches, containing life-size figures of the four evangelists. The extreme height of the central turret is 150 feet. A lofty west window, immediately above the entrance, divided in six lights, terminates in tracery. The spacious gothic entrance, upwards of eight feet in width, is surmounted by an elaborately-carved crocketted gablet, and flanked on each side with full length sculptured figures of St. Thomas of Canterbury, and St. Alban. The ridge of the nave is un-broken from the west turret to the metal cross on the apex of the apse at the east end, where the lines are carried down to the angles of the octagon. The Church over all measures 110 feet in length, and is 60 feet wide. It consists of the nave, 30 feet in width, which opens into two lateral aisles of 13 feet in width each, the aisles being divided from the nave by six gothic arches on either side, springing from stone columns of a light and graceful character. Transverse arches act as principals across the aisles. The arcading columns dividing the nave from the aisles being the reverse of massive, the whole ground area of the Church is open, and the high altar can be seen from every part of the aisles. The altar and taber-nacle present a fine specimen of ornamental work, gothic in design. It is richly carved, having a profuse intro-duction of marbles, and is surmounted by a canopy of elaborate construction. Standing within niches around the chancel apse on each side of the altar are full length figures of the apostles in Caen stone, whilst above these, in five compartments, are large frescoes, illustrative of scriptural subjects. The dwarf screen in front of the high altar, separating the nave from the chancel, is entirely composed of marbles of varied colours, the screen also being continued on each side of the chancel, ex-tending the full width of the Church, on the north and south sides, and enclosing the two side altars facing the aisles. The base of the screen is composed of blocks of

Sicilian marble, upon which rest a range of gothic arches, having alabaster shafts, the screen being surmounted by a massive white marble coping. In addition to the high altar the two side altars are likewise very ornamental and artistic. One of them, which is dedicated to St. Joseph, was the gift of Joseph Pyke, Esq. The other is dedicated to the Blessed Virgin, the gift of the late Mr. Greenhalgh. The pulpit is also a specially artistic feature in the internal decorations of the edifice. It is octagonal in form, and is composed entirely of marbles and alabaster. It rests on a series of six red marble columns, the octagonal front being faced with deeply recessed gothic arches, springing from brown marble shafts, between which are ornamental piers crowned with crocketted finials or turrets, the whole surmounted by a white marble coping or shelf. The Church was opened with much ceremony on the 12th of December, 1867, the consecrating bishop being the Right Rev. Dr. Goss, who laid the foundation stone in May of the previous year. Attached to the Church, on the north side, and communicating with it by a corridor, is the clergy's house, a spacious and substantial brick building. On the south side are the schools, with accommodation for upwards of 1,600 children.

ST. JOSEPH'S CHURCH, RIBBLETON.

This edifice, which was erected and opened in 1874, from the designs of Mr. O'Byrne, architect, of Liverpool, is a spacious structure in the gothic style of architecture, externally faced with brick and stone dressings. Its elaborate and costly internal arrangements and decorations more especially entitle it to notice amongst the other distinctive ecclesiastical structures in the town. It is 115 feet in length, exclusive of the entrance porch at the west end, 56 feet in width, and 60 feet in height to the apex of the ceiling. It is arcaded in four lofty bays, gothic arches, which are carried up to the base of the waggon-headed nave ceiling, springing from polished Aberdeen granite columns. The edifice is lighted on the north and south sides by lofty triple lancet windows, in addition to the massive windows at the east and west ends. Although not yet completed the several altar fittings and decorations strikingly harmonise with the gorgeous ceremonial of the Roman Catholic Church. The reredos at the high altar within the chancel, extends the entire width of the chancel. It contains eight niches, in which are placed statues six feet in height. These statues consist of full length figures of St. Alphonsus, St. Clara, St. Teresa, St. John, St. Cuthbert, the Venerable Bede, St. Joseph, and Our Lady. The altar of St. Joseph, on the south side of the high altar, is a fine specimen of carving and sculpture. It is representative of the death of St. Joseph, in Caen stone, the tabernacle being in alabaster. It is the work of Mr. Sharratt, of Preston, and cost £200, being the gift of a local farm labourer in the neighbourhood of Ribbleton. The north chapel or altar, which is also in Caen stone, and dedicated to Our Lady, is the gift of Mr. Carr. Another chapel is at present in course of construction immediately adjoining the present edifice, which is intended to be dedicated to Our Lady of Perpetual Succour. It is the gift of Mr. Ralph Pearson, and is being built for the reception of a painting which has just arrived from Rome. The painting is a copy of the original picture which is held in veneration by the church of the Redemptionists at Rome. The picture is the gift of Mr. Geldart. There are two stained glass windows in St. Joseph's Chapel and one in that of Our Lady, the gift of Mr. Henry Holden, of Ribbleton Lane. The stained glass window at the east end, over the high altar, is by Meyer & Co., of Munich. There is a large and powerful organ at the west end of the church, which was built by Mr. Henry Ainscough, of Preston, and has been pronounced by several musical professors to be one of the finest toned instruments in the town. It has three manuals and 34 stops. The Presbytery is connected with the church by a covered corridor, with ornamentally laid out grounds in front; and attached to the church are the schools, having accommodation for upwards of 1,000 children.

THE ENVIRONS AND THEIR ATTRACTIONS.

WITHIN a comparatively short distance of the town there are several outlying and suburban districts, not more than half an hour or an hour's ride from Preston, which are well worth a visit. Amongst these, on the west side, are the Lancashire watering places, all of which are situated much nearer to Preston than to any other town in the county, with the exception of the small towns of Kirkham and Poulton. A railway journey of little more than twelve miles in length, brings the visitor, in from twenty minutes or half an hour, to

LYTHAM,

one of the most charming and enjoyable sea side resorts in the north of England. Being so easy of access, Lytham, in addition to its character as a watering place, is largely patronised as a residential locality, by professional gentlemen, merchants, and tradesmen, who carry on their respective avocations in Preston, many of the villas and other houses so owned and occupied, being of a highly

palatial character, and standing in their own grounds.
Lytham is of ancient origin, and may be traced back to
the Norman Conquest, when it was designated *Lidum.*
In the reign of King John, however, its name appears to
have been changed to *Lethum,* and in the early ages was
the seat of a monastery, for about the close of the twelfth
century it is recorded that Richard Fitz Roger gave his
lands in *Lethum,* together with the church, to the monks
in Durham, and a monastery was established at *Lethum,*
to the honour of St. Mary and St. Cuthbert, and the
latter remains the name of the Parish Church of Lytham
to the present day.   The monastery was erected on the
site of what is now Lytham Hall, as is shown by some of
the monastic walls which are still preserved.   The Priors
of Durham and subsequently the Priors of *Lethum,*
exercised all rights as the Lords of the manor, until about
the middle of the sixteenth century, when in 1554, Queen
Mary granted the domain and manor of Lytham to Sir
Thomas Holcroft, who, in 1606, transferred his rights and
lands in Lytham to Sir Cuthbert Clifton, in exchange for
other estates on the opposite side of the river Ribble, and
since that period the Cliftons have been Lords of the
manor of Lytham.   In the year 1770, St. Cuthbert's
Church was re-built, and the edifice as so re-erected stood
until the year 1834, when it was again re-built, the late
Thomas Clifton, Esq., then head of the House of Clifton,
laying the foundation stone.   The Cliftons from the time
they became possessed of the Lytham domain, and for
several generations afterwards, were amongst the leading
Lancashire families belonging to the Roman Catholic
Church, but notwithstanding their creed St. Cuthbert's
Parish Church has from the earliest times been their
place of sepulture, as the several mural monuments in the
church in memory of members of the family reveal.   The
late Mr. Thomas Clifton, above referred to, was the first
member of the family who seceded from Rome, and
embraced the Church of England.   Amongst the
memorials in the church is a tablet and cross in memory
of the Rev. Richard Barton Robinson, (son of the late·

Dr. Robinson, of Preston,) who was incumbent of Lytham
for 36 years, and who died in August, 1872. All the
windows in the church are filled in with stained glass,
and several of them have from time to time been erected
in memory of Preston families. Amongst others the
windows contain memorials of the late Mr. Henry Miller,
and also of members of the Stevenson family, formerly
resident in Preston, but who subsequently settled in
Lytham. A ramble amongst the tombs in the church
yard will well repay the time so occupied. There are
numerous beautifully executed memorials of visitors and
others who have been interred there. One of the most
recent interments at Lytham was that of the late Sir
John Holker, who resigned his seat as member of
Parliament for Preston in January, 1882, on being appointed a Lord Justice of Appeal by Mr. Gladstone, the
Prime Minister. He died on the 24th of May following,
and the funeral took place on Tuesday, the 30th of May,
when the mayor and corporation of Preston, representatives from several other public bodies in the town, and a
large number of the inhabitants were present. In addition
officers and members of several associations in Manchester,
Bury, and other Lancashire towns, were in attendance.
The following eloquent and touching eulogium which was
passed on the late eminent lawyer, on Friday, May 26th,
by Lord Chief Justice Coleridge, in the Court of Appeal,
must have a special local interest. His Lordship said :—

· Mr. Attorney General, Mr. Solicitor General, and gentlemen of the
  Bar, I did not know until late last night, on the information of my
  learned brother, Lord Justice Brett, that there was any desire that
  I should be here this morning and say anything of the great loss
  we have all sustained, and I really feel that, being here present with
  you to-day, I am rather here for the purpose of inviting you to
  express your respect for the character of him whom we have lost,
  your estimate of his great powers, and your sorrow for his loss,
  than to express my own, not that I do not feel sorrow, deep
  and true, but especially Mr. Solicitor General, and some I see here,
  knew him much better than I did. Your opportunities of judging
  of his character and powers were far larger than any chances of the
  profession ever brought to my share. Yet, as I am here, perhaps
  this very circumstance is not without its value, because it enables ·

me to give my independent and peculiar testimony to the quickness
and greatness of his professional career, for I myself left the Bar
late in 1873, and at that time Sir John Holker had hardly opened
his lips in the House of Commons, and he was but little known in
the Courts of London. I know now that he was very eminent in
his own circuit, and now, after scarcely more than the lapse of eight
years, we meet together to lament the loss of a man who in the
meanwhile had filled with universal applause the offices of Solicitor
General and Attorney General, and who at the time of his death
stood, by universal consent, in the very first rank of his profession,
both as an advocate and a lawyer. Looking back over my own
recollection I cannot call to mind another instance of professional
success at once so rapid and so enduring. You and I know the
fame he won was fairly won, and that he deserved to win it, because
you and I know that the profession to which we all belong judges
generously and almost always judges justly, and if it agrees, as it
does in the case of Sir John Holker, unanimously to admire and
respect him, it is because the man is thoroughly worthy of its
admiration and respect. But it is not only, perhaps it is not chiefly,
the great advocate and sound lawyer whose loss we lament to-day.
It is the friend, the companion, the genial man whose memory will
live as long as any one of us lives, and who has left behind him a
void which cannot adequately be filled. I myself know some—
very likely there are those whom I address know many more—acts
of almost princely kindness done by him, simply, independently,
without any ostentation, without effort and display, and so far as he
was concerned, apparently as a matter of course. I do believe
there never beat a kindlier heart in any man's breast. I do believe
a truer, manlier nature than Sir John Holker's never existed in the
world. He has gone from us, and we who are left behind must
recollect what he was—that no success ever spoilt him—that no
elevation ever puffed him up. He remained the same quiet,
simple, unpretending man—unassuming without a single atom of
vanity, selfishness, or self-assertion. I am sure I shall be forgiven,
and may, among friends, use the same endearing title by which he
was known at the Bar, when I say he was the same "dear Jack
Holker" from beginning to end (subdued applause). But not
only in this respect, but as a Judge we have to consider him. The
short time he was on the bench was spent in illness and in sickness,
and the decay, not of mental, but of physical powers, rendered the
effort to use his mental powers greater than he could bear, and
what he would have become ultimately as a Judge it is impossible
for any of us to say. In that respect he must remain one of the
heroes of an unfulfilled destiny, of which there are so many, and
his fate must lead a man to regret it with sadness, and to reflect on
what his career might have been had he lived. Mr. Gladstone,
who was no bad judge of character, had said he considered Sir John
Holker one of the keenest, closest, legal reasoners he had ever
listened to, and it was to Sir John Holker's peculiar qualification

that the just recognition of his great professional eminence came from one who, it was a satisfaction to Sir John Holker to know, had no political bias to disturb his recognition. Certainly, if learning, if a vigorous understanding, strong grasp of facts and principles, transparent honesty, sweet temper, and unvarying courtesy towards all with whom he was brought in contact—if these things were the great qualities of a Judge, those qualities Sir John Holker had in the largest measure. We may regret that the exercise of these great powers has been cut short by one with whom it is useless to reason, and whom we cannot resist ; but he, at least, has left behind him an unstained reputation, a memory which will live and will be cherished by us as long as life is left to us, and it is at least left to us to try as best we may to imitate his virtues."

In consequence of the increased number of residents and visitors, within the last few years, the church is about to be enlarged by the erection of an additional aisle on the north side.

The first Lytham Hall was erected in 1606, by Sir Cuthbert Clifton, when he came into possession of the lordship of the manor on exchanging lands with Sir Thomas Holcroft. The erection of the present hall was commenced in the year 1757, by Thomas Clifton, Esq., and it occupied seven years in construction, not having been completed until the year 1764.

About the year 1825, the marine frontage was levelled, and the present beautiful velvet greensward, of which few other watering places can boast, was formed. It is now about two miles long, with a marine esplanade on the margin of the shore, running its entire length. Although in the height of the season the beach and esplanade are alive with animation, and the numerous marine residences are largely occupied by visitors, Lytham has never been distinguished for attracting the labouring population, its visitors and settlers being for the most part composed of the opulent and well to do classes. The " unwashed " and the masses ' from the Lancashire and Yorkshire inland towns, have not been encouraged as visitors, so that the incursions of this class of the community have never been so frequent at Lytham as at its Blackpool neighbour. There was no material increase in the resident population of Lytham until about the year 1840, for up to that period there was little inducement held out either to the private or speculative builder in consequence of the leases being limited to 40 years.   In the year above named, however, these leases were extended to 60 years, which had the effect of giving a considerable impetus to building ; and within the last few years the Lord of the manor and his agents have seen the wisdom of developing this pleasant and salubrious watering place by offering to lessees for building purposes, terms of 99 and 999 years.   This step was accompanied by the laying out of several wide and handsome new streets and roads, in which numerous residences of an ornamental character have, from time to time been erected, many of these thoroughfares partaking of the boulevard type, by the plantation of trees along the footpaths.   The area and resident population of Lytham has thus very materially expanded, more especially within the last two decades, which may to a large extent be attributed to the opening of the coast line of railway between Preston, Lytham, and Blackpool, which took place in the year 1863.   In 1861, the population was 3189, whereas the census of 1881 showed that it had increased to upwards of 8,000.

Amongst the public buildings and institutions are the Market Hall, erected in 1848.   The Baths and Assembly Rooms, at the eastern end of the town, facing the beach, were erected in 1863.   The buildings, in addition to the baths and assembly room, include a news and reading room, together with a capacious saloon, which will accommodate 350 persons, and which is utilised for concerts, balls, and other entertainments.   In 1871, a Cottage Hospital was erected at the extreme east end of the town, at the expense of J. Talbot Clifton, Esq., the Lord of the manor.   It is in the gothic style of architecture, and stands within its own grounds, three acres in extent.   In April, 1865, a marine pier and promenade, 914 feet in length, was opened with much ceremony by Lady Eleanor Cecilia Clifton.   Lytham was *en fete* during the day, and amongst those present were

the Mayor and Corporation of Preston; the directors of
the Ribble Navigation Company; and the directors of
the Blackpool and Southport Pier Companies; these
several bodies walking in procession along the Pier when
Lady Clifton declared it open. In 1879, the Lytham
Institute, a large and handsome building erected in Clifton
Street, was opened for the use of the inhabitants. It
contains large and convenient news and reading rooms,
lecture room, and billiard and smoking rooms; and
refreshments on the temperance principle are also provided.
Amongst other attractions which Lytham possesses are
the Lowther Gardens, facing the west end of the beach,
which were laid out a few years ago, for recreation
purposes. It was not until the year 1850, that public gas
lamps were introduced in the several streets and thoroughfares. This followed upon the formation of the Local
Board of Health, which was constituted in 1847.

The places of worship, in addition to St. Cuthbert's
Parish Church, already referred to, include St. John's
Church, opposite the East Beach, which was erected in
1849. This edifice contains several memorial stained
glass windows, one of which is in memory of the late Mr.
Thomas Miller, of Preston. The organ was presented by
Mr. W. Bradshaw Swainson, of Cooper Hill, near Preston,
" as a tribute of affection in memory of his mother,
Catharine Swainson, who died at Lytham, on the 1st of
February, 1848." At the extreme east end of Clifton
Street, on the south side, stands St. Peter's Roman
Catholic Church, which was first erected in 1839. Up to
this date the Roman Catholics had no separate and
distinct place of worship of their own in Lytham. Until
the edifice in Clifton Street was opened, the small chapel
at Lytham Hall, which had superseded the domestic
oratory of the Cliftons, in the days when they belonged
to the Roman Catholic Church, had been placed at the
disposal of those professing the Roman Catholic Church
in Lytham, and it was here they worshipped. The edifice
in Clifton Street was re-built and enlarged, and a priest's
residence attached, a few years ago. In 1863, a new

Congregational Church was opened in. Banister Street;
and in 1867, a large new Wesleyan Chapel was erected at
the corner of Park and Westby Streets. This was in lieu
of a smaller chapel, which had for some years previous
been in use.*

On the opposite or south side of the estuary of the
Ribble, which can be reached by a sail of about five
miles from Lytham, is

SOUTHPORT

which, originally a small watering place consisting of
little more than a single street of houses (Lord Street),
running east and west, has, within the last two decades,
enormously expanded its dimensions, having now grown
into a large municipal borough, with a population of
npwards of 30,000 inhabitants. Notwithstanding, however, that it may now be regarded as one of the great
Lancashire centres of business, with its miles of streets,
and numerous palatial public buildings, it still retains its
original character as a sea-side resort, and within the
last few years the municipal authorities have done much
to make it attractive to visitors, whilst numerous public
companies, by the erection of buildings of a varied
character for instruction, entertainment, and recreation,
have adorned the town with ornamental architectural
structures, of which few watering places can boast.
Amongst other edifices of this class are the spacious
Winter Garden Buildings, and Theatre, with their beautifully laid-out grounds, which are daily frequented by
large numbers of the resident population as well as
visitors. The Cambridge Hall, which was formally
opened about three years ago, by the Duke of Cambridge,
is a noble and handsome architectural structure.

---

* It is believed that what is now known as the Horse Bank—dreaded by
mariners—between Lytham and Southport, was formerly a hamlet called Waddam
Thorp, once situated on the coast off Lytham, and fenced from the sea as a broad area
of pasture land. The village is stated to have been swallowed up by the fury of the sea.

Southport, likewise, can justly pride itself upon the possession of one of the largest and best arranged wholesale and retail markets in the north of England. These markets were publicly opened by the Earl of Derby, on the 7th of September, 1881, the day being kept as a complete holiday. The markets, which are situated in East Bank Street, are erected in the Italian style of architecture. They are bounded by streets on three sides, from which there are thirteen entrances, the centre entrance to East Bank Street having pilasters and columns, supporting figures of Flora and Ceres. Surrounding the East Bank Street frontage of the structure is a large octagonal dome, carved with zinc, of fish scale pattern. The central entrance in King Street is surmounted by a bell turret, supported by Tuscan columns and pilasters. The market is spanned by five bays of principals supported on iron columns and lattice girders. The portion of the market set apart for the poulterers, butchers, provision dealers, and green grocers, occupies an area of about 2,660 square yards, and to these several trades 70 stalls or shops are allotted. The fish market occupies an area of 719 square yards, and contains 27 stalls, fitted with earthenware sinks, with water supply over the same, and grid underneath, together with marble fish slabs. The wholesale portion of the market, which is at the rear of the fish market, contains an area of 824 square yards. The whole of the three elevations are faced with stone, from the Longridge quarries, near Preston. The entire cost of the markets amounted to £40,000, of which £25,000 was absorbed in the buildings themselves, and £15,000 in the purchase of the land. The markets were erected from the designs of Messrs. Mellor and Sutton, architects, of Southport, and the builders were Messrs. Bridge and Son, of Southport and Burscough.

On the same day on which the Earl of Derby opened the markets, the Earl of Lathom inaugurated the new Marine Promenade, which is an extension northwards of the promenade as it existed in 1879. The ground upon which the new Promenade is formed cost £8,000, and the contract for its reclamation, including the formation and paving of road and footways, amounted to £32,000. The contractors were Messrs. Gripper and Baylis, of London, who occupied about two years in the work.   In the construction of the works 48 acres were reclaimed from the sea, and built up as a continuation of the promenade, which now extends close up to Hesketh Park, the entire promenade being about a mile and a half in length, of which the extension is three quarters of a mile.

Notwithstanding the great artistic taste which has been displaced in laying out and beautifying the several streets and thoroughfares, which form so well deserved an attraction to visitors, it must be confessed that there is, after all, one great draw back to Southport as a seaside resort.   During the last few years the water has receded very considerably from the Southport shore, thus rendering bathing difficult, if not impossible, except by going a long distance along the shore seaward, more especially during the neap tides, when the bathing cars, with their immersion freight, are under the necessity of traversing something near a mile before arriving at the " briny."

The fine promenade pier, which some few years ago, was considerably extended, and is now upwards of a mile in length, is a favourite place of resort, and much frequented.   A tramway runs its entire length, thus affording to visitors vehicular as well as pedestrian exercise and recreation.

Birkdale, at the south end of the borough, which some few years ago, was little more than a small suburb, . may now be said to have become a part of Southport, the two places being joined together by continuous streets and buildings.   Birkdale Park, which is very artistically laid out, is several acres in extent.

Church and Chapel building have been carried out very largely for several years past, in order to meet the requirements of the constantly increasing population, and the influx of visitors, and there are at present about twenty of these edifices in the town.   There are also numerous hotels, many of them large and handsome palatial structures. The Palace Hydropathic and Spa Hotel, at Birkdale, a new wing to which was opened simultaneously with the opening of the Markets and the new Promenade, last year, is an extensive establishment of notable architectural design and proportions. In addition to the usual coffee rooms, dining rooms, private rooms, and other apartments, in high-class hotels, this establishment contains a spacious recreation room, which is stated to be one of the largest rooms of the kind in the kingdom, being 80 feet long, 40 feet wide, and 25 feet high. Amongst other purposes to which this apartment is applied, are concerts, amateur theatricals, and other entertainments and amusements. The hotel is also supplied with ladies' and gentlemen's baths of various kinds, many of them in marble. At the end of one of the corridors is the Turkish bath, a lofty room terminating at one end with an apse, into which stained glass lights are introduced. There are likewise salt water, medicated, electro-magnetic, shampooing, and douche baths, the accommodation provided also including an inhaling room.

Southport owes much of its success and prosperity to the support which it receives from the two great Lancashire cities, Liverpool and Manchester. Preston, however, is its nearest neighbour, from which it is now only 15 miles distant by the new coast line of railway, *via* Longton and Hesketh Bank, which is not more than half an hour's ride.

Returning to Lytham we proceed by the coast railway to

ST. ANNE'S ON THE SEA,

another new watering place on the Lancashire coast, nearly midway between Lytham and Blackpool, and about three miles north-west of the former, on the Irish sea. St. Anne's on the Sea was founded about seven

years ago, its promoters being a body of capitalists from
the neighbourhood of Manchester, who obtained a lease
of a large area of waste lands known as the Star Hills,
consisting of about 3,000 acres. The land was leased to
the company for a term of 1,100 years, by John Talbot
Clifton, Esq., the Lord of the Manor, and on the 31st of
March, 1875, the ceremony of laying the first stone of
the future watering-place was performed by Master John
Talbot Clifton, grandson of the Lord of the Manor, and
eldest son of the late T. H. Clifton, Esq., who was for
some years M.P. for North Lancashire. The laying of this
memorial stone was the commencement of a large hotel,
some short time afterwards completed and occupied, and
now surrounded by numerous villa and other residences,
which have since been erected. Immediately on the lessees
obtaining possession of the land, large numbers of labourers
were set to work to clear away the sand hills of a considerable area and level it, preparatory to its being laid out for
building upon. This task was entrusted to Messrs. Maxwell
and Tute, architects, of Bury, who formed several broad
streets, having gentle curves, and intersecting each other,
and the place is now in course of active development. There
are some special stipulations as to building, a condition
being that the houses fronting the beach and the river,
and also those in certain other streets, are either to be
detached or in pairs, and in no case will any block be
allowed to consist of more than six houses, with spacious
gardens in front of each. Already upwards of 200 houses
have been erected, many of them of the villa class, and
building is now actively going forward. An esplanade
3000 feet in length, and 180 feet in width, has been
formed; asphalted, immediately on the edge of the shore,
upwards of 20 feet in width, and extending its entire
length. A handsome pier, extending about 900 feet seaward, has also just been completed, and is now open to
the public, and beyond this pier, in a north westerly
direction towards Blackpool, the asphalted promenade
has been extended along the estate, upwards of half a
mile in length. The new watering place has likewise

been selected as a life boat station, and a spacious life boat house and buildings in connexion with it have been erected. Water and Gas Works have been erected, and the sanitary condition and government of St. Anne's is now in the hands of a Local Board, which was formed about three years since. From its favourable situation, commanding a fine view of the sea, and so easy of access by railway from the great Lancashire and Yorkshire towns, it is predicted that St. Anne's on the Sea will at no distant day be one of the most popular watering places on the north west coast of England.

Continuing the journey by the coast line of railway, a short ride of between four and five miles, brings the visitor to

BLACKPOOL,

which, like Southport, has made prodigious strides, more especially within the last decade. There is little in the early history of Blackpool possessing any special features of interest. Its chief, and indeed solitary claim to historical distinction, is that at Foxhalls, or, as it has been designated, " Foxholes," near Blackpool, in the reign of Charles the Second, Edward the son of Sir Thomas Tyldesley, who was killed at the battle of Wigan Lane, in 1651, built a small residence as a summer retreat for his family, having been led to expect a grant of the lands of Layton Hawes, from King Charles, after the Restoration, in return for his own and his father's adherence to the royal cause. But the expected grant was never made by the king to the Tyldesley family. At the time he built this summer retreat Edward Tyldesley surrounded the hall with a high and strong wall as a protection considered necessary in those days of internal disturbance and anarchy ; and it is worthy of record that a considerable portion of this wall remains standing to the present day, in an almost perfect state of preservation, in spite of the numerous hurricanes and furious seas which have from time to time dashed over and against it for upwards of two centuries. It was in the year 1690, that Thomas Tyldesley prepared a secret chamber for the dethroned monarch James the Second, on his invading Ireland in the hope of regaining his crown. The closet or hiding place was afterwards known as "the King's Cupboard." Tradition states that a fox secured by a chain was daily permitted to take his rambles in front of the doorway of the hall, and that the hall took its name from that circumstance. The designation "Blackpool" was given to the place owing to the existence of a pool at the north end of the then hamlet. This pool is stated to have been half a mile in length, in which black and chocolate coloured waters accumulated from Martin Mere and the turf fields in the neighbourhood called the "moss." These accumulations of water remained until the currents were diverted when they finally disappeared. It is recorded that about the period above referred to, Blackpool, with the exception of Fox Hall, was nothing more than a hamlet of rude and clustering huts; and that the first lodging house erected in the place was in the year 1735, and occupied by Ethart á Whiteside, who had a wife possessing great skill in cookery, the consequence being that the cottage in which they resided attracted nu-merous visitors in the summer. The Whitesides were very clean, and popular with their visitors, who flocked down in large numbers, from different parts of Lancashire, summer after summer. After the Whitesides' death, however, the favourite cottage seems to have lost its popularity, which is not surprising, inasmuch as a noted character of the day, called "Tom the Cobbler" became its presiding genius. This rather eccentric individual converted the cottage into an Inn for the sale of liquors, but in his general management and personal habits the "cobbler" does not appear to have been impressed with the scriptural maxim that "clean-liness is next to godliness." Presiding, at the dinner table over his guests, the cobbler host was in the habit of taking his seat at the head of the table, in working

costume, and from his resined leather apron, assisted by
equally resined and unwashed digits, distributing the
bread to each of his patrons.   As may be well imagined,
such an unsavoury trait in the character of this disciple
of St. Crispin did not commend itself to the unqualified
admiration of his visitors, and in a brief period the
hitherto neat and trim hostelrie collapsed.   For a period
of nearly forty years from the date already referred to—
1735—Blackpool made little progress, for in 1769 there
were only 28 dwellings in the hamlet, and these for the
most part consisted of thatched cottages, four only having
slated roofs.   In this year a change took place in the face
of the hamlet, some enterprise and public spirit being
manifested in the erection of a better class of houses.   At
the period there were two Inns, one called Bonny's, but
better known by its designation of "Old Margery's."
The contrast between the cost of living at the present
time and the period referred to, is worth recording.   The
charge for board and lodging at Bonny's Hotel, was from
eight pence to ten pence per day, although it is only fair
to say that a shilling in those days represented a much
higher value than it does at present.   In the year 1788,
the number of houses had increased to about 35, and the
estimated number of visitors in the busiest part of the
season, was set down at about 400, the number of Inns
having at this time increased to four.   The bathing
arrangements of the period were of a singularly primitive,
if not an amusing character, and are worthy of special
record.   The modern bathing machine of the present day
not having been introduced at the time, huge boxes were
placed along the shore, in which bathers undressed and
dressed, and for the purpose of separating the sexes and
promoting decency the following contrivance was adopted.
In the marine ablutions of the visitors pre cedence was
given to the ladies, and in carrying out this arrangement
a bell, rung when it was nearly high water, was the signal
for all the gentlemen to retire from the shore, to their
inns or apartments, which they were compelled to do
under a penalty of a bottle of wine.   When the shore

became clear the ladies rushed to the boxes on the shore,
and prepared for, and completed their ablutions, and
when this had been accomplished, and they had retired
to their homes, the bell rang a second time, when the
sterner sex made their appearance, and in turn disported
themselves in the briny element.   The cost of residing at
the inns had now increased materially, the modest sum of
eight pence and ten pence per day for board and lodging,
having been followed by a charge of three shillings and
four pence per day, in hotels of the first class, exclusive of
liquors ; whilst at the second class inns two shillings and
sixpence per day was the tariff.   From 1788, to about the
commencement of the present century, Blackpool had
made little progress as regards its building or population,
for we find that in 1801 the number of houses were limited
to 40, whilst the inhabitants did not exceed 473.   A
narrow minded and mistaken policy appears, up to this
time, to have prevented the developement of the place.
Large capitalists were not wanting, ready to invest
extensively in the erection of new residences for the
accommodation of visitors; who were now constantly
increasing, but they were prevented from carrying out
their intentions in consequence of being unable to obtain
the necessary land, which to a large extent belonged to
the several hotel proprietors, and who refused to sell it
for building upon, under the apprehension that the
erection of commodious houses and apartments for visitors
would interfere with the patronage of their inns.   These
objections, however, were eventually overcome, and
greater facilities having been given for obtaining land,
building proceeded, attended by a corresponding expansion
of the locality, and the increase of its resident and visiting
population.   In the year 1816, coaches first began to run
between Preston and Blackpool, the communication
between the two places having previously been by means
of pack horses and private vehicles.   For several years
Sunday fairs were held in Blackpool, but in consequence
of the disorderly scenes by which they were accompanied
the fairs were abolished in the year 1830.   It was about

the year 1836 when the first great impetus was given to Blackpool by building on a large scale, and from that time the town has rapidly expanded, until at the present period it possesses miles of streets adorned by palatial dwellings, and numerous public buildings. In the ten years between 1831 and 1841,, the population had doubled itself. In 1844, a public market was.erected, and eighteen years afterwards, in 1872, it was enlarged to double its original dimensions. The branch railway from Poulton to Blackpool was opened in April, 1846, thus adding another stimulus to the development and progress of the town. In 1862, the north pier was erected, at a cost of £12,000. Its length is 1405 feet, and the width of the main portion 28 feet, but at the head it is 55 feet wide. In 1867, an extension or jetty was added, at a cost of £6,000, and in 1869, a new entrance was constructed, the cost of which was £2,700. A further enlargement was again effected in 1874, the pier head being extended by putting out two wings, designed by E. Birch, Esq., C.E. This enlargement involved an outlay of £14,000. The south wing is 130 feet in length, and at one end there is a platform or orchestra, with accommodation for 30 performers. On the east and west sides there are two other buildings, 62 feet by 27 feet, that on the east side forming a restaurant, whilst that to the west is for the sale of fancy goods. On the north wing of the pier there is a spacious pavilion, 130 feet long and 90 feet wide, which will hold an audience of 1200 persons. This portion of the structure, around which there is a promenade, is supplied with an orchestra and refreshment rooms. It likewise is used as a concert room, and serves as a marine lounge. The total cost of the pier and the several buildings upon it has amounted to upwards of £45,000. Amongst the many noble residential buildings which have been erected within the last few years, some fine terraces on the high ground at the north end are especially prominent. These several blocks, from which there is a commanding view of the sea, were erected by a company of capitalists, who purchased a large quantity of land for the purpose. In the centre of the block stands what was originally called the Imperial Hotel, but is now designated the Hydropathic Hotel. The houses, which are in terraces, are respectively designated Stanley Villas, Wilton Parade, Imperial Terrace, and Lansdowne Crescent. In the year 1867 the construction of a pier at the south end of the town was commenced, and it was completed and opened in the following year. The total length of this pier is 1,518 feet, the main promenade being 1,118 feet long, and the lower promenade 400 feet. In 1868 a fine block of buildings, called the Arcade and Assembly Rooms, was erected in Talbot Street. The buildings, in addition to the Assembly Rooms, contain a restaurant, and refreshment rooms, a billiard room, and a spacious saloon, surrounded within by a gallery, and furnished with a stage for theatrical representations. A short distance from the town is Raikes Hall, which for many years was one of the seats of the Hornby family, but which is now the property of a company, who have converted it into a place of recreation and entertainment, under the name of the Raikes Hall Park, Gardens, and Aquarium, the area of the grounds being 40 acres in extent. In 1873, a new cemetery, containing an area of nearly nine acres, was formed and opened. Mr. Gorst, surveyor to the Local Board, laid out the grounds, and Messrs. Garlick, Park, and Sykes, of Preston, furnished the designs for the cemetery buildings. Amongst the numerous companies which have been formed in Blackpool within the last ten or twelve years is the Sea Water Company, which was established in 1872, with a capital of £10,000. The company have pipes laid down in the several thoroughfares, from which salt water is supplied to the houses. In August, 1875, what was known as the Bank Hey estate, the property of W. H. Cocker, Esq., was purchased from that gentlemen for £23,000, with the intention of erecting a Winter Garden and Pavilion, of large dimensions, on the site. The building, which was opened in 1879, is a structure of noble architectural design, containing concert rooms, promenades, conservatory, and other apartments providing entainments of almost every imaginable character. The various companies having building for their object may be described as legion, and include, amongst many others, the Lane Ends Estate Company; the Blackpool Land, Building, and Hotel Company; the Lansdowne Estate Company; the Blackpool Central Property Company; the Clifton Arms Hotel and Pier Company; and the South Blackpool Jetty Company. In January, 1876, a charter of incorporation was granted to the town, and it may be observed as showing the enormous increase in the number of houses and the population, that during the enquiry held by Major Donnelly, the commissioner sent down by the Privy Council, prior to the charter being granted, it was stated that the rateable value of the town had increased from £17,489 in 1863, to £73,035 in 1875. On the occasion of the first election of members of the corporation after the charter was granted, Mr. William Porter, of Fleetwood and Blackpool, proprietor of the *Fleetwood Chronicle*, and one of the oldest inhabitants, was appointed the returning officer. The election took place on the 11th of April, 1876, and in the following week, namely on the 19th of April, the first meeting of the council was held, when alderman William Henry Cocker had the honour of being appointed the first mayor of the newly constituted borough. Amidst the progress which Blackpool has made during the last half century it is somewhat to its discredit that until the year 1821 there was neither Church nor Chapel in the place where the inhabitants and visitors could assemble for public worship. About the year 1790, however, a large room at one of the hotels began to be used for this purpose, the ministers being obtained from the neighbouring parish churches of Bispham and Poulton. In the year 1821 St. John's Church was built, and in 1832 it was enlarged, a further enlargement again taking place in 1847. A chancel was added in 1851, and in 1866 a new tower was built, and a peal of bells introduced. In 1881 the Church was taken down, and an entirely new edifice, of much larger dimensions, was erected. The structure is a handsome building in the gothic style of architecture, from the designs of Messrs. Garlick, Park, and Sykes, of Preston. It is built of Yorkshire parpoint stone, with Longridge stone dressings. The cost of the edifice was £12,000. There are also three other Churches, namely, Christ Church; Holy Trinity Church, at the south end of the town, formerly known as South Shore, but now united to, and forming a part of Blackpool ; and St. Peter's Mission Church. There are also eight other places of worship in the borough, including a large and gorgeously decorated Roman Catholic Church, in the Talbot Road, erected from the designs of Mr. Welby Pugin, at a cost of £12,000. There are likewise a Wesleyan Chapel, and other Chapels connected respectively with the Independent, Baptist, United Methodist, Primitive Methodist, Ebenezar Wesleyan, and Unitarian denominations.

The expenditure incurred in the erection of public buildings and other works at Blackpool during the last eight years amounts to no less than £700,000, and includes £70,000 on the Promenade of two miles in length ; the Clifton Arms Hotel, £18,000 ; the new Parish Church, £12,000 ; the Lane Ends Hotel and block of buildings in connexion, £100,000 ; Sea Water Pumping Station, £10,000 ; Cemetery and Chapels, £5,000 ; South Jetty, £50,000 ; Tyldesly Terrace, £18,000 ; Eaves Terrace, £8,000 ; and Read's Baths, £2,000 ; all of which were carried out by Messrs. Garlick, Park, and Sykes, of Preston. The Winter Gardens and Pavilion, which were erected from the designs of Mr. Mitchell, of Manchester, cost £120,000 ; the North Pier and buildings in connexion, £65,000. ; Palatine Hotel, £50,000 ; Aquarium, £40,000 ; Assembly Rooms, £30,000 ; Roman Catholic Church, £12,000 ; Bailey's Hotel, £30,000 ; Imperial Hotel, £45,000 ; and Claremont Park, £15,000.

Since the year 1876, when the corporation was formed, building has increased at a rate unparalleled in any former period of Blackpool's history, and the town continues rapidly to expand, new streets being formed and houses erected in the interior leading from the promenade, which from north to south is now between three and four miles in length. What the future of Blackpool may be it would be hazardous to phophecy, but from present appearances there seems no limit to its expansion.

FLEETWOOD.

Considerably less than half a century ago, the site upon which the town and port of Fleetwood now stands was nothing more than a rabbit warren, the warrener's cottage being the only dwelling place upon it, with the exception of a few fishermans' huts. The town owes its origin to the enterprise and public spirit of the late Sir Hesketh Fleetwood, the Lord of the Manor, who first conceived the idea of founding the town, and converting the wild waste designated the rabbit warren into a watering-place and sea-port. Sir Hesketh Fleetwood at the time was one of the Members of Parliament for Preston, but the undertaking was by many persons resident in the locality considered impracticable and, indeed, utopian. Sir Hesketh, however, associated himself with engineers and others who had confidence in the project, and the result was that under the supervision of the late Mr. Decimus Burton, architect, of London, streets were laid out, and in the year 1836 the erection of houses was commenced, the first dwelling completed and occupied being that now owned and inhabited by Mr. Richard Warbrick, an extensive outfitter. The Fleetwood Arms Hotel in Dock Street, was erected shortly afterwards, along with a number of private houses and shops, and a mercantile character having already been given to the place by a line of steamships, running between Fleetwood and Scotland, and also between Fleetwood and Belfast, and likewise the Isle of Man, a considerable population

was attracted to the newly-formed town. Railway communication with the place was projected much about the
same period, and on the 15th of July, 1840, a line between
Preston and Fleetwood was opened, constructed by a
company designated the "Preston and Wyre Railway,
Harbour, and Dock-Company," of which Sir Hesketh
Fleetwood was understood to be the heaviest shareholder.
The opening of the railway gave a considerable impetus
to the trade and commerce of the new town and port,
and during the years 1840-41 house building and the
erection of other public works and buildings proceeded
with such activity that numerous cottages had to be
erected for the special accommodation of labourers and
others.   Amongst other buildings which were erected at
this period was the North Euston Hotel, built at a great
cost, from the designs of Mr. Decimus Burton, and at the
expense of Sir Hesketh Fleetwood.   The Crown Hotel
and the Victoria Hotel were likewise erected about the
the same time.   A New Market Hall was also erected in
the latter part of 1840, whilst in 1841 St. Peter's Parish
Church, and likewise a Roman Catholic Church, were
built and opened.   Some years later the last named
building was turned into a school on a much larger Roman Catholic Church being erected.   In the year 1842 a
Town Improvement Act was obtained, and under it a
Local Board was appointed.   In the year 1841 two shore
lighthouses were erected, at a cost of about £3,000. One
of these lighthouses is 90 feet above high water mark,
and the other 104 feet above half tide level.   Although
the establishment of Fleetwood as a sea-port was the
main object of Sir Hesketh Fleetwood and those associated with him, the want of dock accommodation acted
as a great drawback to the carrying out of this intention,
and from 1841 to about 1845 it partook more of the
character of a sea-side resort.   Large numbers of strangers
from Preston, Manchester, and other places in Lancashire
were amongst the visitors during the summer months,
and sea bathing was a prominent feature in the attractions of the place, numerous bathing machines being

ranged along that part of the shore near the recreation
ground known as "The Mount." It was calculated that
in the year 1844 upwards of 60,000 persons visited the
town in this capacity, some being excursionists, whilst
others remained at the hotels and lodging houses for
longer periods. In this year the Mayor and Corporation
of Preston paid an official visit to Fleetwood, under circumstances which turned out somewhat disastrous to the
municipal body. The party embarked at Preston on the
steamer "Lily," no doubt in the hope of enjoying a
pleasant marine outing, but as the result proved they
painfully experienced the reverse. The weather was very
unfavourable, the whole of the passage from Preston to
Fleetwood being made under the adverse conditions of
storm and rain, and most of the unfortunate members of
the local Parliament suffering, during the whole of the
journey, from that dreaded marine discomfort which the
reader will understand. On approaching the lighthouse at
the mouth of the Wyre, the "Lily" became disabled, and
the mayor and his colleagues were taken on board the
steamer "Empress," and by that vessel landed in safety at
Fleetwood, the municipal party, " in their gorgeous robes
and liveries," but now wan and dejected, walking in procession to the North Euston Hotel to dine, pitiable-looking
victims of *mal de mer*. On the repeal of the corn laws
in 1846 the whole of the workpeople in the employ of the
late Mr. Cobden visited Fleetwood to celebrate the
triumph of free trade principles in Parliament, the
entire expenses being defrayed by the great free trader.
Each of the operatives, and others amongst the party,
numbering about 1,300, wore a free trade medal.

In August, 1846, the erection of the "Fleetwood
Testimonial Schools" was commenced, the late Charles
Swainson, Esq., of Preston, laying the foundation stone.
In the cavity of the stone was placed the following in-
scription on parchment :—" The first stone of these schools
which are to be erected as the fittest testimonial to the
beneficent founder of this town, Sir Hesketh Fleetwood
M.P., was laid by Charles Swainson, Esq., of Preston

this 26th day of August, 1846." On a slab inserted in the wall, in the front elevation of the schools, is a similar inscription.

On Monday, the 20th of September, 1847, Her Majesty Queen Victoria, accompanied by their royal highnesses the Prince Consort, the Prince of Wales, and the Princess Royal, landed at Fleetwood, *en route* from Scotland to London. The Queen and the Royal Party came into Fleetwood harbour in the *Victoria and Albert* yacht, the accompanying vessels forming the royal squadron consisting of the *Black Eagle*, the *Fairy*, the *Garland*, and the *Undine*. An address was presented on the occasion by Sir P. Hesketh Fleetwood, M.P. for Preston ; J. Wilson Patten, Esq., M.P., then high sheriff of the county ; and others. This was the first time that the Queen had ever landed in Lancashire, and one paragraph in the address was as follows:—"We rejoice to think that it has fallen to our happy lot to be the first to welcome the Queen of England to her own royal patrimony in the Duchy of Lancaster." The Queen slept on board the *Victoria and Albert* during the night, and on the following morning at ten o'clock, left Fleetwood for London, travelling by the Preston and Wyre and the London and North Western Railways. Enormous numbers of strangers—estimated at 10,000—from Preston, Manchester, and other Lancashire towns, visited Fleetwood on the occasion.

Although it was solely through Sir Hesketh Fleetwood's energy and public spirit that the town was founded, Sir Hesketh himself, like many others in a similar position, was a serious sufferer owing to having embarked on the enterprise. His losses in the railway, in which he held so large a stake, were understood to be very large, and he also sacrificed an enormous amount in the North Euston Hotel and other undertakings, which eventually necessitated his making over his Rossall and other estates.

For something like ten or fifteen years, from 1855 to 1870, Fleetwood may be described as under a cloud, for in the absence of docks little or no progress was made as regards shipping, whilst the completion of the railway system between London and Edinburgh and Glasgow, completely destroyed the steam boat passenger traffic between Fleetwood and Scotland. The railway between Preston and Fleetwood became almost valueless as a property, until at length the line was leased in perpetuity to the Lancashire and Yorkshire and London and North Western Companies, and those two companies now continue to work it, the result being that the prospects at Fleetwood are now brighter and more encouraging than they have been for many years past. On the 2nd of June, 1869, the first sod of a new dock was cut by H. S. Styan, Esq., of London, the surviving trustee of the estate under the will of the late Sir Hesketh Fleetwood, who died in 1866. The dock was to have been constructed by the Fleetwood Dock Company, but within six months after the first sod was cut the works were stopped. In the year 1871 the Lancashire and Yorkshire Railway Company obtained parliamentary powers to construct a dock on a much larger scale than that originally intended, and these works were finished and the dock and a large timber pond were opened, about three years since. The dock is 1,000 feet in length, and 400 feet in width, and contains an area of ten acres in extent. The timber pond adjoining is 17 acres. There are spacious wharves and sheds around the dock, and large new warehouses are at present in course of erection on the north side of the dock. In addition to these warehouses the Lancashire and Yorkshire Company are also erecting an extensive new passenger station at Fleetwood, which will be in immediate connexion with the pier and the steam-ships trading between Fleetwood and Belfast.

In 1859 the North Euston Hotel was sold to the government, and for some years was used as a School of Musketry. In 1867 several new buildings were added, and the hotel was converted into a barracks, to which purpose it continues to be applied.

In 1861 the population of Fleetwood was 4,000; in 1871, 4,428; and the last census returns show the population to have increased to about 7,000.

Returning to Preston from a visit which may have been made to the several marine localities on the west, which we have endeavoured to describe, the stranger or tourist will be amply repaid by spending what leisure time he may have in a visit to the interesting country stretching for several miles east of the town, where he will have an opportunity of enjoying an abundance of charming and enchanting inland scenery, opening out to him in succession as he pursues his journey, whilst at the same time he will find himself in the midst of numerous historic structures, full of interest, and abounding with antiquity.   Amongst other places which may be enumerated is Stonyhurst College, for many centuries the home of the Sherburnes, one of the oldest and most historic Lancashire families, but now, and for nearly a century past, the chief seat of Roman Catholic education in England.   Stonyhurst may be reached from Preston by two distinct routes, either of which the tourist can choose at pleasure.   He may avail himself of the railway from Preston to Longridge, and thence proceed by conveyance, or on foot, from the last named place to Hurst Green and Stonyhurst, a distance altogether, from Preston, of about 15 miles, or he may proceed by railway from Preston, *via* Blackburn to Whalley, from which there is a pleasant and most interesting walk of about five miles in length, when the grey towers of Stonyhurst are opened out to view.   We should advise the last named route, as Hoghton Tower may, by adopting it, be one of the first places of interest to be inspected, amongst other ancient structures, before Stonyhurst is reached.   Assuming this route to be taken the tourist will take the railway from Preston to Hoghton station, where he will break the journey, and on arriving at the station will find himself immediately under the heights of

HOGHTON TOWER,

the ancient baronial mansion, where James the First was

so hospitably entertained by Sir Henry Hoghton, an ancestor of the present baronet, and to which reference has already been made in an earlier portion of our narrative. For many years after the royal visit just referred to the historical old mansion was not occupied by the Hoghton family, and was unfortunately allowed to go to ruin, after having been sacked, and to a considerable extent dismantled during the political conflicts which took place in the middle ages. The general public had full and unlimited access to the dilapidated old structure until within the last ten or twelve years, but this privilege has now for some time been withdrawn, and the mansion, which is at present gradually undergoing restoration, is once more in the occupation of the Hoghton family, being the seat of Sir Charles de Hoghton, the present baronet. It may be interesting to add that in the structural and internal restorations of the mansion many of the old material relics remain, including the ancient kitchen fire grate which cooked the loin of beef said to have been knighted by King James. It stands on the cresting of one of the loftiest heights in Lancashire, and commands a magnificent view of the valley of the Ribble, and the country around, to the extent of upwards of forty or fifty miles, Liverpool and other places in that locality being visible on a clear day. Notwithstanding that the ancient mansion is now closed to the public, admission may be obtained, at stated periods, by orders, which are freely and courteously issued by Sir Charles.

WHALLEY.

Having completed his visit to Hoghton Tower, the tourist can continue his railway journey to Whalley, which is within an hour's ride, including the delay which has often to be made at Blackburn. Although on arriving at Whalley, and looking around, the visitor may reasonably conclude that it is nothing more than a village, or at the best a small country town, the parish is the most

extensive in Lancashire, embracing 49 townships, with an
area of upwards of 100,000 acres of land, and a population
of more than 150,000.   It is pleasantly situated on the
banks of the Calder, one of the tributaries of the Ribble.
The appearance of the place, with one long street, and a
number of clean and comfortable inns, well patronised by
visitors, is charmingly rural.   The main features which
Whalley possesses, and which from time to time attract
large numbers of strangers, consist of the ruins of its once
grand and magnificent abbey, and its ancient parish
church.

WHALLEY ABBEY

has a special history of its own.   It was magnificent in its
structural grandeur;   distinguished for hospitality and
alms-giving, in its prosperity and greatness; and associated
with vandalism, and royal perfidy and plunder in its fall
and ruin.   For a full description of what the Abbey was
in former days, and for the associations connected with it,
from its origin to its suppression, we must refer the reader
to the Rev. Dr. Whitaker's interesting and exhaustive
History of Whalley.   It is sufficient for our present purpose to give a brief sketch.   The original residence of the
Abbots of Whalley, and their Priors and Monks, of the
Cistercian order, was at Stanlaw Abbey, in Cheshire, but
on the 4th of April, 1296, Gregory de Northbury, the
eighth Abbot of Stanlaw, and his Monks, took possession of
Whalley, Pope Nicholas the Fourth having, in 1289, in
answer to their petition to be permitted to remove to
Whalley, finally issued a bull authorising such removal,
and empowering them to appropriate the revenues of
Whalley Church and its dependencies, on condition of
their endowing the rectory on the first opportunity, and
this was done in 1294, on the death of Peter de Cestria,
the last secular rector of Whalley.   Two years afterwards,
as already stated, the Monks took possession of their new
home at Whalley, and on the 12th of June, in the same

year, the foundation stone of the new Abbey was laid by
Henry de Lacey, Earl of Lincoln, the great great grandson of the founder of Stanlaw Abbey, this same Henry de
Lacey, who on the death of his father came into possession
of large estates in Lancashire and Yorkshire, having
added to the previous benefactions of the Abbey the
advowson of Whalley Church.   Whilst the Abbey was
in course of erection the residence of the Abbot and the
brotherhood was at the old deanery.   Ten years after the
foundation stone was laid the Abbey was first occupied
by the Monks, but only a comparatively small portion of
the building had at that period been completed.   The
consecration took place on the 28th of April, 1306.   New
buildings continued to be added, and it was not until 142
years after the foundation stone was laid—nearly a century
and a half—that the structure approached completion,
during the lifetime of Abbot Eccles.   Dr. Whitaker
records that the original cost of the Abbey was £3,000,
which in the present day seems little more than a nominal
sum ; bnt it must be remembered that in those times the
wages of skilled artisans did not exceed two-pence a day,
whilst the timber required during the process of erection
was obtained without any further cost than felling and
cartage from the neighbouring woods and forests; the
stone was obtained on the same terms and conditions
from quarries in the locality on the lands belonging to
the brotherhood.
   In the days of its prosperity and power the hospitalities of the Abbey were boundless, and alms-giving
to the poor and other acts of charity, were carried out on
a scale of the most generous liberality ; whilst gifts were
extended to the great ones of the land. In Dr. Whitaker's
history there is a statement of the receipts and expenditure
of the Abbey in the years 1478 and 1521 respectively.
In 1478 Abbot Holden was in power, and in 1521 John
Paslew, the last Abbot was the superior.   Dr. Whitaker
states that in 1478 the income from the Abbey property
was £687 11s. 1d., and in 1521 £987 11s. 9d. In the
same years the outgoings amounted respectively to

£685 4s. 6d., and £839 11s. 5d. Taking the relative value of money at that period and the present day the figures we have quoted would seem to indicate that they represent the then annual income and expenditure of the Abbey as equal to from £8,500 to £12,000 per annum at the present time. In this statement several of the nobility, amongst others, are recorded as being indebted to the bounty of the brotherhood. The names given are those of Lords Monteagle and Stanley, as also those of the Talbot, Pilkington, and other well known Lancashire families. The travelling expenses of the Abbot and Monks, and the cost of the clothing for the brotherhood are also among the items, which likewise embraces charges for the Abbey minstrels. The fee of 3s. 4d. to a doctor from Lancaster is a curious item amongst the rest. It would be interesting to know what the disciple of Esculapius paid for his conveyance from and to Lancaster, and what was the nett amount of the fee. In 1531, during the time of Abbot Paslew, Dr. Whitaker sets down the entire number of residents in the Abbey at 120, consisting of the Abbot, the Prior, and about 20 Monks, besides an uncertain number of novices; 20 servants belonging to the Abbot, and 70 in the general service of the house. In addition to these the learned doctor observes that the demesnes and revenues of the Abbey had to sustain a daily, though uncertain and irresistable influx of guests of every rank, from the sovereign to the beggar, whose stay, if it exceeded not three days, was never considered as oppressive. "The average yearly consumption of the house," he adds, "may be stated in round numbers, on the authority of the two preceding accounts as, wheat, 200 quarters; malt, 150 quarters; wine, 8 pipes. For the Abbot's table, oxen and cows, 75; sheep, 80; calves, 40; lambs, 20; porkers, 4. And for the refectory and inferior tables within the house, oxen and cows, 57; sheep, 40; calves, 20; lambs, 10. From this statement may be inferred a great disproportion in the quantity of animal food, when compared with the other necessaries of life, to modern habits; for, in this table of expenses, it may be made clearly to appear that the value of shambles meat consumed was, to that of wheat and of malt, in a much higher ratio than at present. The latter circumstance leaves a very favourable impression with respect to the sobriety of religious houses." Entertaining the numerous pilgrims and others, payments in pensions, alms to the poor, and maintenance of novices at the universities, appears to have been a heavy drain on the resources of the Abbey.

During the two centuries since the foundation of the Abbey, in 1306, and extending down to the year 1500, sixteen Abbots had presided over it.   William Rede, the sixteenth Abbot, died in the year 1506, and was succeeded by John Paslew, the seventeenth, and last of the Abbots, for with his untimely and ignominous death the work of the Abbey was brought to a close, and the succour which the brotherhood, for more than two hundred years, had been enabled to extend to those around them in education, alms-giving, and boundless acts of charity, was ruthlessly terminated by a licentious monarch, actuated by avarice, and regardless of morals.   John Paslew, the last Abbot of Whalley, whose eventful career in connexion with the grand old monastery of which he was the ruler, belonged to a well known family of that name, residing at Wiswall, in Whalley parish.   For some time before his elevation to the abbacy he had held the office of Prior.   He took a great interest not only in the educational and other work of the Abbey, but in the material grandeur of the fabric itself, and soon after he became Abbot he caused several additions to be made, one of these being a new lady chapel, and the other the quadrangular building known as the Abbot's Lodgings, in which the Assheton family for some years resided after the dissolution of the monastery.   The western gateway, one of the finest portions of the ruins of the Abbey which remain, is also said to have been erected under the auspices of Abbot Paslew. Dr. Whitaker, in speaking of Paslew's time, says :—" The first twenty years of this Abbot passed like those of his predecessors, in the duties of his choir, in the exercise of

hospitality, in attention to the extensive possessions of
his house, or in the improvement of its buildings; but a
storm was now approaching, before which either conscience
or bigotry prevented him from bending, and which
brought quick and premature destruction on him and his
house." It was in the year 1534, that Henry the Eighth
and his Parliament first determined upon the crusade
against the monasteries, and charges of a varied nature
were made against them by Henry and his advisers, many
of whom, there is too much reason to believe, were
parasites of the king, willing to pander to his cupidity,
and to share with him in the spoils and plunder which
would follow upon the destruction of the religious houses.
The charges made against the monks were manifold, it
being alleged that the discipline of the abbeys was lax
and immoral, and that the monks had been unmindful of
their vows. Notwithstanding that this was strongly
denied, the king appointed a commission to visit the
abbeys, with instructions to report as to the manner in
which they were conducted. There are many who hold
that this commission was little more than a mockery, and
that, judging by the antecedents of the king, his motive
in appointing it was a sordid one, the suppression of the
monasteries having already been resolved upon by Henry,
with the sole view of seizing upon their property and
possessions. The visit to the different abbeys was made
in 1535, and upon the report of the commission an act
was passed suppressing the smaller monasteries, with
incomes of less than £200 a year, and providing for the
reversion of their revenues to the crown. This act was
passed in 1536, and the preamble is worthy of being
recorded as shewing the questionable character of the
subsequent attack upon Whalley and the other great
abbeys throughout the country. The preamble recites
that "manifest sin, vicious, carnal, and abominable living
is daily used and committed among the little and small
abbeys, priories, and other religious houses." The
preamble, however, goes on to make the admission— and
this is noteworthy—that "in the great monasteries of

this realm *religion is right well kept and observed.*"
Under this Act all the monastic foundations in the county
of Lancaster, with the exception of two—Whalley and
Furness—were suppressed. The entire number in England, was three hundred and seventy-eight, having an
aggregate annual revenue of £32,000, which in the
present day represents between £350,000 and £400,000
per annum, and this large sum the king took from the
monks, and added it to his own already princely income.
Moreover, not content with this act of spoliation, the
whole of their plate and jewels were taken from the
monks, which it is stated represented upwards of three
times the annual revenue already stated. Amongst the
monasteries suppressed were several in Preston and the
immediate neighbourhood. Those in Preston were the
Grey Friars, and the Magdalen Hospital, on the site of
the latter of which St. Walburgh's Church now stands.
They also included the monasteries at Penwortham,.
Lytham, Burscough, Warrington, Upholland, and Lancaster. The lands belonging to these religious houses
were in many instances sold for the benefit of the crown,
whilst the remaining portions were made grants of to the
favorites of the king. In the following year the larger
abbeys and their lands and other property were similarly
attacked by the king and his selfishly interested advisers,
notwithstanding the preamble in the Act of 1536 that in
the "great monasteries of this realm religion is right
well kept and observed." Whalley was included amongst
those wealthier foundations, all of which were now so
shortly to be swept away at the bidding of a grasping and
capricious monarch, and a corrupt court. Whalley was.
one of the abbeys against which no charge was made by
the visitors, preceding the Act of 1536, and, adverting to
the absence of any such accusation, Dr. Whitaker observes
that "charity should incline us to think no evil of an
institution, professedly religious, against which no specific
evidence appears." The attempt to take possession of
the great abbeys was resisted by the abbots and monks,
more especially those connected with the northern

foundations, and in this they were supported by many families of the laity, who had been connected with the abbeys as their founders and benefactors, and who, whatever reforms they might have considered desirable in the internal economy and management of these ancient religious houses, were nevertheless averse to their rude extinction, and the confiscation of their property and estates. The king's demand led to an uprising and a rebellion, which rapidly spread over the north of England. This rebellion developed itself in what at the time was known as the "Pilgrimage of Grace," headed by a Yorkshire gentleman named Robert Aske, and this insurrection had the active sympathy of large numbers in all classes of society. "Every element," says Froude, "necessary for a great revolt was in motion—wounded superstition, real suffering, caused by real injustice, with their attendant train of phantoms. The clergy in the north were disaffected to a man." In this movement the Abbot of Whalley and the members of the brotherhood joined, but the rising was quickly subdued and overpowered by the king's forces, after which the leaders of the insurrection were arrested and tried on a charge of high treason. Amongst them were John Paslew, Abbot of Whalley, and John Eastgate and William Haydock, two of the monks. They were tried at Lancaster on the 10th of March, 1537, and were found guilty and sentenced to death. After the trial they were conveyed to Whalley Abbey under guard, and on the morning of the 12th of March, Paslew and Eastgate were executed near a spot called the Holehouses, at the foot of Whalley Nab, immediately facing the place of Paslew's birth. Haydock was taken to Padiham, where he was hanged on the following day.

Such was the end of the last Abbot of Whalley, and of the glory, hospitalities, and charities, of the magnificent Abbey over which he presided. About three months after his death all the landed possessions and properties of the Abbey were taken possession of, and were eventually sold for the benefit of the crown, the Assheton and Bradyll families becoming the owners. For nearly two centuries after the fall of the Abbey the Assheton family resided in that part of the building known as the Abbot's Lodgings. The monks who had formed the brotherhood met with a hard fate. All their property and effects were seized on behalf of the king, and they themselves were driven from the Abbey penniless, suffering the greatest of privations. Some of them remained about the locality, earning a scanty living by teaching, whilst others settled in France. The history of one of them is specially interesting. Thomas Holden, a younger son of Gilbert Holden, of Holden, a respectable Lancashire family, said to be the last surviving monk, on the dissolution of the Abbey, returned to his native place of Holden. Dr. Whitaker says of him :—" In 1559 I meet with him once more under the title of Sir Thomas Holden, curate of Hasling-den ; and in 1574 he was licensed to the same cure at the metropolitical visitation of Archbishop Grindall, held at Preston, by the style of 'Thomas Holden, clerk, of sober life and competent learning.' "

Adverting to the disastrous fortunes and ultimate fall of the Abbey, Dr. Whitaker says :—" It continued for two centuries and a half to exercise unbounded hospitality and charity, to adorn the site which had been chosen with a suecession of magnificent buildings, to protect the tenants of its ample domains in the enjoyment of inde-pendence and plenty, to educate and provide for their children, to employ, clothe, feed, and pay many labourers, herdsmen, and shepherds, and to exercise the arts, and cultivate the learning of the times." Such was the establishment which, in the name of religion, hypocriti-cally paraded, one of the most licentious of monarchs was chiefly instrumental in destroying. His ignoble reign, stained and degraded by sensuality and lust, was rendered still more hateful by the spoliation of an ancient religious institution, under the influence of a spirit of avarice and greed.

The Abbey and grounds, exclusive of the estate, covered an area of upwards of 36 acres, the buildings themselves occupying between five and six acres. It originally consisted of three quadrangles, the west quadrangle forming the cloisters and court; the nave and conventual church, the north quadrangle; and the chapter house and vestry the east quadrangle. Dr. Whitaker states that the conventual church exceeded many cathedrals in extent. Of this portion of the Abbey nothing now remains above ground, but Dr. Whitaker states that he ascertained its dimensions by excavating the site, when he found the foundations of the walls, and the bases of the various pillars, and was thus enabled to ascertain its extent and character. The church, and cloister court remained 120 years after the dissolution of the abbey, and it is stated were only demolished by Sir Richard Assheton in 1661, when Queen Mary attempted to restore the religious houses. Amongst other portions of the Abbey which still remain are the chapter house and vestry, in the east quadrangle.; the dormitory in the west quadrangle; and the refectory and kitchens are likewise still standing, so far as regards the walls, and the two huge fire places. With the exception of what is believed to have been the Abbot's house, no roofs remain. Embracing other parts of the venerable building still standing are the gateways, a conspicuous feature being the massive west gateway said to have been erected by the ill-fated John Paslew, the last of the abbots. It will thus be seen that there are still many interesting ruins, sufficient to attract the lovers of antiquity and the archæologist to this once magnificent Abbey, of which we must now take leave, and invite the tourist to pay a visit to the neighbouring ancient church.

WHALLEY PARISH CHURCH,

hard by the abbey, is one of the most ancient ecclesiastical structures in England, having been first built in the early part of the 7th century, namely, in the year 628. In 1283 it was rebuilt by Peter de Cestria, the last rector before the appropriation of the church and the rectory to the

abbey authorities. Additions and alterations appear to
have been made in the building between the thirteenth
century and the period of the Reformation. The interior
of the old edifice possesses several features of interest,
suggestive of its ancient origin and character. It consists
of a nave, and side aisles, and an unusually long choir
and chancel, the stalls in the choir being in oak, and
richly carved. These stalls, which are upwards of 400
years old, were taken from the abbey at the time of its
suppression. They are eighteen in number, each of them
having carved folding seats, the carving being of a quaint
and singularly grotesque character. The principal stall
is what was the abbot's seat when in the abbey church.
The inscription on the seat, in old English characters,
is:—"Semper gaudentes sint ista sede sedentes," or as
translated "Ever gladsome may they be who occupy this
seat." The seat is also ornamented with sculptured vine
wreaths and clustering grapes. The seats of all the other
stalls are likewise attractive for the odd and antique
carving which is their distinguishing feature. One of
them represents a satyr making love to a rustic maid,
who laughs and makes merry at his proposals. Another
represents a husband on his knees before his wife, the
latter beating her lord with a ladle. Of these curious
carved representations Dr. Whitaker suggests that they
"perhaps might be intended to console the monks for the
privations of love and marriage." Perhaps the most
ludicrously whimsical of them all is the carving on one of
the seats, which represents a man shoeing a goose, under
which is the couplet in old English characters

> "Wo so melles hy : of yt : al me : dos
> Let hy : com here and shoe ye gos."

the suggested meaning of which is that those persons
who meddle with other men's business are employed in
as foolish a work as shoeing a goose, or, as some have
put it

> "That fool to shoe a goose should try
> "Who pokes his nose in each man's pie."

The ancient carved oak pews in the body of the church

are likewise a special feature of the interior. Two of these pews, which stand out in bold relief from the rest, are very elaborately carved, and are well worth a minute examination. They are much higher than those around them, being carried up to a height of upwards of nine feet, and surmounted by a canopy resting upon richly carved pillars, an inscription on lattice work at the sides recording that one of them was constructed by Roger Nowell, Esq., in 1534, and the other in 1610, by Roger Nowell, his son. According to tradition these pews have a singular history. It is said that there was a dispute in reference to the sittings in the church, and that this dispute was referred to the arbitration of Sir John Towneley, who in those days was the most influential person in the parish. His decision is stated to have been given in the following cppigramatic and sententious language:—" My man Shuttleworth, of Hacking, made this form, and here will I sit when I come, and my cousin Nowell may take one behind me if he please, and my sonne Sherburne shall make one on the other side, and Mr. Catterall another behind him ; and for the residue the use shall be, first come first speed, and that will make the proud wives of Whalley rise betimes to come to church."

The monuments and tablets in the ancient edifice are amongst its chief attractions. In a niche on the north side of the chancel is a recumbent figure, in Sicilian marble, of the Rev. Dr. Whitaker, the distinguished historian of Whalley, and for many years its vicar. It must not, however, be inferred that Dr. Whitaker's remains are deposited here, for he was interred at Holme Chapel, in the family vault of his ancestors. John Paslew, the last unfortunate Abbot of Whalley, is said to be buried within the church, although there is no absolute evidence in confirmation of Whalley having been the place of his interment. There is, however, a memorial stone in the north aisle, which is believed to be over the abbot's grave. On the surface of the stone there is a carved floriated cross, together with the representation of a chalice and

paten, typical of his sacred calling, with the inscription
in old English characters :—"Jhs. fili Dei misereri mei."*
Amongst the other tomb stones in the church is that of
Christopher Smith, the last Prior of Whalley, having on
its surface a floriated cross; also another tomb stone
recording that the remains of Thomas Lawe, a monk,
rest beneath it, with an inscription asking for prayers for
the repose of his soul.   In the north or Mitton chapel, on
one of the pillars, is a brass plate, and engraved on it are
the figures of a man aud a woman kneeling before a desk.
These are the figures of the father and mother of the
children represented behind them.   Behind the father are
nine sons, and behind the mother eleven daughters, and
beneath is the following inscription, in old English
characters :—" of youre charitie pray for the soules of
Raphe Catterall, Esquer, and Elizabeth his wyfe, whiche
bodies lyeth before this pillar, and for all their childers'
soules, whiche Raphe deceased the 20th day o' December,
in the yere o' Lord God, 1515, and on whose soules Jesu
have mercie.   Amen."   This plate is associated with a
strange and romantic history.   It appears to have been
abstracted from the church about the middle of the seventeenth century, and was only discovered between the
years 1818 and 1823, when it was restored to its original
place in the church, where it may now be inspected.   Dr.
Whitaker, in a historical description of the parish of
Garstang, gives the following explanation as to the long
missing relic.   He says :—" In the neighbouring house of
Catterall, which stands on the site of the ancient house
of the Catteralls, I found a brass plate, of which the
account given is that it was dug up in the churchyard of
Garstang.   However that may be it is the identical plate,
transcribed by Dugdale, in the church of Whalley, and
recording Raphe Catterall, of this place, and of Little
Mitton, Esquire, and Elizabeth, his wife, with the figures
of twenty children, nine sons behind the father, and
eleven daughters behind the mother.   It is difficult to

---

* Jesus, Son of God, have mercy upon me.

conjecture how it came to be removed hither, but the names, the date, and every circumstance about it, identify it with that which is known to have existed at Whalley, where Raphe Catterall is known to have been interred, having died at his manor of Little Mitton. It has since been restored to its original situation in Whalley Church." Amongst other memorials in the church is a monumental brass, recording the death, in 1693, of the Rev. Stephen Grey, a former vicar of the parish. The hearthstone in the vestry, which is said to be six hundred years old, consists of an ornamental tomb stone, which is believed to have been in memory of some divine of high rank belonging to the church.

There are likewise many interesting memorials and relics in the churchyard, amongst which are three stone crosses of the sixth century. These crosses are believed to have been erected to commemorate the preaching of St. Paulinus, the Apostle of the North. During the period of the Commonwealth, when Puritan zeal ran to wild and extravagant excess, Dr. Webster, a prominent adherent of the Puritan zealots, at the head of a party of his followers, caused the three crosses to be removed from the churchyard, and after such removal they were utilised, says Mr. Crossley, in his Notes on Witchcraft, "as a boundary fence of some adjoining fields. After the Restoration, and when his religious views had become sobered and settled, he (Dr. Webster) is said, in an eager desire to atone for the desecration of which he had been guilty, to have purchased the crosses from the person who was then in possession of them, and to have been at the cost of re-erecting them on their present site, from which no sacrilegious hand will, I trust, ever again remove them."

There are some odd and singularly curious entries in the accounts of the churchwardens of Whalley. These accounts, still preserved, date so far back as the early part. of the seventeenth century, and amongst other entries there are payments for "whipping dogs" out of the church and churchyard. There are likewise entries of the sums paid for "mossing" the church, by which is meant covering the roof with moss. Amongst other items set out in the accounts are the travelling expenses of the churchwardens, one entry being a payment of 1s. 4d. for "a quart of sack for the committee" on the occasion of the churchwardens paying a visit to Preston, in 1647, to have an interview with the "committee," who sat at Preston during the period of the Commonwealth, for the purpose of superintending ecclesiastical business.

Leaving Whalley the walk towards Mitton and Stonyhurst is through a charmingly picturesque country. The far extending and beautiful vale is intersected by the Ribble, the Hodder, and the Calder, the three rivers converging in the valley near Little Mitton Hall, as the local rhymer of the district sings,

> "Hodder, Calder, Ribble, and rain,
> Mingle together in Mitton domain."

Mitton is between two and three miles from Whalley, on the route to Stonyhurst. One portion of Mitton is in Lancashire, and the other in Yorkshire, the river Ribble dividing the two parts of the parish. Before crossing the Ribble, Little Mitton Hall is seen on the left. It is an interesting old mansion in the Tudor style of architecture, one of its chief features being an ancient gothic gallery of the period of Henry the Seventh. After crossing over the Ribble we notice Great Mitton Hall, which is also in the Tudor style of architecture, and proceeding a short distance further, on rising ground, we come to

MITTON CHURCH,

an interesting old structure of the period of Edward the Third. The most attractive feature in this ancient ecclesiastical edifice is the Sherburne Chapel, on the north side of the church. This chapel was founded by Hugh Sherburne in the fifteenth century, the present chapel having been erected by Sir Richard Sherburne in the reign of Queen Elizabeth. It was for more than two centuries

the place of interment of the Sherburne family, but has
for many years past been closed, a member of the Weld
family, who were the lineal descendants of the Sherburnes,
being the last person interred there.   The memorials
within the chapel consist of white marble recumbent
figures of the Sherburne knights, and their ladies and
families, which rest on the surface of four tomb stones
and enclosures at an elevation of some four feet above the
ground floor of the chapel.   The most ancient of these
tombs is that of Sir Richard Sherburne, the original
owner of what is now Stonyhurst College, which he built,
and resided at as his mansion, and other members of his
family after him, for many generations.   The figures on
this tomb are those of Sir Richard Sherburne and his
wife, the latter of whom pre deceased her husband by
seven years.   Sir Richard died in July, 1594, the inscription on the tomb recording that he was Master Forester
of the Forest of Bowland ; Steward of the Manor of
Slaidburn ; Lieutenant of the Isle of Man ; and one of
her Majesty's Deputy Lieutenants of the county of Lancaster.   The adjoining tombs and memorial figures are
those of four succeeding Sir Richard Sherburnes and their
families.   That next to the tomb of the above named first
Sir Richard Sherburne is the tomb of Sir Richard his son,
and his wife, who died in child-bed of twins, during the
time that her husband was Captain of the Isle of Man, in
the year 1591.   The monument to Sir Richard and his
wife is mural, and represents them on the wall of the
chapel as kneeling opposite each other at an altar, in
prayer.   On compartments beneath are the representations
of twins in bed, with their nurses watching by their side;
and adjoining are figures of monks praying for the soul
of the dead mother of the twins.   The inscription on the
tomb and the recumbent monumental figure of the next
heir—another Richard—records that he was " an eminent
sufferer for his loyal fidelity to King Charles, of ever
blessed memory, and departed this life February 11th,
A.D. 1667, aged 81 years."   On the adjoining tomb stone
of a succeeding Richard, and his wife Isabel, there is an

inscription which states that "he built the alms house
and school upon Hurst Green, and left divers charitable
gifts yearly," and that "he died in prison for loyalty to his
sovereign, (James the Second), at Manchester, in 1689."
There is likewise a similar memorial to the last Richard;
together with a further monument to the memory of Sir
Nicholas Sherburne. He died without male issue, the
title thus expiring, but he left a daughter, who was
married to the eighth Duke of Norfolk. She also died
without issue, when the Stonyhurst estate passed to her
aunt, then married to William Weld, son and heir of Sir
John Weld, of Lulworth. The estate in after years
became the property of Thomas Weld, Esq., (grandson of
the wife of William Weld), who, in the year 1794, gave
the Jesuits possession of the ancient mansion at Stonyhurst, together with the large estates belonging to it.
Within the chapel there are also monuments in memory
of Sir Nicholas Sherburne and Lady Sherburne his wife,
also buried there. The former died on December 15,
1717, and the latter on January 27, 1772. There are
lengthy inscriptions on these monuments, which were
placed in the chapel by the Duchess, and on which the
many virtues of her parents are recorded. The conclusion
of the inscription on the memorial to Sir Nicholas states
that "this monument was set up by the Dowager Duchess
of Northfolk, in memory of the best of fathers and
mothers, and in this vault designs to be interred herself
whenever it pleases God to take her out of this world."
In addition to the several family memorials above described, there is also another in memory of a juvenile
member of the Sherburne family, which is invested with
a special if not a melancholy interest. It consists of an
alto relievo of white marble, and is in commemoration of
the last direct male descendant of the Sherburnes, who
died whilst a boy, in the ninth year of his age. Tradition
has it that the deceased boy was poisoned by eating yew-
berries in the grounds of Stonyhurst. On the monument
are represented a figure of the youthful heir to the Stonyhurst estates, whilst on each side of him are the figures

of two boys, supposed to represent his playfellows, weeping
for the loss of their young companion.

There are several objects of interest in the chancel
of the old church, amongst others the "chained books,"
comprising some thick and massive volumes enclosed in
an oak case, with glass covering.   They were formerly
fastened by chains on the top of an old oak table.   The
books are all of a religious and theological character, and
appear to have been intended for the perusal and benefit
of the inhabitants of the village, for on the title page on
one of them—" Barkitt's Expository Notes "—there is the
following autograph and record :—" Bought by William
Johnson, vicar of Mitton, for ye use of ye parishioners."
The carved oak cover of the baptismal font shews the
ancient character of the old edifice.   It bears the date of
1593.   It will thus be seen that Mitton Church possesses
many memorials and relics of antiquity, which cannot
fail to be of interest to the tourist.   Leaving Mitton and
proceeding along the highway, a walk of about three
miles opens out to view the historical building and
lofty cupolas of

STONYHURST COLLEGE,

And here it may be incidentally remarked that before
reaching this great Lancashire School of Roman Catholic
education by our present route, we have to pass out of
Lancashire into Yorkshire, and again out of the last named
county into the former.   The river first crossed on the
road from Whalley to Stonyhurst is the Ribble, and the
tongue of land lying between this river and the river
Hodder, which is crossed nearer Stonyhurst, is a part of
Yorkshire.   Hence in crossing the Hodder from Whalley
to Stonyhurst, we again pass out of Yorkshire into
Lancashire.   Shortly after crossing the Hodder the grey
turrets of Stonyhurst are seen as prominent objects
in the immediate distance, and in a short time
the tourist finds himself within the grounds and precincts

of the principal educational institution of the Roman Catholics in England. Like Oxford and Cambridge, in relation to the English Church, Stonyhurst has now, for something like a century past, been the *alma mater* of those professing the Roman Catholic faith, not only in this country, but on the continent and abroad. Many of the chief dignitaries of the church have been educated there, as well as several of the Roman Catholic nobility, and also those who, in after years, have from time to time distinguished themselves in the various walks of professional, literary, and public life. Amongst others may be enumerated Charles Waterton, the naturalist, (the well-known author of "Waterton's Wanderings,") who has enriched the museum at the college by the presentation of a rare and valuable collection of foreign birds. Richard Lalor Sheil was also a student at Stonyhurst; likewise the late Mr. Justice Shee, Sir Charles Tempest, the Hon. C. Langdale, Lord Clifford, John Talbot, the sixteenth Earl of Shrewsbury; Richard Vaughan Barnewall, barrister, author of "Barnewall's Reports;" and many others of distinction, now passed away, including the celebrated tragedian John Vandenhoff. Of other celebrities who were educated at Stonyhurst may be included Judge Ball, ex Lord Chancellor of Ireland; the Right Hon. Richard More O'Ferrall, Admiral Jerningham, Percy Fitzgerald, Alfred Austin, Dr. Vaughan, Roman Catholic Bishop of Salford; The O'Donoghue, Lord Arundell, of Wardour, &c.

Stonyhurst was founded as an educational establishment in the year 1794. It was in that year that the Jesuits were driven from their college at Liege, in Belgium, during the fury of the French Revolution. England then became their home, and Stonyhurst was placed at their disposal by Thomas Weld, Esq. (father of Cardinal Weld), who was then in possession of the mansion and estates, after they had passed from the Sherburne family. In the first instance the Jesuits occupied it at a nominal rent, and some years afterwards the mansion and grounds, and the whole of the lands, were conveyed to the order on easy terms. The estate at present comprises upwards of 2,060 acres, the whole of this large area being farmed by the Jesuits themselves, with the assistance of their agents and other servants. There have been seventeen rectors since the college was first established, the present rector being the Rev. Father Eyre. A visit to this ancient seat of learning is well worth undertaking, for it is not only the college itself, but the gardens and grounds adjacent, which combine to form a most interesting attraction. The rector, and all the college authorities are exceedingly hospitable, and show a kindly readiness in conducting visitors through the college buildings, the numerous and varied apartments in which possess several features of historic interest. Amongst others, worthy of a minute inspection, is the Refectory Room for the special use of the Community. It is a spacious apartment, containing several portraits of distinguished men belonging to the Roman Catholic Church, including those of the late and present Popes, Cardinal Manning, Cardinal Newman, and others. A certain set of apartments in the college are limited to the exclusive use of the "Philosophers," consisting, for the most part, the sons of wealthy parents in the higher ranks of life, who are sent to the college for the purpose of securing a good training, and laying the foundation of a university career. They occupy a similar position to the undergraduates of Oxford and Cambridge. They have the benefit of a special reference library, in addition to the general library of the college, which contains upwards of 30,000 volumes, many of them in black letter, and of great value, in addition to MMS. An inspection of the "Infirmary Corridor," as it is called, should on no account be omitted. It is adorned with numerous valuable paintings, including portraits of the Jesuit Fathers, who were put to death in England for their religion. They represent the Martyrdom of Catholics "chiefly in the reign," observes the author of *Stonyhurst College, Past and Present*, "of that wholesale marauder and inflated tyrant Henry the Eighth." The "Sodality Chapel" is a magnificent apartment. It is of modern construction, having been erected so recently as 1859. It is richly and gorgeously decorated, the altar being of alabaster and Caen stone. It is only used occasionally by a select few of the elder students. We now come to the Students' Refectory, a magnificent apartment, 90 feet in length, and 27 feet in width, the entire floor of which is paved with white marble. This ancient baronial hall was formerly the great dining room of the Sherburnes. There is an old table in the apartment, on which it is stated that Oliver Cromwell slept, when he stayed at Stonyhurst on the night of the 16th of August, 1648, the day before he moved on to Ribbleton and Walton, near Preston, where a battle was fought on the following day. There are many other apartments within the college which will afford the visitor much pleasurable interest and instruction, foremost amongst which are the library and the museum. The College Church, which is not only for the use of the college itself, but for the entire district around Stonyhurst, was erected in 1834, in the Tudor style of architecture, the interior being richly and most elaborately decorated. Astronomy forms one of the leading studies at the college. This branch is under the superintendence of the Rev. S. Perry, who is the Astronomical Professor at the College, and who has been appointed by the Government director of the expedition to Madagascar to witness and report upon the approaching transit of Venus. He is accompanied by two others from the College as assistants, and the party have just set out on the journey.

The blocks forming the educational department of the college were erected by the Fathers between the years 1803 and 1815, after they came into possession of the property, and these having now been found altogether inadequate to the college requirements, are at present being entirely re-built, at an outlay of upwards of £150,000. When completed the new buildings will form one of the noblest architectural structures of the kind in the country. And here it may be observed that the administration of the college estates has been so successful as to have provided for the support and maintenance of the establish-

ment for many years past. This has admitted of the
bulk of the payments made by the students to accumulate,
and it is said that it is out of these accumulations that
the cost of the palatial new buildings now in progress
will be to a large extent defrayed. The work is being
carried out in sections, and as one section of the building
is completed and opened, the old educational blocks are
in succession taken down, and the new buildings proceeded
with in continuation.

The plans of the buildings, which are Elizabethan in
character, were prepared by Messrs. Dunn and Hansom,
of Newcastle. When completed they will contain
accommodation for 250 students, in addition to the rooms
of the teaching staff. The buildings, which are in the
form of a parallelogram, face the south, and are 600 feet
in length from west to east, by about 300 feet in width,
in the narrowest part. They are open on three sides to
the gardens and surrounding country, thus having a
cheerful and pleasant aspect. That portion of the frontage
nearest the main college buildings facing the west, is in
the form of a quadrangle, being flanked by two wings on
the east and west sides. The west wing, which communicates by a cloister with the parochial church, is entirely
set apart for the private rooms of the Community, and is
joined at right angles with the main building by the chapel
and connecting corridors, so as to form another open
quadrangle, facing the west, 95 feet in width. This wing
contains 36 rooms, nine on each storey, with well lighted
corridors at the back. It is terminated by massive
pavilions, having bay windows of bold projection, with
cornices and parapets around them, with ornamental
shafts at the angles, up to the full height of the building.
The intervening space is also broken by smaller bays to
give the necessary light and shade demanded by the
great length of the line of building.

The new college chapel forms a special feature in
this section of the new buildings. It is 90 feet by 35 feet
inside. It is in the perpendicular style, with moulded
and carved roof, and panelled ceiling. One side of the

chapel has a row of confessionals, treated externally like the corridors, with flat roof, and ornamental parapet, and above are six large windows, filled with rich and delicate perpendicular tracery. On the opposite side of the chapel are the tribunes, to which access is given from the west wing, this building containing the professor's rooms. The east end of the chapel is almost entirely filled in by an elaborate reredos, reaching to the roof. It contains a large amount of niche work and sculptured panels, representing various scenes from the Passion of our Lord, the figures on the rood crowning all, and rising into the central arch of the roof. In this design it is intended to combine the "retables" which are such striking objects in Spanish churches, and the magnificent reredos of the Perpendicular period in England, some of which are preserved to us at All Souls and Magdalene Chapels, Oxford. Externally the effect will be very rich. The elaborate tracery windows are well set back under deeply moulded arches, between which are buttresses of 12 feet projection in the lower storey, and the space between the buttresses is thrown into the lavatory. Confessionals occupy this position on the level of the chapel floor, while above, the chapel walls appear some ten feet further back, and are finished at the top by a panelled and embattled parapet, broken by pinnacles which crown each of the buttresses.

The chapel forms one side of what is called the Priest's Quadrangle. This new chapel is most conveniently situated for both the students and the professors, and it may be added that the old chapel, when the chapel in progress is finished, will be added to the college library, which is rapidly out-growing the accommodation for books.* The idea is to build the new edifice as much as possible by subscriptions raised amongst the old Stony-hurst scholars, so as to make it a memorial chapel. The names of the subscribers are to be engraved on tablets to be placed in the sacristy. When completed it is said

---

* It has nearly 50,000 volumes, including black letter productions and numerous MS.

that it will be one of the most splendid chapels in the country.

The main quadrangle is set back 100 feet from the wings, and its chief feature is the grand central study hall, 90 feet by 35 feet, and of proportionate height, supported on an open and elegant arcade, and flanked by turrets of Elizabethan type, which rise to a height of 95 feet. The space between them is filled in with niches and statuary, and rich mouldings, the whole being surmounted by a pierced parapet. The rest of the quadrangle is more simple; but is relieved by ample bays. The east wing, which is on the same line as the west, is principally occupied by the academy room, or exhibition hall, a fine apartment 95 feet by 40 feet, and 28 feet high. It is treated with pannelled walls and ceiling, and contains tiers of seats for the audience at one end, and a permanent stage at the other. Externally its pavilion and bays are in keeping with those of the west wing. With the exception of the chapel, the roofs of all the several blocks forming the new buildings are flat, covered with seyssel asphalte, and enclosed by stone parapets over the pavilions and bay windows. They form a pleasing promenade, and judging from those portions of the buildings already completed they command an extensive view of the surrounding country. The fine and hard stone of which the buildings are being erected is all obtained from the quarries on the College Estate.

One of the best features of the interior of the buildings consists of the lofty rooms which are in course of being provided for both the students and professors. The building is entered from the old quadrangle by a broad flight of stone steps, leading to a handsome gallery, 120 feet in length, and 20 feet in width, lighted by large windows on the south side, and leading, at the west end, by the cloisters, to the parochial church. At its east end, on the left, is the grand staircase, leading to the chapel, the refectory, the long room, and the schools. On the right is the entrance to the lavatory beneath the chapel, an apartment 90 feet by 35 feet. A corridor 14 feet in width, and well lighted from the north, runs from this part the whole length of the building, and along it, on the right, are two spare school rooms, 30 feet by 25 feet; the Prefect's room, two large shoe rooms, the playground underneath the hall, two reading rooms, 45 feet by 25 feet; and three play rooms, respectively 63 feet by 40 feet, 70 feet by 30 feet, and 60 feet by 25 feet. In the basement of the east wing is the drawing school, 40 feet by 30 feet; also rooms for the music masters, and a large room for music practice, divided by glass partitions, with a pianoforte in each compartment. On this floor there are also dancing and fencing rooms.

On the first floor, and on the same line with the long room, refectory, and chapel, there is a reference library, with space for 10,000 volumes for the " Philosophers "; a billiard room, and a community recreation room, all looking into the west quadrangle. On the north-east side of the main quadrangle are nine school rooms, each 17 feet in height, and well lighted from the south. The study hall and academy room, also occupy the east wing. At the back of the study room, and opposite to the playground entrance is another grand staircase leading to the second floor, which is devoted to dormitory accommodation. The dormitories occupy the whole width of the building, and are 19 feet in height. When the several buildings now in course of erection are completed, the dormitory accommodation will be 370 feet in length, with cross ventilation throughout. The third staircase occupies the east angle of the principal quadrangle, and leads again to the dormitories and the magazine of store for the boys' clothes, over the academy room. There are also coal and luggage lifts, and a ventilating shaft to draw off the foul air from all the rooms.

All the school rooms are furnished with fire places, but in addition the whole of the boys' department will be heated upon the hot water system, each room containing coils in the window recesses, covered by seats, and capable of being turned off at pleasure in any room, independently of other rooms, which is an exceedingly advantageous

feature in the sanitary arrangements of the college.
A description of Stonyhurst would be incomplete
unless accompanied by a notice of the other educational
establishments in connection with the main building. These
consist of the buildings known as the Seminary, and the
Preparatory School called Hodder House, both of which
are within the precincts of the college estates.   The
former is the residence of those students who, having
finished their educational course in the college, and who
have determined upon entering the priesthood, enter the
Seminary at the close of their Noviciate, in order to study
logic, metaphysics, moral philosophy, and other cognate
subjects.   The Rev. Father Perry, the astronomical
professor at the college, is the Superior of the Seminary,
but subject to the authority of the Rev. Father Eyre, the
rector of Stonyhurst, and the head of the entire establishment.   On an average there are about fifty students
residing at the Seminary.   The building was some time
ago very considerably enlarged by the addition of two
wings, each 90 feet by 60 feet.

Hodder House, the Preparatory School, is situated
in the centre of charmingly picturesque grounds, about a
mile to the east of the college.   It originally belonged to
Mr. Emmett, a manufacturer, residing in the neighbourhood, but was ultimately purchased by Thomas Weld,
Esq., who presented it to the Jesuit Fathers shortly after
they took possession of Stonyhurst, and in 1804 it was
appropriated as their Noviciate for England, remaining
as such until the year 1854, when Beaumont Lodge, near
Windsor, was purchased for this purpose, and on the
Noviciate being transferred to Windsor, Hodder House
was converted into a Preparatory School in connection
with Stonyhurst.   Some time before the year 1871 the
accommodation for pupils had been found to be inadequate,
and in that year the establishment underwent a considerable enlargement, several class rooms having been added,
together with the erection of a new chapel, forty feet in
length, by eighteen feet in width; and also a spacious
dormitory, ninety-six feet by thirty-four feet, the old dormi-

tories being converted into an infirmary, entirely separated
from the rest of the building.   The number of boys at
Hodder average from 80 to 100, the age of admission
being from eight to twelve years.   The course of studies
is uniform with that taught in the lowest class at the
college; religious instruction, however, being a special
characteristic in the training of the boys, who are here,
with much thoughtful care and attention, prepared for
their first communion.   So strict is the discipline in this
respect that no boy is allowed promotion from Hodder to
the College until his training in the profession and
practice of religious duties is well assured.

Such is the extent and magnitude of this great
historical Lancashire seat of learning, which, within the
last century, has become one of the most renowned
educational establishments in the country, not only as
regards its material grandeur, but in respect of those
varied and elevated features of instruction which form
its distinguishing characteristics.

CLITHEROE CASTLE, SAWLEY ABBEY, AND RIBCHESTER.

There are several other interesting historical localities
within a radius of a few miles around Stonyhurst which,
should the tourist have time and leisure, he may pay a
visit to with profit.   Amongst these may be included the
borough of Clitheroe, with the ruins of its ancient castle,
from which there is a magnificent panoramic view of the
country, in almost every direction, for many miles around.
On the south-east side Pendle rears its lofty and majestic
head; while at its western end rises Whalley Nab,
immediately above the beautiful Vale of Whalley, and its
ruined abbey, and ancient church.   To the north-west is
one of the most enchanting landscapes of which Lancashire
can boast.   It includes the valleys of the Calder and the
Ribble, the prospect extending as far as the Irish sea, and
prominent amongst the views being the towers, spires,
and other lofty buildings in Preston.   From Clitheroe
the tourist might continue his journey to visit Sawley

Abbey. It is about three miles from Clitheroe, but a short railway ride to Clitheroe brings him within a mile-and-a-half of the old abbey. It was founded in the year 1147, by William Baron Percy, grandson of that William de Perci, who accompanied the Norman Conqueror to England, and obtained from him large possessions in Craven. William Trafford, its last abbot, took part in the " Pilgrimage of Grace," for which, like John Paslew, the last abbot of Whalley, he was tried at the Lancaster Assizes, found guilty, and executed on the 10th of March, 1538. A visit to Ribchester should, if possible, be undertaken whilst the tourist is in the district. It is one of the oldest places in England, and is believed to have been founded by the Romans in the year 79, when, according Tacitus, Agricola conquered this part of England. It is about three miles and a half from the Wilpshire station on that section of the Lancashire and Yorkshire railway between Preston and Whalley. The scenery between Wilpshire and Ribchester—the course of the Ribble being ever present along the route—is very delightful.

Should the tourist be indisposed to pursue his journey beyond Stonyhurst, but determine on returning to Preston after his visit to the college, he may agreeably vary the return route by proceeding in the direction of Longridge, taking his leave of Stonyhurst along the straight carriage drive in front of the college buildings, which will bring him to Hurst Green. Thence he may either walk or, if he prefers it, take a conveyance by road, from Hurst Green to Longridge, from which the railway will once more land him in Preston. The scenery from Hurst Green to Longridge is well worth the six or seven miles walk, between the two places, to see. The road way is undoubtedly " up hill and down dale," but the physical toil which the pedestrian may have to endure will be amply compensated by the beautiful scenery of which the elevated portions of the road in succession command a view.

H. OAKEY, Printer, Caxton House, 36, Fishergate, Preston.

BIBLIOLIFE

Old Books Deserve a New Life
www.bibliolife.com

Did you know that you can get most of our titles in our trademark **EasyScript**™
print format? **EasyScript**™ provides readers with a larger than average
typeface, for a reading experience that's easier on the eyes.

Did you know that we have an ever-growing collection of books in
many languages?

Order online:
www.bibliolife.com/store

Or to exclusively browse our **EasyScript**™ collection:
www.bibliogrande.com

At BiblioLife, we aim to make knowledge more accessible by
making thousands of titles available to you – quickly and affordably.

Contact us:
BiblioLife
PO Box 21206
Charleston, SC 29413

CPSIA information can be obtained at www.ICGtesting.com
Printed in the USA
LVOW102111100212

268132LV00017B/36/A

9 781103 089710